Now the long trick's over

A British merchant seaman's life from 1932

Captain Arthur Mathison

Published by Dead Good Publications
Newport,
East Yorkshire
HU15 2RF

Front cover
My last command, m.v. "Naworth", built by Cammell Lairds of Birkenhead
in 1973 and owned by R.S. Dalgliesh Limited of Newcastle upon Tyne.
(Photograph Captain Arthur Mathison).

ISBN 978-0-9546937-7-0

Published by Dead Good Publications
Newport,
East Yorkshire
HU15 2RF

Contents

Foreword

Before my father, Captain Arthur Mathison, passed away in 1993, he wrote the story of his life at sea from the age of 15 in 1932, when he joined the s.s. 'Saranac' at Saltend on the River Humber. It is a fascinating insight into a maritime era that has long gone. The tale starts in the years of the Great Depression, with the Spartan conditions endured by able seamen on merchant ships, many of which dated from the Great War. The Second World War years are here, with my father's work at Scapa Flow, and subsequent voyages in North Atlantic convoys. After the war, the majority of his time was initially spent in the tramp steamer trade, going from port to port wherever there was a cargo. At one point the trade took him away from his hometown of Hull for seventeen months! Arthur gained his master's certificate in 1949, and he subsequently worked for Bolton Steamship Company of London until 1961, when a disagreement left him out of a job. He then turned his hand to shop keeping, followed by taxi driving, but he longed to return to the sea. Initially, much to his chagrin, he could only obtain employment on the coastal trade. However, in 1965, he joined R.S. Dalgliesh Limited of Newcastle upon Tyne. The work consisted mostly of the iron ore trade, which took him to Murmansk in Russia and Churchill in Canada. Following two heart attacks, he finally retired from the sea in 1977 on ill health grounds. So ended a seafaring career spanning 45 years, his working life taking him from being a humble deck boy and A.B., to master of the then recently launched m.v. 'Naworth'.

Phil Mathison

April 2009

Incidentally, the 'trick' mentioned in the title refers to an old maritime term, meaning " A period of two of the helmsman at the wheel. A turn or spell of duty". I would like to thank Captain A C Douglas, Editor of 'Seabreezes' and Nigel Lawrence, Editor of 'Shipping, Today & Yesterday' for their research into this archaic term.

The book is dedicated to a great dad, much missed.

Me in September 1940

The opening pages of my first discharge book

Chapter 1.
Pre-sea life.

My earliest recollections of my life before I went to sea are that Granddad and father both were seafarers. The former being a ship's Carpenter and the latter, a ship's Steward. Sadly, neither of them ever spoke to me about their voyages. Their long spells away from home remained a mystery to me. Granddad served on foreign-going tramp ships, and as a result of this he would be away for up to three years at a time. Father served in ships registered in Norway, yet owned by a British company, so you see flags of convenience are not something new to British shipowners. Despite the fact that his voyages were to and from the Scandinavian countries, carrying coal from the U.K., and bringing back timber, we saw very little of him.

In fact I can only remember seeing him about three times before he was lost at sea in a terrible storm in the Baltic Sea in December 1926.

Grandma, who had a little corner shop close to the gates of Victoria Dock in Drypool, Hull, had got a house on mortgage for Mam and us four children. However, failing business and the loss of father's earnings, made it impossible to meet the mortgage.

As a result, the house was repossessed, and we all moved in with Grandma. She had got another house, in Trinity Square, after leaving the shop.

The house was No.7 Trinity Square, Anlaby Road, property owned by the Trinity House, the World renowned sea training school for future Merchant Navy Officers.

This shift of home took me quite a long way from my primary school, but I used to roller skate there and back each day. I had tried another school nearer home but could not settle, so I went back to Blenkin Street School.

Living in Drypool had brought me close to ships which discharged their cargoes of timber in Victoria Dock, and the docks area became our playground after the work had ceased for the day.

Several of us kids would gang up and go and raid the barges loaded with groundnuts (Peanuts), or Locust Beans, or bungy as we used to call it.

These commodities were imported for the oil-seed crushing mills, for which Hull was noted. Most of these sort of cargoes being for British Oil and Cake Mills, (B.O.C.M.) whose works were down Wincolmlee, a street running parallel and close to the River Hull. The barges sailed from the docks into the River Hull, and up it to the factories which had berths on the riverside.

After these raids on the barges, we would come away with our pockets bulging with peanuts and/or bungy, which we ate with relish, and as far as I am aware, none of us ever suffered any ill-effects from eating the peanuts or Locust.

At the end of the street where Grandma had her shop was United Molasses storage tanks, where tankers came and filled up with raw molasses. As they left the depot we kids would chase after them to get a handful of the raw black treacle from the filling pipe.

This we licked from our hands with great relish as it was so sweet. None of us ever needed any laxatives, the black treacle took care of that.

Another of the pranks we got up to was to stand at the dock gates and "Bread left", which meant that as the dockers left work we would ask them if they had any bread left.

Many of them would have food left over from their lunches and this they would give to any lad asking them "Any bread left Mr?"

To many of the kids this was a meal they would not have had at home, Drypool was a very poor area of Hull in those days.

My parents would have been horrified if they had known that I took part in that game, as I was fairly well fed at home. Even so I enjoyed eating some of the spoils of the game along with the rest of the lads, especially when it happened to be a bit of apple.

At school, my favourite subject had always been geography. I hated arithmetic and geometry, but talk to me about those far away places with strange sounding names and I was in seventh heaven.

During such lessons, my mind conjured up images of the places being discussed. For instance, I remember the teacher telling us that Canada produced tremendous amounts of salmon.

As he put it, "The Canadians eat what they can, and can what they can't".

He then went on to say how a lot of the canned salmon came to Britain. In my mind I saw thousands of salmon being netted and packed in cans for this country to enjoy, if you could afford a tin.

A talk about Zanzibar and all its spices brought to my mind the smell of those sweet smelling spices used at home.

In a way, it was fitting that I would eventually go to sea in the hopes that I might see for myself all those wonderfully described places around the world.

As stated earlier, December 1926 was a black month for mother, for the ship father was on, The s.s. "Rodney", sank with the loss of all hands in a storm of intense ferocity in the Baltic Sea. She was on her way back to Britain with a cargo of timber.

The only trace of her ever found was one upturned lifeboat, and a lifebelt.

Mother made a claim for compensation for the loss of her husband, which was fiercely contested by the owner, Sir James Bell, it was his contention that as the ship was registered under the Norwegian flag, mother would have to apply to the courts in Norway for compensation.

This was a clever move by the owner, for he knew full well that a working class family could not afford lawyer's fees to follow this up. Mother sought the help of her local Member of Parliament, one Commander Kenworthy, (Who later became Lord Strabolgi).

He took up the case with great zeal, and as a result mother was awarded one hundred pounds, (The limit of the shipowner's liability at that time, fortunately long since abolished and replaced by more realistic amounts of money in such cases).

In 1926 a man's life was apparently worth only £100!

Grandma and mother battled on trying to keep the family together, but with four children, and no child allowances in those days, it became impossible.

In 1928, entry to an orphanage appeared to be the only solution, and to this end application was made for us four children to be taken in at the Newland Orphanage, on Cottingham Road, Hull.

My two sisters, and my brother, then aged about four, entered the orphanage. I stayed at home for some time after that, then I was taken to the Hesslewood Orphanage on the outskirts of Hull.

I remember only too well the horrible shock of being stripped of my own clothing, being put in a large bath and tubbed, then having all my hair shaved off, and finally being dressed in the prison garb of the Orphanage.

I do not remember too much of the time I was in there, but I do remember that one day my mother came and I was given my own clothes back and told to get dressed in them. Then I was taken from the Orphanage and back home.

No reason was given to me why I had been removed from the orphanage, and I was surprised to learn that my sisters and brother would not be coming back home to join me.

It was to be many years later that I learned that you can put your natural born children in an orphanage, but you cannot put an adopted child in a home. I had been an adopted child, the people I thought were my parents and grand parents were not my blood relatives at all. This knowledge had devastating effects on me because I found out that my natural mother was unmarried when she gave birth to me. In other words I was illegitimate.

This knowledge, for many years gave me a great inferiority complex. I finally overcame the complex and vowed to prove myself equal as the next man.

I only saw my sisters and brother once in all the years they were in Newland Orphan Homes, and that once was to be the last time. I saw my eldest sister, who died in the home, aged about 12.

After the three children were admitted to the Home, mother went out to work. The job was a six-day week one, so it fell on Grandma to make the weekly visit to the Orphanage.

Every Saturday afternoon, without fail, for 12 years she visited my sister and brother, always taking a paper carrier with some small items of sweets and/or fruit for them. Such things had to be handed to the House Matron, and they were shared out with the less fortunate children who had no visitors.

I think Grandma had delusions of grandeur, because one day she took me to see the Principal of the Trinity House Navigation School, in the hopes of getting me enrolled there to learn to be a ship's officer. As things were hard, I don't know how she was going to find the money needed to clothe me in the school's uniform. Any way, it didn't come to that, I was too small to be accepted, 5 feet was the minimum height for entry, and I was only 4 ft.11 inches tall.

"Bring him back in a year's time, he'll have grown that inch by then", that was the summing up by the Principal.

I did go back there ten years later as an adult pupil, but a lot of things happened before that occasion.

I left school at the age of 14, the then legal age for leaving school and going out into the cold cruel world to try and earn a living. The year was 1930, and the world was in the grips of the "Depression". Jobs were scarce and very poorly paid.

The best I could get was an errand boy's job on the princely sum of 5/- (25p per week) for 48 hours!

Next I was taken on as an apprentice at Brigham and Cowan's ship repair yard on Hedon Road, Hull. In reality, apprentices were cheap labour, but I enjoyed the work. At first I was put in the machine shop stores, where I had to clean up hundreds of bolts and nuts used in ship repair work. I later was transferred to the joiners and pattern maker's shop. This I really enjoyed because I got the chance to go aboard lots of ships undergoing repairs, and it was then that my desire to go to sea started to grow.

I used to talk to the members of the crews about their voyages, and they were willing to tell me all sorts of stories. Many I suspect, were greatly enhanced for my benefit, but made me even more determined to find a job at sea.

One of the ships I was on was a "banana boat". She had just come from the West Indies with her cargo of stalks of bananas.

The Chief Steward saw my covetous look at the hands of bananas in the pantry. He took down a hand of them and gave them to me, and then had a yarn with me. Whilst he was talking, I could visualise an island covered in banana palms waiting to be picked and eaten. That was the life for me. Imagination is a wonderful thing!

The problem was how to get to sea, apart from stowing away, which I did not relish. My prayers were answered by a friend of the family, for he worked in a shipping agents office in Hull.

Part of his job was to find the crews for ships for whom they were acting as agents. Having been informed of my desire to go to sea, he said he would keep an eye open for a berth for me.

Some little time later he came round and said that he had a job for me. A tanker was arriving at Salt End Oil Terminus to discharge her cargo of crude oil.

Her Captain had radioed in that he needed certain crew members, one of which was an Ordinary Seaman. The job was mine if I wanted it.

This was a dream come true, a job for me at sea. Little did I know that such a rating was the lowest form of humanity at sea, and little did I care, I was going to sea!

I was told to attend at the office at 10 a.m. on the 3rd April 1932. I was there on time and taken to the Mercantile Marine Office in Posterngate, close by the office, where I was to be signed on the ship's Articles of Agreement as Ordinary Seaman.

There were three or four other men to be signed on the ship, and the procedure was all Greek to me.

The shipping Master read out the salient points of the Articles to us all, and then got each of the men to append their signatures to the Articles. This made them legally members of the crew of the ship the "Saranac".

When it came to my turn, he took great pains to explain to me what all this was about, as I was a "first tripper".

He explained that the Articles were a legal and binding agreement between the Captain of the ship and the crew.

My rating was noted in the Articles, so was my monthly rate of pay, which was to be Four Pounds Ten Shilling per calendar month, whatever a calendar month was.

I'd never heard the expression before. Anyway, I was rich beyond my wildest dreams, I was to be paid 3/- a day, 21/- a week, as against the 5/- a week earned ashore.

The shipping Master went on to define the voyage limits - "The vessel not to trade beyond the limits of 70 degrees North, nor 60 degrees South Latitude, and I was to report on board complete with gear for the voyage at "One minute past midnight on the 4th April".

Having appended my signature to the Articles, I was now free to go home and get my gear packed ready to join the ship.

The rest of the day was spent rounding up and packing what it was thought that I would need on voyage.

I remember packing a battered old suitcase with a couple of clean shirts, a change of underwear, a towel, face flannel, some soap, my overalls, socks, and a pair of shoes. Then a bed sheet and a worn blanket and a pillow case was added to the contents of the case, and finally it was topped off with a packet of sandwiches for my supper that first night aboard a ship.

Chapter 2.
I join the "Saranac".

About 7.30 p.m. that evening I was bundled into a taxi along with my mother, grandmother and an aunt who were going to see me off to join the ship. It was lying at the Salt End oil terminal jetty.

The taxi wasn't able to get alongside the ship as there is a long wooden jetty from the shore, and at that time was not intended to take the weight of cars or lorries.

That meant I had the long walk from the taxi to the ship, and it seemed miles away when I stepped out of the car.

I said my goodbyes, picked up my case and strode away bravely to a completely new world and life. I turned and waved to my relatives and then saw the taxi turning to leave the scene.

I was on my own now. Reaching the gangway of the ship after the long walk along that jetty, I paused and looked at the size of her, she seemed ginormous to a little chap like me standing on the quayside.

Nothing daunted, I made my way up the steep gangway steps to the deck of the ship. As I stepped aboard, I was stopped by the ship's watchman, who demanded to know what my business aboard the ship was.

"I'm the new Ordinary Seaman", I announced with pride.

"O.K., your accommodation is up for'ard on the starboard side", he pointed me in the direction of the fo'castle head.

I'd learned enough at the ship repair yard to know that the starboard side was the right-hand side of the ship.

I made my way along what seemed miles of steel deck before reaching the entrance to the fo'castle.

Entry was by means of a scuttle, I went inside the right-hand one and saw a long flight of stairs leading down to the accommodation.

Descending the stairway, I came to the open fo'castle, a huge space lined on both the inboard and the outboard sides with bunks, three tiers high. Many of the bunks had bedding and clothes strewn on them, but there was nobody in the fo'castle.

Down the centre of the space was a long white wooden table and either side of it was a wooden bench. As I had no idea which was to be my bunk, I just sat down and weighed up the world I had come to join, this was going to be my home, but for how long?

Shortly afterwards, I heard someone coming down the stairs, a man entered the fo'castle, and seeing me there, wanted to know what I was doing in the Sailor's accommodation.

I told him I was the new Ordinary Seaman.

"Oh, that's O.K. then, can't be too careful these days".

"Got yourself a bunk then"? He asked.

"No, I don't know which one I can take", I answered.

"Where's your donkey's breakfast"?

"Where's my what"?

"Your bed", he replied.

"Er, I haven't got one".

"Your first trip is it"?

I told him it was. In the meantime, he looked around the fo'castle, then pointed out a bunk to me.

"Take that bunk kid, the man who's left has left his mattress and pillow, you might as well use them seeing as you ain't brought your own".

I thanked him and dropped my gear on the bunk and opened the case to get my blanket, sheet and pillow case out.

I made the bed up to the best of my ability, not being in the habit of making up my own bed. The sailor and I exchanged a little patter whilst I was doing this, and when I'd finished, he asked me if I'd like a mug of tea.

Just what I needed to finish off the day, I could have my sandwiches, and then " hit the hay".

I learned that that saying came from the bedding down on the seamen's straw filled mattresses.

He made a pot of tea with water from a hot water boiler at the end of he accommodation.

"Where's yer mug then"? He asked me.

I hadn't one, no one had told me that ships did not supply seamen with eating and drinking utensils.

My shipmate didn't need telling that I'd neither mug, plate, spoon, knife or fork.

"Yer proper schooner rigged ain't you", he said, going over to a locker, he produced an enamel mug and plate, a knife, fork and spoon.

"These 'ave been left by fellas who left the ship, give 'em a good wash and keep them for the voyage", he handed them to me.

I did as he had said, I washed them in the sink in hot water.

I had my mug of tea and my sandwiches, and felt like bed, it was now late in the evening, and past my normal bedtime.

My shipmate pointed out a locker to me, saying "Keep your gear in that locker, it's yours for the voyage".

Having put the utensils away, I then started to get undressed for bed. I felt a little abashed in the presence of someone I didn't know.

He sensed this, and said "It's alright lad, we're used to seeing one another bollock naked, you'll get used to it as well".

I donned my pyjamas and got into the bunk, and within minutes I was dead to the world. The sleep of the innocent and the just!

Some time later, I was awakened by the noise of members of the crew coming down into the fo'castle.

All were a little worse for wear, having obviously just rolled out of the pubs. Most of them just crash landed in their bunks in their shore going gear, to sleep off the effects of the booze before sailing time.

At 6.30 a.m. came the clarion call from the watchman.

"Wakey, wakey, rise and shine, six-thirty and coffee's on the table".

I heard grunts and groans from the various bunks as the occupants slowly re-entered this world.

I got up and wanted to get washed, but were did one do their ablutions? There were no wash basins or even a bathroom in sight.

I was to learn that ablutions were done in a galvanised 2 gallon bucket, which I was told I would have to get from the Bosun.

The bathroom, such as it was, was a steel house on the upper deck, this also served as the toilets as well.

The deck of it was simply concrete covered and had a wooden duck board on which to stand when sluicing yourself down.

No one except the Captain had a bath in which to clean oneself.

Fortunately, fresh water was plentiful and was obtained on tap from a large tank over the accommodation, which it turned out was my duty to see was filled up every morning.

That was to be one of my daily tasks, attend to the filling of all the fresh water tanks, one for the officers, one for the engineers and one for the sailors and firemen.

About an hour later, the Bosun called down the hatchway.

"Alright lads, stand-by fore and aft".

We all trooped out of the fo'castle and up onto the deck, where the Bosun detailed several men to go to the after station.

The rest, including me were to stay on the fo'castle head, to attend the fo'ward moorings. I stood to one side whilst the men flaked down an 8" rope ready for the tug to tow the ship off the quay.

A call from the bridge came, "Single up to headline and a spring".

Such orders were over my head, so I just watched the procedure.

All ropes except one were let go ashore and heaved in by the sailors. Then the tow rope was put out through the fairlead for the tug to take onto his hook. Unaware of the danger, I was stood in one of the bights of the rope as it started to run out.

The next thing I knew was being thrown arse over tip by the huge beefy hand of one of the Able Seamen.

As I picked myself up from the deck, he said "Kid, never, ever stand in the bight of a running rope".

I had learned lesson No.1 at sea, self-preservation.

When the tug was made fast, it started to pull the ship off the quay, at the same time swinging her round head out to sea.

Ships always moored head up river when mooring in a tidal berth, this was because the strongest tide is the ebb tide in the Humber.

Shortly afterwards the tug was cast off and the "Saranac" headed down river under Pilotage. I helped stow the mooring ropes away, though I had difficulty in getting my small hands around an 8" manilla rope.

The Bosun then told me that I would be the Petty Officer's "Peggy", that meant that I would fetch and carry for them. I was taught how to make up a bed, this I had to do for the Bosun and Carpenter each morning. In addition, I had to set the meal table and fetch the food from the galley each meal time.

The galley was right aft, and quite a long walk from the forward accommodation. In fine weather it wasn't so bad getting the food forward, but in dirty weather it was no fun.

For the first couple of days, the weather was beautifully warm and calm, and I was in my element, then we met the heavy swell from the Atlantic as we approached Land's End

It was then that my stomach rebelled and I started to be violently sick. This state of affairs was not helped by the smell of the oil fumes from the open oil tanks.

I'd be alright first thing in the morning when I got up from a night's sleep, but when I went to the galley for the P.O.s' breakfasts, the sight of the bowl of burgoo (Porridge) which I had to carry back for breakfast was enough to make me puke all over again.

It was four days before I got over the mal de mar (sea sickness).

In the meantime, I swore that as soon as I got home and ashore again, I'd never go to sea again. That was how bad I felt at the time.

After the first few days, when the sickness had gone, I felt on top of the world. I enjoyed every moment of my working day.

During my bouts of sickness, the Chief Cook was a great help, he insisted that I had to eat something otherwise I'd strain my stomach with retching. He'd have an apple for me to eat each time I went to the galley for the P.O.s' meals. Those apples were a great help in settling me down.

Our loading port, I was told, was to be a place called Talara, a fairly new oil port on the NW coast of Peru. That meant that I would be going through the Panama Canal on my first voyage to sea. I would see the wonder that I had only previously read about in books at school. I'd see how the ships were lifted up 72 feet above the level of the Atlantic Ocean so as to steam through the lakes to the other set of locks which would lower the ship down to the level of the Pacific Ocean. All this, I learned, was done by gravity, water flowing from the higher levels into the lower locks, thus lifting the ship up to the level of the next lock.

At the Pacific side it was done in reverse, the water was allowed to run into the lower lock till it was level and then the gates opened for the vessel to steam into the next lock. This was then repeated until the vessel was down to sea level and could steam out into the ocean.

I fully understood why it was known as the New World, to me it was a new world, the sight of all those tropical forests and vegetation was a sight to behold. I remember well the Culebra Cut, the most dangerous and narrow part of the canal, cut through the side of a mountain.

They were still working on widening it at the time we went through it. I believe that today, the largest ships in the world can now pass through that cutting.

I was looking forward to getting ashore at the loading port, in the hopes of enjoying the sights of a foreign land.

After tea on the day we arrived at Talara, all the crew were getting ready to go ashore for the evening. I asked them if I could go with them, and they agreed to let me accompany them ashore.

It was about a mile walk from the ship to the nearest habitation, not that there was much to be seen.

The first port of call, as one would expect of seamen in from an ocean passage, was the bar.

The crew ordered bottles of beer for themselves and lemonade for me. After they had had two bottles each, they said they were going to see someone. They told me to stay in the bar until they returned, under no circumstances was I to try following them. They gave the barkeeper some money and told him to keep me in bottles of lemonade until they came back.

By the time they came back I was awash with lemonade. I was to learn later that the person or persons they had been to see, were the local prostitutes, hence the reason they did not want me with them. Having sown their wild oats, they returned to the bar for more light liquid refreshments before returning to the ship.

So my first trip ashore in a foreign land was a bit of an anticlimax, all I had seen was the dark road to the town and the dingy bar. Whilst I was in the bar, one sexy dame made eyes at me, but at the age of just under 16, I wasn't enamoured by her efforts. Such pleasures of the flesh came on later voyages.

We sailed from Talara the next morning, back to Hull with our cargo of crude oil. By now I was a seasoned seaman and the sickness had long since gone. I'd got my sealegs now and all I wanted to do was to stay at sea.

On arrival back at Salt End Jetty, I was paid my wages for the voyage and signed on for another voyage, but not before the National Union of Seamen's delegate had got me to become a member of the Union. According to him, I would not be allowed to sign on the ship again unless I was a member of the said Union, so I paid my 10/- entrance fee and several weeks subscriptions of 6d per week, and was given my Union card No.118614. That Union number is still marked in my Discharge Book.

I went home and gave my parents some of my wages and then went out to buy gear I needed for the next voyage. I made sure that I had all the things that I did not have on my first voyage. I now knew what things a seaman needed to take with him. It had been a hard lesson to learn. I was no longer schooner rigged when we sailed for my second voyage, which was across to Galveston, Texas for more crude oil back to Hull.

I did not get ashore at Galveston as we were too far from the town at the loading berth.

On arrival in Hull on the 3rd July 1932, I left the "Saranac", why I do not really know, but I did. That was the termination of my voyages 1 and 2.

Chapter 3.
s.s. "Chelsea".

A month after leaving the "Saranac", I obtained a job as Deck Boy on a Hull owned and registered ship. She was the " Chelsea ", owned by William Brown Atkinson, whose office was in Scale Lane, Hull.

To join her, I had to travel down to Barry Docks where she was to load a cargo of coal. This rail journey was of course at my own expense. Shipowners did not pay for travel in the 1930s as they have to in this day and age. This time I was no longer schooner rigged, I'd learned from my previous experience what I needed in the way of gear when joining a ship. Having reported aboard the ship and deposited my gear in the fo'cstle, I then went and bought my donkey's breakfast and straw pillow, an enamel mug and plate, a knife, fork and spoon and some tablets of Lifebuoy soap.

Lifebuoy soap being a great favourite amongst seamen for washing and bathing. Strangely enough, it could also be used in place of currency in places like Spain, as I was to find out later.

The accommodation aboard the "Chelsea" left a lot to be desired, for it was extremely small. It was situated under the fo'cstle head, as usual. There was a centre alleyway under there, and on the port side was the sailors' accommodation and to starboard was the firemen's. Each had a very small messroom, the only fittings in them being a scrubbed wooden table and two wooden bench seats, an iron pot bellied stove to serve as the heating system in cold weather. Lighting was by means of a paraffin dynamo, in other words, an oil lamp. I was soon to learn the art of trimming an oil lamp so as to get the best lighting possible from a double burner oil lamp. Believe it or not, there is an art to it. If not done properly, the lamp will smoke and blacken the chimney, (the glass).

In each fo'cstle, which measured about 14 feet lengthwise by about a mean of 10 feet breadth there were fitted eight steel framed bunks, nine in the case of the firemen's fo'cstle. There was a small wooden locker, 18"x18"x24", these were the only space allocated for each man for his personal possessions. No provision had been made for hanging up clothes. The result was that your wardrobe was made by placing your clothes on a hanger, putting an old shirt over them, and then hanging them over the end of your bunk. As bad as the sailor's accommodation was, the Bosun and Carpenter who had to share a room, were far worse off. Their room was right at the fore end of the fo'sctle space, in consequence it was a tiny narrow room, too small to swing the proverbial cat. To make matters worse, they had no separate space in which to have their meals. They had to make do eating from a small folding table. I'm surprised that the ship ever managed to get anyone to live in such squalid conditions.

In the 1930's, jobs were so scarce it was a case of Hobson's choice, and you took whatever job you could get. The "Chelsea" was a typical tramp ship of the 1930s, a three island ship, with a well deck forward and aft of the bridge and centre castle. On the fore deck was No.1 and 2 hatches, No.3 hatch was between the bridge and stokehold. No.4 and 5 hatches on the well deck aft. To finish off was the poop deck, with the storage space known as the lazarette. It was in there that the vegetables for the voyage were stored, bags of potatoes covered in lime to keep the rats from eating them! The bags of dried codfish were also stored in there, that stuff known as bacalau and was as hard as a board. To make it edible it had to be soaked in water for about 24 hours. This also removed a lot of the salt from it. Despite that, it still tasted awful unless you had a Cook who knew how to make it into a tasty meal. Most Cooks served it for breakfast every Friday morning with a dollop of what was known as Jessie's dream poured over it. That was a tasteless white sauce. Only once in all my time at sea did I sail with a Cook who could make a really tasty meal from dried cod. He managed it by begging, borrowing or stealing, a tin of canned tomatoes. He then poured the tomatoes into a pan in which he was boiling the fish. The result was a tasty fish breakfast.

I found that by joining as a Deck Boy, my monthly salary went down by 30/- (£1.50 in today's currency), but I was not too concerned, I had a job.

It was on the "Chelsea" that I was to really learn all about being a seaman. I learnt about all I would need to know for the rest of my time on deck as a Deck Boy, an Able Seaman and on to being an Officer some years later. Much of what I learned as Deck Boy on the "Chelsea" stood me in good stead for all time. For that I have to thank the sailors of those days, who were real sailors, capable of turning their hand to anything the ship might need, come hell or high water.

For instance, I have watched so called seamen trying to bowse a stage in alongside the ship when painting over the bow. These days they want the stage hauled in by a guy rope attached to a winch. We were taught to fasten the inboard end of the guy to a cleat, then get on the stage and haul in the slack of the rope at each end of the stage. Having hauled it as tight as possible, we would then start to lower the stage. As we did this, the stage would be pulled hard up against the ship's side. There was no bowsing in for us over the side of the ship when overside painting. Access to the staging was by means of a "Jacob's ladder", made from 14" lengths of broom handles inserted into lengths of 2" rope, and spaced 12" apart. There was even an art in climbing one of those ladders, and that was to get one leg on one side of the ladder, and one on the other side. This way you could get up the ladder, whereas if you tried to climb it when it was lying against the ship's side you could not get a foothold on the rungs. If you were using an ordinary Pilot ladder, the rungs were about 5" wide and could easily be climbed holding on to the side ropes. As stated earlier, the " Chelsea " was in Barry Docks, she was to load a full cargo of coal for Savona, in the Gulf of Genoa, Italy. It was mid August when we sailed from Barry and we had fine calm weather all the way there.

Going through the Straits of Gibraltar at night, I was amazed at the number of tuna fishing boats there were. There must have been hundreds of them, and most of them sailing without lights. As a ship approached them there would be a frantic lighting of a paraffin flare, waved to warn a ship of their presence. I have often wondered how many of those small boats were from time to time run down by a passing steamer.

Savona turned out to be a pleasant surprise to me, the town appeared to be built on a hillside, so the streets were terraced. I quite enjoyed our stay at that port discharging the coal. It was hot, dusty and thirsty work for all concerned. Despite the hot weather, it was necessary to keep the ports and doors closed to try and keep the coal dust out of the accommodation. It was a fruitless effort, the coal dust got into everything, but so far as we, the deck crowd were concerned, the worst part was to come.

As the coal was discharged, we had to go down on top of the cargo and sweep the overhead stringers and beams, to clear them of coal and dust, we also had to sweep down the ship's sides as well. We more or less followed the coal as it went down during the discharge. When the stevedores finally got down to the last of the coal cargo we would be shovelling coal towards the centre of the hold for them to put into the grabs. That way it saved us a lot of work when it came to cleaning the holds ready for the next cargo. This we heard was to be a full cargo of dried peas to be loaded at Constanza in Roumania.

This meant that the holds had to be washed down with sea water after we had had a bilge-diving operation. This job, as usual, fell to the two Apprentices and me. The Carpenter would remove the limber boards and we would have to climb into the small bilge space and sweep it out, then move on to the next bay and do the same again until we reached the strum bay. That is the aftermost bay of the bilges, and it contains the bilge suction pipe, which is surrounded by a perforated metal box. The idea of the box being to stop any large pieces of material being sucked into and fouling the bilge pump in the engineroom.

If by any chance there was any water in the bilges and any grain from a previous cargo mixed in that water, then the stench was unbelievable. It stunk to high heaven, and it was not unusual to sweep up a dead rat or two, not an enviable task at the best of times. Holds swept and washed down, the limber boards would be put back in place. Any spaces between the boards would be packed with oakum and then the whole lot covered over with burlap, (a loose woven type of sacking), which was held in place by means of thin wooden laths nailed in place. The holds were now ready for the cargo of dried peas at the next port.

Our stay in Constanza was pleasant, as the weather was fine and very warm, so much so that sleeping in the small forecastle was almost impossible at night because of the heat. Most of us slept up on the forecastle head under the canvas awnings. Even up there in the more or less cool of the night, sleep was hard to come by, as we were pestered by myriads of bloodthirsty mosquitoes. Leaving Constanza, we sailed back through the Bosphorus and Dardenelles back into the Mediterranean towards the Straits of Gibraltar and on to the port of Antwerp, Belgium.

When we arrived there, it was getting extremely cold. I remember that standing on the poop at my docking station, I was nearly frozen in the keen brisk breeze. To add insult to injury, or so it seemed, the port authorities berthed us in Siberia Dock, one of the very large docks in Antwerp.

It was in Antwerp that I had my first taste of going into the "Red-light" district, not that I made any use of it, but like most other seamen, I was pestered by a number of "ladies of easy virtue", all who promised you a very good time at a reasonable rate, whatever that was. Looking at some of their faces, I decided that I would sooner remain a virgin sailor!

Schipper Straat was in those days the red-light district and the haunt of most of foreign seamen. The next time I saw Schipper Straat was after the war. Gone were the bars and the hoards of prostitutes. It was a deserted area down by the docklands. It bore no resemblance to the place I had seen in 1932.

Leaving Antwerp we sailed up to Immingham on the Humber to sign-off, re- sign for the next voyage with various changes of crew. My second voyage in the "Chelsea" turned out to be my first around the World trip, and lasting some seven months. On sailing from Immingham we proceeded to Huelva on the Southern coast of Spain. There we lay at anchor in the Rio Tinto for a couple of weeks whilst we loaded a full cargo of copper pyrites. The cargo was brought out to us each day by barges and loaded aboard using tubs and the winches. In those days, the town of Huelva was a quiet and friendly place. I spent many pleasant hours ashore there when the day's work was done. To get ashore we had our own "jolly boat" in the water and there was always someone not going ashore who was willing to man the boat.

When all who had been ashore returned to the ship, we had to lift the boat well out of the water on the davits. The idea being that the boat would not be stolen during the night, or break adrift and be lost in the tideway.

After a very pleasant stay in Huelva we sailed for Capetown, South Africa, calling en route at St.Vincent, Cape Verde Islands for coal bunkers and water, not that they could spare much water. Water was at a premium in the Cape Verde Islands, the whole place looked as though it had just popped up from the bottom of the Atlantic Ocean. There was little or no signs of vegetation anywhere, all I could see was volcanic rock. Nevertheless, it was a busy and important coaling station for steamers on their way to South America or South Africa. Coaling and oil bunkers, were as far as I know, the only trade the Islanders had to support them. I have often wondered what happened when ships went over to diesel engines and had no need to call at Cape Verde for bunkers. Still, if oil was cheaper there than other ports, the shipowner would have his ships calling there so as to save money.

Of all business people, shipowners were noted for their penny-pinching. It was reflected in their ships and the accommodation for crew and Officers. They were too mean when building a ship to have a dynamo fitted to give electric lights for navigation and the Officer's rooms, and much less the crew. The fitting of such a dynamo would have meant a great deal to those who sailed in the ships.

For instance, they could have had refrigerators fitted, which would have meant fresh meat would be fresh meat. I have seen meat come out of the icebox which most tramp steamers had to carry meat and fish in, coated with a lovely greenish mould.

Penicillin on the hoof to say the least!

When taking fresh stores, the icebox would be layered on the bottom with ice, the meat and or fish would then be put into the box and packed around with ice. Unfortunately, the ice would only last effectively for about ten days, especially if the ship was going South into the warmer climates.

I've watched the cook wash a link of sausages, which the crew were to have for tea, in a solution of Condy's crystals (Permanganate of Potash). This is a powerful disinfectant, but at least it made the sausages edible, without giving any of us food poisoning. Somehow or other, we all survived the grub that was dished up to us.

On the "Chelsea", we had Arab firemen and they were a bit wiser so far as fresh meat was concerned. When they knew that we had a long sea passage ahead of us, such as Durban to Australia, they would buy a couple of live sheep and a store of food for them.

The sheep would be tethered on the deck somewhere fairly safe. The firemen would water and feed them each day until the so-called fresh meat supplied by the ship ran out. At this point, one of the firemen, usually the one who acted as the prayer leader, would slaughter one of the sheep. I found it a bit disturbing when I saw him slit the throat of a sheep and let it bleed to death.

After this he would skin and dress the carcass ready for cooking.

This way they had really fresh meat when everybody else on board was making do with the salt beef or pork. Many of those barrels of salted meat had been packed for many years before being opened for use. At least the firemen were generous enough to always offer some of the fresh meat to us sailors.

It was in the "Chelsea" that I learned how meagre the weekly food rations for seamen were, as provided according to the Merchant Shipping Acts of 1906.

The average shipowner didn't believe in giving any more than he was legally obliged to.

The weekly scale, per man, was as follows:-

Fresh water, 7 gallons. Soft Bread, 3 lbs. Biscuits, 4lbs.

Biscuits did not mean fancy types, only hard Water biscuits in place of bread, these were often the home of weevils, and they had to be knocked out before eating them. Such biscuits were issued when the weather prevented the Cook from baking bread for the crew. They were as hard as rock and the only way to eat them was to dunk them in your coffee or tea.

Salt Beef, 3lbs. Salt Pork, 2 lbs. Preserved Meat, (Corned Beef), 2.5 lbs. Fish, 0.75 lb. Potatoes, 6 lbs. Dried vegetables, 0.5 lb.

Peas, split, 2/3 pint. Peas green, 1/3 pint. Haricot beans, 1/3 pint.

Flour, 2 lbs. Rice, 1/2 lb. Oatmeal, 8 ozs. Tea, 1.75 ozs. Coffee, 4 ozs.

Sugar, 1.25 lbs., of which the ship kept back 0.25 lb. ostensibly for cooking purposes, or so they said. Milk, condensed, 1/3 lb. (This meant that we got one tin of milk per man once every 3 weeks).

Butter, 0.5 lb. Marmalade or Jam, 1 lb. (Actually we never saw jam, that was reserved for the Officers).

Syrup, 0.5 lb. Suet, 4 ozs. Pickles, 1/2 pint. Dried fruit, 5 ozs.

Fine salt, 2 ozs. Mustard, 0.25 oz. Pepper, 0.25 oz. Curry powder, 0.25 oz. Onions, 3 ozs.

Our greatest need was sugar, milk and tea. These were items that were not sufficient for a man's weekly ration. To eke out the tea ration, we used to work out how many times tea would be mashed per day, multiply by 7, and that would be the number of little paper bags of tea we would make up. Old newspaper was used to make conical bags. One bag being used to make the tea for the entire Deck crew. As the tea was mashed in a 7lb. butter tin, it was rather weak. We overcame that by the addition of a teaspoonful of sugar, which drew out the strength in the so-called tea.

One way or another, we seemed to get by on our rations. Water, of course was another thing of which we were kept very short. The average tramp ship only had one tank capable of holding only 25 to 30 tons of water, which equals 5,600 to 6,720 gallons of potable water. For this reason, as soon as the ship sailed on a long passage, the water pump was locked up so that only water for the galley, cooking and drinking could be obtained.

Water for washing yourself had to be had from the "hotwell" in the engineroom, and only then with the permission of the Engineer on duty. This water was condensed from the exhaust steam from the engine, consequently it was very soft and always had an oily smell about it. Ships did carry a condenser in the engineroom, capable of producing drinkable water from sea water if necessary. Such apparatus was never used, the excuse being that the cost in fuel was too great per ton of water so produced. The same old story of penny-pinching again. Sod the crew but save the shipowner money for him or be out of a job! To become a better sailor, I naturally wanted to go to the wheel and learn how to steer properly. When I went to the bridge to ask the Chief Officer if I could go to the wheel, the Captain was there too. He asked me if I could "box the compass". I told him I couldn't. His reply was that I should first learn to box the compass and then he would allow me at the wheel. That meant that I had to learn all the 32 points of the compass and be able to recite them in correct order right round the compass. In addition, I had to memorise all the quarter points as well and to be able to say them in reverse order. That is, to say them from North by quarter points round through West to South to East and back to North.

When I was able to do this I went back to see the Captain and he listened to me boxing the compass. Thus satisfied, he let me go to the wheel to learn how to steer a ship. Of course, I initially had an Able Seaman standing alongside me to put me right if I made an error and didn't put the helm on the right way to keep the ship on a straight track. In the meantime the Officer of the Watch would be keeping a beady eye on the wake of the ship. By this he could tell how well or badly I was steering the ship.

Before long, I became a proficient helmsman, doing longer and longer spells at the wheel in my spare time off duty. At that time, I was on daywork, that meant that I started work at 6 a.m. and worked to 8 a.m., then 9 a.m. to 12 noon, then 1 p.m. to 5 p.m., when I knocked off for the day. I also finished work at 1 p.m. on a Saturday afternoon until 6 a.m. on the Monday morning.

The watch-keepers, on the other hand worked 4 hours on and 4 hours off, because there were only two watches on deck whereas the firemen had three watches. That meant that they had 4 hours on and 8 hours off duty. It wasn't until January 1st 1937 that the National Union of Seamen managed to get three watches for the deck crowd. My keenness to steer a ship was to be my loss, on a long passage I was put into one of the watches, thus releasing one A.B. so that the Chief Officer could get more work done. Not that I minded initially, but it meant that I was now doing 84 hours work a week for the paltry sum of £3 a month.

Imagine, 12 hours a day, 30 days a month, that is 360 hours.

That works out at 6 hours work for every shilling (5p) of my wages! How many people would work for that these days - the answer is none, they wouldn't be so daft!

Having bunkered at St.Vincent, we proceeded down to Capetown, our discharge port. What a marvellous sight it was approaching the port. The Table Mountain had the cloud covering the plateau at the top. This I was told was known as the Tablecloth. Passing the penal settlement on Robin Island, we picked up our Pilot and steamed into port. I found Capetown a really marvellous place to go ashore. In the days I am speaking of there was no such thing as Apartheid, though there were places where Whites and Blacks could not mix. There was segregation of the two, but there was little trouble for foreign seamen on their visits ashore at night. In fact, the females of the coloured people used to be allowed on the docks and to board the ships to flaunt their wares to any seaman wanting to indulge in a little sexual relief.

The average fee for their services was 2/6, (13p), provided they were disease free. That was value for money! As condoms were not issued or even carried aboard ships in those days, seamen took great chances with their health. However, there is a saying that a standing prick has no conscience. After a long sea passage, men put aside all conscience when it comes to fulfilling sexual needs. Not infrequently, some of them had reasons to regret their foolish actions. There was no penicillin or M and B tablets for the treatment of V.D. at that time. Treatment aboard ship was crude but ashore it was brutal to say the least, from what I heard from those who had had such treatment.

After discharging in Capetown, we then proceeded round the coast to Durban, where we stored and bunkered for the long run across the Indian Ocean to Sydney, Australia, calling next at Freemantle for further coal bunkers, On this run we headed on what was known as a composite Great Circle course.

A Great Circle course is the shortest distance between two places in the world. However, to take the full Great Circle course from South Africa to Australia, would take a ship too far South into Latitudes where Antarctic ice could be encountered. To avoid this, the composite course is followed. This means that the ship started off on the Great Circle and continued until it reached Latitude 41 degrees South, when it would continue along that Latitude until it reached a point where it could rejoin the Great Circle to its destination.

The run from South Africa to Australia is a long and very lonely one, just thousands of miles of ocean. The only life around were the albatrosses, the dolphins and the flying fish.

All of these are a pleasure to behold, dolphins playing in the bow wave of the ship, albatrosses gliding along at the speed of the ship without the use of their wings except to float on the air currents. Flying fish are marvellous to watch as they take to the air from the water when they are disturbed. Their scales are iridescent and beautiful to see. Not infrequently some of them would land on our decks during the night, those that did were rapidly collected by members of the crew. Cleaned and gutted they made a really tasty meal when fried. I know, I have savoured them when I have been fortunate enough to get there before any other member of the crew. The sad thing about those fish is the fact that when they die, the gorgeous colouring of the scales also dies with them. I have seen many a sailor try to perform taxidermy with a flying fish, in the hopes that he can take one home as a souvenir. No one ever succeeded in keeping them with their wonderful rainbow like colouring.

After a short spell in Freemantle for water and coal, we steamed away again to round Cape Luewin, to head East across the Great Australian Bight, a distance of some 1,200 miles to the Bass Straits, and then up the coast to Sydney.

The weather across the Australian Bight is very unpredictable, it can be reasonable, but most times it is unfriendly. We were very fortunate and had a reasonable run across it to the Bass Straits between Tasmania and the southern coast of Australia.

Arriving off Sydney Heads, the high cliffs at the entrance to Sydney harbour, a Pilot boarded us from a very old Pilot boat, the "James Cook".

Once through the heads the beauty of the sight of Sydney harbour became visible. There was the newly opened Sydney Harbour Bridge, built by the British firm of Dorman and Longs, spanning the harbour from Circular Quay to a point close to Taronga Park on the Northern side of the harbour.

We steamed under the bridge to berth at a place called Glebe Island, where we were to load a full cargo of bagged wheat for China. As we had several days there loading, I made a point of walking ashore and going for a walk across the bridge I had heard so much about. I have sailed under that bridge many times since that day, but I never walked across it again.

It was whilst we were berthed at Glebe Island that I saw the full impact of the "Great Depression". Every day whilst we were there, we would have several men coming down to the ship carrying small cans. They would sit outside the forecastle door and beg us to give them any morsels of food that we had left over from our somewhat meagre meals. They were doing this to try and feed their families, things were bad in Great Britain, but not as bad as out in Australia.

We always made a point of keeping something back from our meals, so as to give it to these poor fellows. Their profuse thanks really brought it home to you what a sad world it was. Even to this day, some 60 years later, I can still visualise those men waiting expectantly for crumbs from our table.

Years later, when talking to Australians during my subsequent voyages there, when told of those days they would not believe that such a state of affairs could have existed in Australia, the land of plenty. It did. I saw it all in the 1930s.

Fully loaded, we sailed from Sydney, for our next destination, Shanghai, some 4900 miles steaming North up through the Barrier Reef, through the Torres Straits and East of the Philippine Islands to the mouth of the Yangtse River.

Arriving there, we were berthed in the river close to the centre of the city, along with dozens of other ships, mostly British tramp steamers loading or discharging their various cargoes. At that time, China was not under Communist rule and seamen could go ashore quite freely, in pursuit of whatever their pleasures were.

We had of course, all the usual Chinese merchants coming aboard to sell us their wares. Seamen usually took advantage of the cheap suits which you could have made-to measure in a few hours. When I say cheap they were.

You could get a well made suit for about 30 Shillings (£1.50), suits of dungarees cost about 5/- or (25p). I actually had two teeth removed and a new palate with two teeth on it made for the sum of 5/-, and this done by one of the travelling Chinese dentists who came aboard and painlessly removed the broken teeth. He did not use any form of anaesthetic before removing those teeth, nevertheless I felt no pain. I can only think that he must have used some form of acupuncture, for which the Chinese are noted.

It might be as well to add that as we steamed out of Sydney harbour and through the Heads, we, the deck crowd, were engaged battening down the No.1 hatch. We had just stretched a new tarpaulin over the hatch when a freak wave climbed aboard over the forecastle head. With it came several tons of water which swept all of us down the decks, depositing us in the scuppers at the after end just below the bridge housing.

The Captain, who had only just rung "Full away", swiftly slowed the ship down so that we could get back and safely secure the No.1 tarpaulins in the cleats around the sides of the hatch coamings.

When this was safely done and all was secure, we proceeded at full speed again on passage. In the meantime we, all soaked to the skin made for the forecastle to strip off our wet clothes and dry ourselves out.

I didn't see any of the City of Shanghai, I confined my runs ashore to going on the liberty boat each evening to The Flying Angels Mission to Seamen, to enjoy the hospitality of that Mission. The boat came around just after tea each evening and brought you back again to your ship about 11 p.m. There was no charge for this service, it was entirely free. The hope was of course that those who took advantage of the service would attend the Mission, even if just for the service there. Most seamen put in a token appearance and then disappeared to take in the more erotic services of the local "girls" and the bars. If you missed the return boat then you had to get a sampan at the cost of about one Shanghai Dollar for the trip. Whilst we were there, a ship called the "Maidenhead" came and tied up astern of us. I knew two of the people on her, namely the Captain and the Chief Engineer.

Dressing up in my new suit of dungarees, I got a sampan to take me to see them. I was made quite welcome but as I was not "decently" dressed, they would not allow me to have tea with them in the ship's saloon. So ended my visit to the ship. I got a sampan back to the "Chelsea". I never saw those people again.

On completion of discharge at Shanghai we sailed for Vancouver, Canada, where we were to load a full cargo of grain. En route we called at a place called Muroran in the Northern Island of Japan for bunkers. I have never forgotten the sight of the snow covered mountains behind the town, set against a clear, deep blue sky. It was a breathtaking sight. As we were to be there a few hours I thought it a good chance to get ashore and try to buy some sugar. That was the stuff that I missed most, having a sweet tooth when it comes to drinking my tea or coffee.

With a few shillings sterling in my pocket I made my way ashore into the small town. Eventually I found a shop which I took to be a grocery store, and found that they had an open bag of sugar on display. I indicated by sign language that I wanted some of it, and the shopkeeper weighed out a quantity for me. I don't know what the weight was in Japanese weights, but there seemed to be about two pounds of it in the bag. I indicated that that was fine, and handed the shopkeeper a Sterling Half-a-crown, he seemed happy with it so the deal was complete. I had my store of sugar and he had been paid for it. As he raised no objection to the money I can only assume he was happy with the currency.

Shortly after I got back to the ship we sailed for the long passage across the North Pacific Ocean, and it was now mid-winter, so we could expect anything in the way of weather.

Fortunately, it was quite calm, but it started snowing and I have never seen so much snow fall continuously for days on end. It seems that we had taken a Great Circle course again, and this was taking the ship up close to the Aleutian Islands, hence all the snow.

Each morning, our first job was to shovel a path from the forecastle head, along the deck to amidships. The snow being up to 5 feet deep on either side of our path. Our little pot-bellied stoves gave us sterling service during that icy cold passage. We kept them going day and night. They were our only means of keeping warm, the side of them was glowing red-hot trying to heat that cold forecastle space we called our quarters.

As we got across the ocean and nearer to Vancouver, the weather became much warmer and wetter. The snow had turned to sleet by the time we berthed in Vancouver. Whilst we were there, we had the usual photographer come aboard trying to sell us a hand coloured picture of the ship entering the harbour.

They have been doing this for years and years as I found out when I visited the place years later. Mind you, they were good pictures and many of the crews of ships bought them if they wanted a reminder of a certain ship they had sailed in.

I remember my grandfather bringing one home of a ship called the "Ferndale", in which he served as ship's carpenter, and was away for two years on that voyage. Being away on voyage for two years was not uncommon in those days, when the Articles of Agreement were for three years duration. They had not as yet moved away from the sort of Articles that would have been signed when joining a sailing ship and could expect extremely long voyages. It was to be very many years before the length of those Articles was be made shorter.

In fact, if I remember rightly, It was after the war that the powers that be reduced it to two years. During our short stay in Vancouver I saw very little of the city, what time I had ashore was mostly spent at the Flying Angels Mission to Seamen.

The main reason for this being the shortage of funds, especially when you are only paid £3 a month. Our cargo was this time destined for Hull, my home town. This pleased me no end, and by the time we reached there I would have, for the first time, gone right around the World, having sailed over more than 32,000 miles of the ocean. We arrived in Hull on the 15th April 1933. I had 2 weeks at home then signed on again for another voyage.

Chapter 4.
More adventures on the "Chelsea"

This time it was to be a comparatively short voyage, light-ship to Nuevitas in Cuba for a cargo of sugar. The actual port was called Pastelillo, which was little better than a mosquito-ridden creek somewhere on the North coast of Cuba.

On arrival there I was made nightwatchman. It was cheaper for the shipowner to have a boy as watchman than a fully qualified Able Seaman. Penny-pinching again, it never ended so far as the shipowner was concerned. He wanted his pound of flesh. Thank heavens the National Union of seamen finally got the rules changed so that no boy could be put to work as a nightwatchman.

That however was many years later, after the war.

Looking back, I think that shipowners were the worst of all employers to give a little, in wages and conditions for the people who sailed in their ships and made them wealthy men. There were of course, exceptions to the rule.

I sailed in one such company, the Bolton S.S. Co. of London. I met up with the crew of one of their ships in 1934 in a Russian port, and the crew spoke very highly of the feeding and accommodation aboard their ship.

In those days, that was indeed an accolade if ever there was one.

At that time, little did I realise that in some future year I would in fact sail in the very ship that I had heard so much good spoken of, but more of that later in this story.

The sugar cargo we were to load was in bags, damned big bags, each one weighed 300 lbs, and these were manhandled by short stumpy stevedores. To carry that sort of weight on your back you needed to be short and stumpy. It was amazing to see the way they handled those bags of sugar, which were brought aboard by the ships winches, then lowered into the holds onto a platform made of bags of sugar. The men would then get a bag on their back and carry it to the far ends of the holds. There, others would place it carefully in position until the floor of the hold was completely covered with bags, and so it went on until the holds were full.

I only went ashore once in that port, I had got another seaman to keep my watch for me whilst I had a look at the place. The only way to the so-called town was by the single railway track from the port, there being no other road to it. Several of us crew walked ashore in the early evening along the track, which went through the main street of the place.

There wasn't very much to see, just the usual bars and shops, so after a quick look around the town we decided to go back to the ship. That is, after a final drink in the local bar. As it was now very dark, the barkeeper told us that it was "Muy malo" to walk back along the railway track. He insisted that for our own safety we should get a taxi back to the ship. We agreed with him and he ordered a so-called taxi for us.

It turned out to be a dilapidated pick-up truck, which was driven along the rail track, bumping over the sleepers on the way.

It was a most uncomfortable ride, but the driver was very used to doing this. On the way back, all we could see in the headlights of the truck, were thousands of green, large ugly and dangerous looking land crabs. We knew then why the barkeeper had said it was Muy malo (very bad) to walk along that track at night. I shudder to think what could have happened to any poor seaman befuddled by drink, falling in his tracks along that way back to his ship. I could not imagine he would be a very pretty sight when found, having seen all those voracious crabs scuttling about.

Our cargo of sugar was for the sugar mills in London, and we moored in the middle of the River Thames and discharged it into barges to be taken ashore. The London dockers used a unique way of discharging. They used a swinging derrick. This entailed setting one derrick up clear of the hatchway on the opposite side to that where the barges would be moored. A wire from the swinging derrick would be led through the head-block of the stationary one, and to it was a weight added in the form of a 40 gallon drum of sand.

When a sling of bags of sugar had been lifted clear of the hatch, the swinging derrick was hove across the ship and overside by winch. The sling was then lowered into the barge and unhooked.

The runner of that winch was then hove in, and as the hook came clear of the bulwarks the weight of the sand barrel would bring the derrick back inboard over the hatch again.

There was a hazard to this method, for if you were walking along the deck and failed to look up for the weight, you were in danger of being clobbered by the descending drum. I know, because I failed to look up as I went along the deck, and the weight caught me on the shoulder and knocked me to the deck. Fortunately I escaped with nothing more than a bruised shoulder. It could have been much worse if it had struck me on my head.

There should have been somebody shouting, the usual recognised signal "Under below" to look up for a falling danger.

When we finished our discharge of the sugar cargo we sailed for West Hartlepool, where we paid-off and signed on for the next voyage. This time we loaded a full cargo of coal for Venice, of all places. I could hardly imagine a place like Venice having heaps of coal.

During the time, several days that we were in Venice, I had chance to walk around the town quite a lot. I've walked over the Rialto Bridge, I saw the Bridge of Sighs, St. Marks Square, the Doges Palace, and the famous Camponile, the bell tower.

The last night we were in Venice, I got lost trying to find my way back to the ship from St.Marks Square. After many vain attempts to ask Italians the way, I was in distress, I knew the ship was due to sail early in the morning, so it was imperative that I got myself back to the ship. When I'd just about given up hope of finding my way back, three sailors came up to me. One of them asked me if I was in trouble. I explained to them that I was lost and didn't know the way back to my ship. They asked me the name of my ship, I told them the "Chelsea". It was then that they told me that their ship was lying just astern of us at the coal quay.

They were from a Yugoslavian ship, all spoke good English, and got me back safely to my ship, and for that they had my undying gratitude.

I made sure after that, that I was always able to find my own way back to my ship after a jaunt ashore.

On finishing discharge and sailing from Venice, the next leg of our voyage was to be the long run, light-ship to Sydney, Australia again. This time it was to be through the Suez Canal, my first run through that famous seaway. At Port Said we were pestered with the usual tribe of salesmen, trying to sell their wares, be they "Feelthy postcards", or "Spanish Fly" to make the girls want you.

I have no idea whether that stuff really worked or not. I did not find out. I did however buy what I thought was a pack of the "Feelthy cards" as shown to me by the Arab. He must have been a past master of the art of sleight of hand. After he'd got my money and disappeared, I found that there was only one dirty picture, the rest the pack were just dirty playing cards. I wonder how many suckers have fallen for that trick over the years when passing through Port Said.

In Port Said we shipped the carbon arc searchlight, a far cry from the modern lights. The light was shipped over the bow, cables from it led to a resistance mat that looked rather like an old wire mattress from a bed. This in turn was coupled up to a steam driven generator. Steam for the generator engine was supplied by the ship through the deck steam lines.

What intrigued me was to see that Egyptian workmen come aboard carrying blankets when it was so hot. Little did I realise how cold it got at night after the sun had gone down. I soon found out as we sailed through the Canal that night, for it was almost freezing by comparison with the daytime temperatures. We changed Pilots at Ismalia, approximately half way through the Canal, and then continued until we reached Suez, where we dropped the Pilot and landed the searchlight and all its fittings into a barge. From there on it was "Full away" for the run down the Gulf of Suez and into the Red Sea. I had hoped that I might be able to see Mount Sinai on the way through the Gulf. No such luck, there was too much haze around to make out the biblical mountain of such note.

The run through the Red Sea was marvellous. The weather was flat calm, the sea like glass. The heat however, was greater than I had ever experienced before at sea. Inside our accommodation was like being in an oven, which it virtually was, being surrounded by steel plating and only the timber decking overhead to help keep the heat off the deckhead.

Passing through Hell's Gate (The Straits of Beb-el Mandeb), we called into Perim to take on the coal bunkers and water necessary for our long run to Australia. We had no chance of going ashore in that place, not that any of us would have wanted to so do. We were not there very long before we were on our way again. What a relief to feel the cool breezes in the Gulf of Aden. From there onwards we would have at least a cooling breeze through our tiny accommodation. Steaming along slightly North of East, we rounded the Horn of Africa and past the island of Socotra.

At that time, I believe, not a particularly friendly place, from what I heard of it.

Ahead of us was some 4,700 miles of steaming, across the Indian Ocean before we would reach Freemantle, Western Australia, our next port of call for bunkers, stores and water. The fresh water pump was locked as soon as we left the port for the long run to Australia. Seven gallons per week per man for drinking, washing and cooking, not a lot when you think about it.

To have a wash down, there was no such thing as having a bath, you needed a bucket of water. A normal bucket is 2 gallons of water, so bathing was kept to the minimum at all times. Nevertheless we all seemed to manage to keep ourselves reasonably clean. The drinking water pump, usually fitted inside or just outside the galley, was kept under lock and key, crew only being allowed to draw water for drinking purposes from it. If the ship was rolling when you tried to carry a 2 gallon bucket full of water all the way up the steel engineroom ladders, it was inevitable that you would spill some of it. The spilled water would cascade down the engineroom, much to the chargrin of the Engineer on duty down there. There would be a loud roar from down below casting aspersions on our legitimacy. Nevertheless it was all taken in good spirit, even though it happened day after day when someone went down below for water.

We eventually arrived at Sydney, and berthed again at Glebe Island berth to load bulk grain for Dublin, Ireland. The turn round this time was much faster than the previous time when we loaded a bagged cargo. I think we were loaded in 48 hours and then were on our way for the 12,000 mile run home.

As we were leaving the berth, the ship went astern and struck a wooden dolphin with a mighty crash. You could hear the timbers of it creak under the pressure of the weight of the ship. A hasty examination of the stern of the "Chelsea" showed no apparent damage to her. The dolphin also appeared to have survived the blow except for a few cracked timbers, so without further ado we sailed down the harbour.

When we finally dropped the Pilot off at Sydney Heads and the Master rang "Full away" on the engineroom telegraph, the Engineers opened up the steam throttle valves. The ship started to pick up speed as the revolutions of the engine increased.

It was then that it became apparent that all was not as well as had been thought. As the engines reached their top revolutions, there was a most uncomfortable vibration set up. It had become apparent that the ship must have bent or broken one of the blades of the propeller. To have gone back into Sydney and had the ship drydocked, as would have been necessary to make a real examination of the situation, would have been a costly job. More so because the ship was fully loaded, and would have needed extra special shoring to support the weight.

It was therefore decided by the Master to continue on passage home. To obviate the vibration problem, the Chief Engineer adjusted the engine revolutions down to a level were the vibration stopped. That was the speed of the engine for the long run back to Ireland.

Our average speed for the passage home was just around 7 knots. It took us 77 days to make the passage. Sailing ships have been known to do it in less time than that.

By the time we got up off the coast of Portugal, it was mid winter in early 1934. When we got into the Bay of Biscay the weather was absolutely atrocious, there was a full storm blowing in from the Western Ocean. The seas were mountainous, and we were hove to.

An idea of the height of the waves can be judged when I tell you that when a Union Castle two funnelled liner dipped into the trough between the seas, we could only see the tops of her masts.

Those seas must have been anywhere up to 70 feet high. All around us were dozens of other ships, all hove to for safety.

Our Radio Officer reported picking up the distress calls from 3 ships out in the Atlantic, all were in sinking condition.

They were the "Usworth" of Newcastle, owned by R.S.Dalgliesh Ltd. ; the "Blairgowrie", owned I think by Nesbitts of Glasgow, and one of Ropners ships and the "Rushpool", I think it was. There was one other ship, a Japanese, who was also in dire straits and calling for assistance to save lives .

Many lives were lost in that atrocious storm, which I have heard said was the worst on record, certainly proving how true the saying is "That Nature in the raw, is seldom mild".

We suffered only one casualty in the Bay, our messroom steward was caught by a sea as he was carrying the Engineers dinner from the galley to their messroom. The sea overtook him as he walked through the port outboard alleyway. It carried him along the deck and dropped him in the middle of No.4 port steam winch.

It was the Engineer, stood waiting for him in the lee of the messroom, who saw him spread-eagled in the bed of the winch. At great personal risk, he dashed down onto the after deck and pulled him out of the winch before another sea could come aboard, and which no doubt would have killed him.

As it was, he was unconscious and very badly lacerated. They carried him to the saloon, were the Captain attended to his injuries as best he could with the available dressings.

On arrival in Dublin there was an ambulance waiting at the berth to take the injured man straight to the hospital. He was still in hospital when we sailed for the Tyne, on completion of our discharge.

On arrival at the River Tyne, the "Chelsea" was moored in the river just off Commissioner's Quay to await orders. It was whilst we were there that we had some Geordies come aboard and ask the Chief Officer if they could clean and sweep the holds for him. They did not want any payment for the service, all they asked was that they could keep any and all grain that they swept up from the holds. This they said was to help feed the chickens they kept at home to provide eggs for their families.

This will give the reader some idea of the desperation of people during the years of the "Depression".

After a few days lying at anchor we received orders to proceed up river to Dunston to load a full cargo of coal. We had to wait a few days, lying at anchor off the coaling berth.

It was whilst we were there that one of the sailors taught me the art of sculling a jolly boat, that is propelling the boat along through the water using only a single oar over the stern of the boat. As it was a tideway, it was an ideal place to learn how to handle the boat. In a day or two I was truly proficient at the art.

As we had a weekend at the anchorage, all the deck crowd except me were ashore on the Saturday afternoon. The shipowner didn't pay to have any crew member on duty at weekends, the only exception being the nightwatchman.

The Captain, Captain Smith, had his wife and child on board and he wanted to get ashore with them. He came forward to see if there was a sailor aboard who would take him and his family ashore in the boat. He saw that I was the only one up forward, and said that he had hoped that there would be a sailor there to get him ashore.

I said that I would take him ashore if he so wished, but he did not think that I was good enough to do the job. After all, so far as he was concerned I was only a Deck Boy, and he didn't consider me capable of handling a boat in the tidal river. I told him I would be glad to take him ashore, he was very hesitant, but I assured him that I could handle the boat as well as any A.B. He then agreed that I could scull him and his family across to the coal jetty. He was more than surprised at the way I put the boat alongside the quay right at the steps for getting ashore.

That was another feather in my cap, and another step to being a good sailor.

I spent my evening going to the pictures, in the cheapest seats available at the local cinema. Whilst we were at Dunston I saw two films I have never forgotten. One was " Hindle Wakes" and the other was" Love on the Dole". If I remember rightly, Gracie Fields starred in the first one. Eventually we loaded our coal cargo, it was for Venice again. I did not get lost in Venice the second time there, I'd learned my lesson the first time at that port.

After discharging the coal, we proceeded to the Black Sea to Poti.

What a desolate port it was and very much under the harsh regime of the Stalin government. Foreign seamen were allowed ashore, but there was a very strict curfew in practice, and all seamen had to be back aboard their ships by midnight.

If not back on board they needed to be off the streets, when they spent the night in some girls small shack. Two of us did just that and spent the night with a female, and returned to the ship in the morning. We got away with it without any bother. Possibly the guard understood the needs of seamen when ashore amongst delectable females. He might once have been a seaman himself.

We each had a pass, which you had to produce to the armed guard at the foot of the gangway as you went ashore. He noted down that you had left the ship at whatever time, on returning you had to produce your pass again and he would tick you off the list as being back aboard the vessel.

If perchance you were challenged to stop on your journey to or from the ship, it was in the interests of your own safety to stop instantly. The guards were trigger happy, one Chief Engineer of a ship failed to stop when so challenged by a guard on the dock.

He did not live to tell the tale, the guard just shot him.

No money was issued to spend ashore, instead we were issued with "Torsin Stamps". These were stamps with varying values in Kopeks or Roubles on them. These could only be used in the "Torsin Store", this was a government run shop especially for foreign seamen or visitors. The resident Russian people could not buy anything from that store. In it was all the things unavailable to the ordinary Russians. All the goods in the store were considered as luxury goods. Things like clothing, perfumes, cosmetics, ladies stockings and underwear. We could also use the stamps in the cafe next door, where we could get drinks or food, and we could also use them at the only place of entertainment for foreigners, the "International Club".

The club, run by the government was hosted by very charming young Russian girls. These girls would act as dance partners at the club.

There was only two other ships in the port of Poti when we arrived. One was a British ship called the "Romney". She was loading a cargo of manganese ore for Baltimore in the United States. I met and talked with several of the crew of her at the club. As usual our conversation got around to what our ships were like for accommodation and most important of all, what did they feed like?

The crew of the "Romney" said they had fairly good accommodation by the standards of those days, and as to food, she was a very good "feeder" and a good ship to serve in.

That was indeed a real accolade for the Owners of the ship, Boltons of London.

Some days after our arrival the "Romney" was due to sail and the last night she was there, the club put on a party for the crew and our crew were also invited to attend the party. The Russians put on quite a spread foodwise for us all. There were the parting farewell speeches, and lots of handshakes as the crew of the "Romney" left the club to return to their ship. With the sailing of the ship, little did I know that ten years later she would play a big part in my life at sea.

In addition to being able to buy things at the store with the stamp, I discovered that I could also buy the sexual favours of a very pretty Russian girl with them. I'd met her after leaving the club early one night, she spoke a reasonable amount of English, which the girls in the club did not appear to do.

This girl made it plain that she would like to obtain some "Torsin" stamps as she could use them to buy things she could not otherwise obtain. She explained that she would be able to use the stamps in the store. This, it seemed, was permissible.

The result was that we ended up in a very deserted street and I had sex for the first time, on the grass verge in that street.

It was worth a couple of the stamps, she was satisfied financially, and I, sexually!

We were invited to visit the other ship in the port, a Russian one. On board, we were made very welcome by the crew, and they showed us around their quarters. I must admit that they were better than ours aboard the "Chelsea". They even had a bathroom with a real bath in it, and they had running water laid on too, which was more than could be said for our British ship.

The main topic of the conversation seemed to be all about our system of health service and unemployment benefits when people were ill or out of work. I realised later that these crewmen were really spies for their government, trying to get all the information possible about Britain. The day our loading was completed and the ship ready for sea, a good number of our ship's personnel went ashore to enjoy the International Club for the evening prior to sailing. They held a small party for us too, but of course there was only the few men from our ship there. When time came for us to leave the Club, the hostesses were at the door to wish us Bon Voyage. I remember saying to one of the girls who I had fancied during our stay there "Goodbye". To my amazement she replied in perfect English "Please don't say goodbye, it is too final and means that we shall never meet again, instead say " Au Revoir".

You could have knocked me down with a feather, those girls had been able to understand every word we said amongst ourselves, such as how we would have liked to screw them given the chance.

No wonder they had often laughed when they heard some of our conversations when we were with them at the Club. It turned out that they could all speak perfect English. So ended our stay at Poti, we had loaded a full cargo of manganese ore for Japan.

Our discharge port was to be a small place called Fushiki, I think the port must in recent years have been renamed. I have not been able to find it marked on any atlas in my possession.

It appeared that on arrival there, our ship was the largest that had ever been to the port. This was for the dignitaries of the town a great occasion, and we had all sorts of visitors down to the ship. One day we had the entire school populace come aboard, each and every one of the children carrying a note book and pencil. I gathered that they had to note down all they saw on our ship and would have to write an essay about their visit to a large foreign ship. The kids swarmed everywhere, they were down the engineroom making copious notes of all they saw. Everybody aboard our ship was very tolerant, after all, children are children whatever their colour, race, or creed.

This much I can say, they were all very well behaved.

It was in Fushiki that the other Deck and I made our first visit to a brothel. When we went ashore, neither of us had many Yen to spend. We did however know that the local Shipchandler was also the ship's agent. We boldly went into his place and asked for a sub of a few Yen. "The Captain will pay" we told him, so he advanced us a few Yen each after we had signed a note saying that we had drawn the sub from him.

With these ill-gotten gains we made our way to the local red light part of the port and made our acquaintance with the local Madam, who put each of us in a room with a kimono clad female. A room, where the bed was simply a straw mat on the floor, the female laid down, resting her neck in one of the traditional blocks which served as a pillow Japanese style. To me it looked hellish uncomfortable, still it was only for a few minutes of the "short time" and then we were on our way back to the ship.

My experience that day, exploded the myth of the "Tramlines running East and West" where the Oriental females are concerned!

The next day, the Captain sent for the two of us Deck Boys, giving us a right dressing down for having the temerity to go and draw cash without his permission. He was right of course, he asked us what we had done with the money. We made some sort of excuse or other, after all I do not think he would have been very chuffed if we had said that we used it to bag-off, as the seaman jargon has it. After a good bollicking he let us go, but warned us never to try and do such a thing again. I noticed a flicker of a smile on his face when we made our excuses as to the use of the Yen. I think he had a good idea of what we had spent it on, after all, he had been a young apprentice when he first went to sea and would have had all the same urges as we had.

Leaving Fushiki, our next port of call was Darien, otherwise known as Port Arthur, in Manchuria.

This place had once been ruled by the Russians, and for all the world was very much Russian. We loaded a full cargo of maize there, which was destined for Hull.

This was my 5th and was to be my final voyage serving in the "Chelsea". We had had a new Chief Officer for this voyage, and for some reason or other he did not seem to like me very much. Throughout the voyage he had tried to give me a dog's life. It seems that he was aware that I knew people in the owner's office, and his idea was that I had been put there as a spy for the company. This of course, was far from true. I was just an ordinary member of the crew of the ship. One fine morning, on the way West across the Indian Ocean, I was at the wheel and I noticed a flashing light on the horizon. I called to the Chief Officer, who was on watch at the time, and told him there was a flashing light right ahead of us. He had a look in the direction I'd indicated, and then turned and said "There's no bloody light there".

Just then the light flashed again and I told him so. He had another look and told me I must be seeing things.

I insisted that there was a bright flashing light ahead, with that he came into the wheelhouse and told me not to be "Bloody well cheeky".

I knew that I had definitely seen a bright flashing light ahead, and I repeated it. With that he raised his hand to give me a backhander across the face. I moved my head to one side and then stepped down from the wheel platform.

"Mr Bowen," I said, "Just you try raising your hand to me again, and it will be the rock you perish on".

He got the message and went out of the wheelhouse, he could have had me up before the Captain on some charge or other and have had me logged. A logging would have cost me five shillings, a lot of money in those days. Worse still, it could have lost me a good discharge from the ship in my Discharge Book.

I had seen the light alright, it was the lighthouse on the island of Minicoy, a well known landmark for ships traversing the Indian Ocean, and the Chief Officer could now see it. It was probably that, which deterred him from making any complaint to the Captain.

After all, it would have cast doubts on the efficiency of his eyesight, if I could see it and he couldn't. Our passage across the Indian Ocean was during the monsoon period, April to September. Most of the way we had a very pleasant passage, but as we got further West and near to the Island of Socotra we felt the full force of the monsoon winds.

These winds come from the Southwest and can be very fierce as we found out. The sea was whipped up into a frenzy just North of Socotra, and our ship got a real hammering, the seas were piling aboard. I don't know what the situation was, but the Captain ordered all hands amidships wearing their life-jackets.

I remember being called out and told to don my lifejacket and get along to the galley. Having got safely along the foredeck, despite the seas crashing over it, I made it to the galley. There was the rest of the deck crowd, all huddled in the galley, awaiting whatever orders might come from the bridge.

We were never told what the emergency was, and I have often wondered, was the Captain in fear of the ship sinking in those awesome seas. Eventually we made the lee of the Horn of Africa, and of course the seas died away as if nothing had ever disturbed it.

Shortly afterwards we arrived at Perim for coal bunkers and some fresh water to take us through the Red Sea to Port Said. There we took a further supply of coal, sufficient to get the ship home to Hull.

The bunkering system at Port Said was unique, all done by hand.

First, the gang would rig stages over the ship's side, each one at a different level until they reached deck level. The barge of coal would come alongside with a large gang of coolies. Some of these would stay on the coal in the barge, others would man the stages at each level, then the bunkering started.

The men on the barge filled small baskets with coal, each basket would hold about 28 lbs. of coal. These would be handed up to the chaps on the first stage, they in turn handed it up to the next stage, and so on until the men on deck grabbed it and dumped it down the bunker hatch.

This may seem a slow method, but in fact it was one of the fastest bunkering stations in the world. There would be hundreds of baskets on the move all the time. As each basket was tipped out, the basket was thrown down onto the barge to be refilled.

The tonnage of coal moved in an hour was simply amazing.

Bunkering finished, we sailed on the final leg of the journey home, arriving in Hull on the 19th September 1934.

We signed off the following morning at the Mercantile Marine Office, so ended my service in the s.s."Chelsea" as Deck Boy.

I had sailed in her for a day or two over two years, in which time I had travelled some 100,000 miles of ocean in her. It was now time to have a spot of unpaid leave before looking for another job.

By a strange quirk of fate, I was to meet that Chief Officer of the "Chelsea" who disliked me so much, at a later date.

I think that he would have preferred that we had not met again, in view of the circumstances, but more about that meeting in a later chapter.

Chapter 5
Three years at sea completed

I see from my Discharge Book, that on leaving the s.s."Chelsea" on the 20th September 1934, I was ashore for a little over a month. During that time I went looking for another job at sea, this meant going down to the Shipping Federation Office in Posterngate to see what ships, if any, were wanting crew members.

One such ship I noted was the s.s. "Lilburn", lying in Alexandra Dock, Hull.

She was wanting some crew, so I then went across the road to the Seaman's Union Office, and asked if they needed an Ordinary Seaman. The Union said she did want one such rating.

I told them I was interested in the job, whereon they asked to see my Union membership card, to check that I was up to date with my subscriptions to the Union. I was, so they issued me with a PC5.

Now a PC5 was an introductory card from the Union to the Master or Chief Officer of a ship when applying for a berth.

Armed with this card, I went down to the ship. I cycled there, that was my only means of transportation, other than a tram to the docks in those days.

I found the ship lying under one of the coal hoist berths, ready for loading. I boarded the ship and saw the Chief Officer, and told him I had been sent down by the Union for the job as an Ordinary Seaman. I was promptly asked for my Discharge Book, which I handed to the Officer. He had a look through it to see what sort of discharges I had entered in the book. Times were tough in 1934, which meant that if any of your discharges were not V.G. (V.G., that is very good for ability and conduct), then you had little chance of getting a job.

In my case, all discharges were V.G. so the Chief Officer said that I could have the job. He signed the card I had handed him on arrival and gave it back to me.

His signature on that PC5 meant that I was provisionally accepted for the job as Ordinary Seaman.

The provisional part of it meaning that if I passed the necessary medical check-up and was available to sign on the ship when she opened her Articles. He told me that the ship would be signing-on the following day, and that I was to be at the Shipping Office at 10 a.m. next morning.

I thanked him and left the ship to cycle back to the Union office to let them know that I had got the job. They in turn handed me a form to take across to the Shipping Federation Office, wherein the Doctor who gave us the medical had his surgery. This form was to request the Doctor to medically examine me prior to being signed on the ship.

These medicals were a bit of a farce really, the Doctor sounded your chest, had you drop your pants. First he would look for any signs of venereal disease, then gently holding your testicles, he would ask you to cough. I have never found out what that proved. Some used to say it was to find out if you had a hernia or not. Then he would produce the chart to test your eyes for colour blindness. This was a card with dozens of coloured dots on it, but somewhere amongst those dots was a couple of numbers. If you could tell him what those figures were, then your colour vision was O.K.

I passed the exam on all counts, so now I was all set to sign on the ship.

Attending the Mercantile Marine Office at the appointed time, I was signed on, Ordinary Seaman. My wages were to be £4.10.0. per month. As usual, all the new crew were ordered to report on board the ship at "One minute past midnight" that day.

In other words, get yourself complete with seagoing gear, aboard the first thing next morning. The ship was not a very large one, she was of about 1,500 tons deadweight.

She was in other words, what is known as a Short Sea trader, owned by a now defunct Company called Smith Hoggs, of West Hartlepool. Her main trade was coal out from Britain to Spain or Portugal and iron ore back to this country. I understand that she also did runs into the Mediterranean to bring back Esparto Grass, used I think for paper making.

I was not fortunate enough to manage one of those runs. We loaded a cargo of coal for Bilboa in Northern Spain. We had several days moored in the river there right opposite a bar, which was much patronised by our crew during the stay in port.

On the Saturday afternoon, I was ashore in the bar with a couple of shipmates and was getting on famously with a very pretty barmaid. It seemed that I was going to be able to date her when she finished work that day. Of course, my intentions were purely sexual, I hoped, if I took her out. My shipmates, it seemed, were not too pleased with my progress with this dame. They kept plying me with drinks, little did I know that they were spiking those drinks with brandy, which was very cheap in Spain at the time.

When it was time to go back to the ship for tea, I could hardly stand, let alone walk.

Somehow or other, my shipmates, responsible for my condition, got me into the jolly boat and back to the ship.

I was however in no condition to climb the ladder over the side.

We did not have a gangway fitted over the side, only a rope ladder. To get me safely aboard they fixed a bowline under my armpits and hauled me aboard that way.

They then took me to my room, which I shared with another seaman, dumped me on my bunk, and left me to sleep off the effects of the booze.

I awoke some time later with a head that felt like a ten gallon piss pot, and I felt bloody awful. When I had fully recovered from the effects, I washed, shaved and dressed for shore going, and went back to the bar. The barmaid didn't want to know me, not after she had seen the state I had been in. So ended what might have been a lovely friendship.

It might have been fun to those shipmates to see me get pissed as a newt, but little did they realise that they had done me a favour, one which was to last me my lifetime.

I swore never ever to get drunk again, and I never did, in fact I became almost a teetotaller, having a small drink only under force majeur. By that, I mean when necessary to act friendly when with other people.

After leaving Bilboa we sailed along the coast to a place called Vivero to load iron ore for home. What a God forsaken place that was. It was simply a small bay in some very high cliffs and the ship had to be moored with all the ropes possible, such was the heavy swell coming in from the Bay of Biscay.

We had to hold the ship under a spout jutting out from the top of the cliff, down which the iron ore poured.

Only one hold could be loaded at a time, so this meant that we were constantly having to move the vessel under the spout into other holds.

This moving process was fraught with danger owing to the surging of the ropes on the drum ends of the windlass or the poop winch. Neither of these were fitted with what are known as whelps, that is, horizontal bars welded to the drum ends. These whelps stopped ropes from running back when a great strain came on them as the ship ranged on the swell rolling in.

In one incident, whilst heaving the ship along to another hold, two surged over the poop winch drum end. This happened just as the 2nd Officer, who was in charge of the moving operation on the poop, was stepping between the ropes. The ropes caught his leg just at the ankle and was towing him into the fairlead.

The loading Foreman saw his plight and dashed to his aid. I have never seen a person wield a knife so fast as he did.

He slashed down and cut the Officers trousers leg free from the rope. He then pulled the 2nd Officer clear as the rope ran out. We the crew, handling the ropes were powerless to hold them against the tremendous weight of the ship surging.

There is no doubt that the speedy action of that Spaniard saved the 2nd Officer from serious injury. Had he been towed into that fairlead, he would probably have lost a leg.

I think it took us about two days to load our cargo of ore, and we were all glad to see the back of that port. It was not possible to go ashore, and in any case there was no town anywhere near the so-called port of Vivero.

Our cargo was for Middlesborough, where we discharged a few days later. The next outward cargo was to be coke from West Hartlepool. This cargo being so light and bulky, meant that we had to have cargo on deck as well as in the holds. To this end we had wire netting fitted above the gunwales of the decks to hold the cargo in place. Staunchions were erected along the deck at the bulwarks, then horizontal timbers were fitted to which the wire netting was fixed, thus forming a big pen in which to pour the coke.

Though they fitted some sort of catwalk for us the crew to get from our accommodation aft to amidships, it was a pretty hazardous job getting along the top of the cinder as the ship rolled at sea. In the English Channel we met rather inclement weather which we then had the rest of the way to Pasajes, a small port on the North coast of Spain.

The weather wasn't much better in the Bay of Biscay, which of course we had to cross to reach the port. We were pitching and rolling something chronic as we approached the coast line. To us, the deck crowd, it seemed as though we were steaming into cliffs about 400 feet high. We could see the seas breaking against the base of the cliffs. Where the hell was the so-called port?

When we were a few hundred yards off the cliffs, a small boat appeared creeping out of a split in the cliffs. This was the pilot boat. With difficulty, the boat made it alongside us and the Pilot came aboard to pilot us in through the "hole in the wall", for that is what it seemed to be. We had to admire the skill of the Pilot in handling the ship, rolling as she was in the Biscay swell.

To make matters worse she was also yawing about all over the place owing to the slow speed at which we were approaching the cliffs. Finally, the Pilot got our nose into the narrow entrance, and I do mean narrow entrance, it was little wider than the beam of the ship. It seemed that at any moment we would hit the base of the high cliffs on either side of the entrance as we slowly gained the harbour.

What a sight, it was as though we had entered another world. There was the quay and a couple of antiquated cranes and the whole town was sort of covered with a film of haze from the various chimneys.

Being in a deep hollow between the high cliffs, the smog could not get away from the town of Pasajes. It didn't take them long to discharge our cargo of coke and we were soon on our way to load at the port of Setubal on the Portugese coast. It was of course ore we loaded for Middlesborough again. Setubal was another of these ports affected by the heavy swell coming in from the Western Ocean. Our mooring was done using the 12" coir springs, to which our mooring ropes were fastened. These coir ropes have a great capacity for stretching when a heavy strain comes on them.

Fortunately for us, there was a mobile belt feed on the quay so this saved us having to shift the ship to facilitate the loading of the holds. This was another place where the town was several miles away from the ship, so very few of us bothered to go ashore.

In any event, I had developed what turned out to be a bad bout of 'flu, and on the way back home I was in a very poor state of health.

On arrival at Middlesborough, the Master of the ship decided that it would be in my best interests to pay off and go home. I heartily agreed with him as I felt bloody awful, so home I went to get treatment from my own Doctor. So that was the end of my stint in the "s.s. Lilburn".

Somehow or other, it seems that I stayed ashore for about three months after getting over the bout of 'flu. Jobs were scarce.

My next ship was the s.s. "Grodno", she belonged to Ellerman's Wilson Line of Hull, and I joined her as an Ordinary Seaman for a voyage into the Mediterranean. The "Grodno" was one of the many of Wilson's ships which traded from Hull with general cargoes for ports in Italy, Yugoslavia, Greece, Turkey. In fact, most ports in the Mediterranean. Our run was Italy and Yugoslavia.

Our cargo consisted of comparatively small parcels of general cargo for umpteen different ports. We carried everything imaginable, from heavy machinery to packages of tea, biscuits, bales of cloth, tools, crockery, you name it, we carried it.

We started off at Genoa with the discharge, then a few hours later sailed for Leghorn, then Carrara, and on to Naples, Messina and round the coast into the Adriatic up to Trieste.

At Trieste we used to have to use our anchor cable for mooring, owing to the terrifically strong Katabatic winds which flowed down from the high mountains around the port. Those winds were called Boreas, which means a wind from a Northerly direction. This was of course true because the mountains were to the North of Trieste, and at certain times of the year these winds come howling down into the bay where the ships were at anchor.

Leaving Trieste we then went to Sebenik, then Split and down to Dubrovnik.

We had a couple of days in Dubrovnik and it was a pleasure to go ashore there to see the very old walled port dating back many centuries. One afternoon I went for a swim in the harbour, I jumped in from the boat-deck and when I entered the water I went down so deep that I thought I'd never reach the surface again.

I swam for the shore, and stepping onto the beach, I stood on a sea anenome and ended up pulling dozens of its quills out of my foot.

At each port, as we discharged cargo we picked up cargo for home. For instance, at a port called Duggerat, in Yugoslavia, we loaded dozens of drums of Carbide for London. Also, on the way back we called at Carrara to pick up slabs of Carrara marble.

In all, we used to visit twenty ports in the month in the Medi.

I remember when we were discharging the drums of Carbide in St.Katherines Dock in London, one drum fell out of the sling of cargo and into the dock waters.

There was panic stations, the Dock Authorities called a diver to go down and find the drum so that it could be brought out of the dock.

When I asked what all the fuss was about, I was told that if they did not get it out of the water, and water got into the drum, there could be a nasty explosion. Such an explosion they said could badly damage the dock wall foundations.

Well, knowing that water on Carbide produces acetylene gas, and being tightly packed in a small drum, I could well imagine there would be an appreciable explosion.

Here in Britain, the Carbide was used to produce acetylene gas for welding purposes, and strange as it may seem, it was also used in cycle lamps in those days. I had one such lamp on my bicycle. You partly filled the lower container with dry carbide, the upper portion of the lamp was a water container, to light the lamp you turned a little valve which let water into the carbide. In a few seconds you had gas coming out of the lamp nozzle, strike a match and you had a gas lamp to light you on your way at night. Those lamps were quite popular with cyclists and cheaper to run than a battery lamp, and also far brighter light than from the old oil lamps used on bicycles.

It was not unusual on ships carrying general cargoes, for there to be a certain amount of broaching, (Stealing) of minor items of cargo. I must admit that the seamen were not beyond a little activity in this matter. On the "Grodno", we members of the deck crowd had raided No.4 hold one evening whilst we were in Trieste. Our haul consisted of a few packets of biscuits and packets of Brooke Bond tea. These we stowed away in our accommodation. The following morning it was noticed by one of the deck Officers that there had obviously been theft of cargo.

Word came aft that there was to be a search of our accommodation.

Panic stations, there was a furious dumping through the port holes of the incriminating evidence, before anyone came aft to make the search.

Imagine our relief when one of the dockers was seen to be stowing yards of material away. He was wrapping it around his waist. That removed all doubts about us, the crew, having anything to do with the broaching of the cargo. It was all put down to the Italians who were engaged in working the cargo out of the ship. So, we had to do without our ill-gotten gains of biscuits with our tea!

At the end of my second voyage in the "Grodno" I had completed my 3 years sea service on deck. This meant that under the Merchant Shipping Acts of 1906, I had become eligible for the rating as an Able Seaman. To get this rating I had to go to the Mercantile Marine Office in Hull and produce my Discharge Book to the Superintendent, to prove my 3 years at sea. He checked all and every discharge and length of each voyage. Having satisfied himself that I had in fact completed the necessary time at sea, he then wrote the endorsement in my book after which he stamped it with the official stamp. I now had the rating of Able Seaman, which meant that on my next ship, my wages would go up to £9. 12. 6. a month. Big deal! All I had to do now was to find a ship requiring an Able Seaman.

Chapter 6
"Cadillac" days

My Able Seaman's endorsement was dated the 1st of October 1935. Three weeks later, on the 22nd October I joined my first ship as an Able Seaman.

By some strange coincidence, the ship was to be the sister ship of the one in which I made my first voyage to sea. The name of the ship was the "Cadillac", another one of Anglo-American Oil Company's tankers. She was in all respects the same as the "Saranac", built about the same time in 1918, and accommodation and conditions were in keeping with those days. I think the only thing that had changed in all those years was the quality of the feeding of the crews. Certainly nothing else had changed, large open fo'castle for the ten members of the deck crew and similar for the Firemen. The voyage was from Salt End oil terminal to Baton Rouge, an oil port on the Mississippi River. The run up that river requires complete attention to the steering of the vessel. I had a two hour spell at the wheel on that passage up river and was congratulated on my steering by the Pilot.

On arrival at Baton Rouge, I was made the nightwatchman, not an enviable job. You were not allowed to smoke on board the ship, if you wanted to have a cigarette you had to go ashore to a little cabin specially designated for smokers. As a smoker, this wasn't much solace to me as nightwatchman, I had to be around the deck all the night. I did manage, when the duty officer went to have his supper, to dash ashore and have a cigarette before he missed my presence on the deck.

The next day I decided to have a look at the town,

I found that you were not even allowed to walk through the installation to get to the town. You had to wait for what they called a Jitney, a bus laid on by the oil company to take crew members and workers to the gates of the oil installation.

I wasn't very impressed with what I saw ashore and I was soon back aboard the ship with my meagre purchases. We sailed shortly afterwards, back to the U.K. This time our discharge port was to be Fawley, near Southampton. On the way home I had a brush with the Chief Officer of the ship. He was a nasty piece of work, and a bit of a megalomaniac. I was at the wheel during one of his bridge watches, and I happened to let my mind wander from my steering.

I got a blast from the Chief Officer, telling me to use less helm. As he was not in the wheelhouse I wondered how he knew that I was applying excess helm to correct my course. What I hadn't noticed was the fact that there was a helm indicator on the bridge telegraphs. In any case looking aft he could see a distinct kink in the wake, whereon he came into the wheelhouse and gave me a blasting, saying he would break my heart before the voyage was over. My reply was "You'll be lucky, Mister".

His next remark was that he would have me logged for insolence to an officer!

At 11 a.m. I was called to the Master's dayroom, were there was the Chief Officer. He made his charge to the Master, who in turn asked me what I had to say.

What was there I could say. Only that I had answered the Chief Officer back when he made the statement he did. The Master was reluctant to make any entry in the Official Log Book, but that bastard of a Mate insisted that I be logged for insolence.

Under those circumstances, the Master had no other option than to back his Chief Officer and make a log entry against me.

The entry in the Official Log book read something like, Number so and so in the Articles, A. Mathison, Able Seaman, for insolence to the Chief Officer, is hereby logged and fined the sum of 5/-.

This entry has been read out to the seaman, and his reply to the charge was "Nothing to say".

The entry was then signed by the Master, and witnessed by the Chief Officer, I was then told to get back to work.

Before we reached Fawley, I was informed by the Bosun that I would not be wanted on the next voyage as I would be paid off there.

On arrival at Fawley we had the Shipping Master on board to make the changes in the crew. When it was my turn to sign off and draw my wages for the voyage, the Shipping Master told me that the Master of the ship could not give me V.G.V.G. in my discharge book. He gave me the option of having V.G. for ability but either Good or D.R. for conduct. I would explain that D.R. means "Decline to report", and such an entry is frowned upon by prospective employers.

I was at a loss to know what to do for the best, when the chap behind me said "Take the Good in your book".

I told the Shipping Master to endorse my book with the Good in the Conduct column, this he did. I am glad the man behind me advised me what to do. A D.R. was known in seagoing jargon, as a burn-down, and with one of those in your discharge book, your chances of a job were nil at a time when jobs were at a premium amongst seafarers.

My period of service in the "Cadillac" had lasted just 1 month and 21 days. I hope Mr. Swann, the Chief Officer was proud of himself for my discharge entry. Fortunately it did not stop me from sitting for my first certificate as a navigating officer.

I did however have to convince the Board of Trade Examiner as to why I had been given that Good instead of V.G. He listened to my explanation, and was in fact rather sympathetic about it. He thought that the said Chief Officer had been a little out of order in the matter. After all, a good dressing down from the Master of the ship would have sufficed to keep me in order.

Having been paid-off, I was given my free railway warrant back to Hull, the port at which I had joined the ship. Even in the 1930s, if you were sacked from a ship, they had to give you free travel back home.

It was the 12th Dec. 1935 when I left the "Cadillac", and after a little while at home, I searched for another job as an A.B.. I had very little success, no one wanted to know me when they saw that "Good" discharge. All the Chief Officers had their doubts about my conduct. In the end I exercised the only option open to me, and that was to ship out as an ordinary Seaman again. It turned out to be a wise move, because at the end of my next voyage I got V.G. and V.G. in both columns of my discharge book.

The ship that I joined as O.S. was the m.v. "Sutherland". She was a brand new ship, and had just arrived in Hull after completing her maiden voyage to Vancouver for grain.

From what I heard, she was the first of the economy class Doxford Diesel engined ships, built by Doxfords on the Tyne. The engine was a three cylindered one, which made for fuel economy.

To carry economy even further, Doxfords had devised a means of using the exhaust gasses from the engine when at sea to heat a small Cochrane boiler. This boiler could provide enough steam to power the steam pumps, heat the accommodation, and provide hot water. In port, when the engine was not being used, the boiler was fired by oil, but it all added up to great economy, so precious to any shipowner. The Sutherland had a fair turn of speed, her normal sea speed was 11 knots in fine weather. The crew's accommodation was a real leap forward, as we were 3 men in a room. In other words one watch to a room, which was of course a good idea. Instead of the usual red asphalt composition on the decks of the rooms, there was timber decking, which we were able to wash and keep clean.

There were of course the usual steel framed bunks, but the room was light and airy. It was fitted with decent lockers for our personal possessions. In addition there was also a settee and a table, something I had never had before in any other ship.

The "Sutherland" had a raised forecastle head and poop, but otherwise she was a flush decked ship. The idea of the raised forecastle head and the crew poop space was so that she could carry deck cargoes of timber.

The rules and regulations stipulate that timber deck cargoes can only be carried on ships so built. The reason for this was to protect the timber from being lifted off the decks in heavy weather. If there was no housing to protect the ends of the stacked timber, seas crashing aboard could lift and shift the cargo.

I understand that the ship was built at a cost of 100,000 Pounds, of which 60,000 Pounds was for the engine and engineroom fittings, the hull therefore cost £40,000.

As she was of about 10,000 D.W. capacity, that works out at £10 per ton.

Today, the cost would be about £1,000 per ton, so a ship of that size would now cost ten million pounds. How times have changed.

As we were to make a light ship passage to Vancouver for grain and timber, the outward passage was very pleasant. Our work as deck crew was normal maintenance work after we had cleaned out the holds ready for a grain cargo. There was the usual cleaning and greasing of the derrick head and heel blocks, runner wires to oil and stow away until we neared the load port. A lot of time was spent on painting the ship, to get a decent thickness of paint on her steelwork to protect it from the salt air.

On arrival at Vancouver we loaded grain so that the holds were about 3/4 full, the remaining space was to be filled with timber to be loaded at Victoria, on Vancouver Island. This was to be the one and only time that I was to visit Victoria. We had a pleasant stay there loading the timber. When the holds were full, then they started loading the deck cargo, and did so until the cargo was about 8 feet high. That was the limit of our deck load height. Then came the lashing down of the timber, using chain and Warwick screws. The lashings were also fitted with Senhouse slips. These are a quick release method, used constantly for ship's lifeboats, where in an emergency the slip can be knocked free, and the boat or the cargo is free to go over the side of the ship.

Along the top of the deck cargo, staunchions were erected to carry lifelines for the use of anyone having to walk over the cargo, such as us the deck crew going from our accommodation to amidships or vice versa. If the ship was rolling heavily they really were lifelines, they prevented anyone from falling over the side into the sea. All these precautions are laid down in the timber deck cargo carrying laws for the safety of the ship and the crews thereof.

In Vancouver, I had bought my usual supply of extra sugar, and stowed it away in my locker. On the way south from Victoria I was in the 4-8 watch, and one morning the Chief Officer asked me to make a pot of tea for the Captain, who wanted to be called at 6 a.m., when we would be passing a certain point on the coast.

The Chief Officer gave me the teapot and some dry tea and off I went to the galley and mashed the tea. On taking it back to the bridge, the Officer discovered that there was no sugar left for the Old Man's cuppa. Apparently, the Captain, like me, liked sweet tea. I, thinking to be a Good Samaritan, told the Officer that I could bring a little of my own stock of sugar, which I did. I took about half a dozen teaspoons of the stuff to the bridge. The Mate thanked me for my generosity, and away I went.

For some reason or other, from that day onwards, the Captain took a great dislike to me, and I couldn't think why.

Then one morning I had occasion to get some of my reserve stock of sugar out for my own use. On opening the packet and about to spoon some into my tea, I noticed some larger than usual crystals on top of the sugar. This puzzled me, I wet my finger end and dipped it into the sugar to get some of the crystals on my finger. I then gingerly tasted the crystals, they were Epsom Salts! Some witty bastard of a shipmate had spiked the sugar with Epsom Salts, and in all probability the sugar I gave for the Captain , was more Salts than sugar.

I knew then why he had taken such a dislike to me, he would naturally think that I had done that purposely. With shipmates like that, who needs enemies! It all turned out O.K. eventually, when I explained to the Captain what had happened. He actually saw the funny side of it. I have had shipmates who have metaphorically given me the shits, but these had tried to do it literally.

It was on that ship that my palate with two front teeth, made in China, came to a sad end. I got into a fight with another crew member who hit me in the mouth, driving the gold clips through my lip and breaking the palate. He didn't get another chance to hit me again, because I floored him with one hefty punch over his heart. He just flopped out cold on the deck.

That incident rather frightened me, to think that I could put a man out with one of my punches. As a result it was to be many, many years before I ever lifted my fists to defend myself against an attacker. That happened when much later I was a Chief Officer of a ship, and one of the crew struck me on the chin whilst full of Dutch courage, but more about that incident in a later chapter.

Our cargo was destined for London, Surrey Commercial Docks, where we all signed off, and left the ship on the 11th July 1936, having been on the ship 3 months and 16 days. In that time we had covered just under 18,000 miles of ocean.

My discharge book was now endorsed with V.G. and V.G.

With that stamped in my book, I could now look for a ship as an Able Seamen again, which I did and 18 days after arriving home, I got such a job on another one of Wilson's ship out of Hull. This time it was the "Gitano". Her regular run was across the Western Ocean, the Atlantic, to New York with general cargo

She was a ship of about 5,700 tons deadweight, not a particularly large ship for the North Atlantic run. I remember that we went up to the Tyne to complete our outward cargo for the States.

We berthed at Jarrow Staithes for the night, when a lot of us crew went ashore. As the weather was a bit on the cool side several of us bought wooden soled clogs to wear around the deck. We knew these would keep our feet warm on passage.

I will always remember the Chief Officer. His name was Mr.Priest. He was known by all the crew as Just Priest, because of his habit of saying "So and so, will you just do this or that". It was always "Just do", whatever it was he wanted done!

Another of his idiosyncrasies, was, come hail, snow, rain or shine, he would have the crew wash the decks down every morning. I've been out on deck struggling with a leather hose pipe, slippery as a butcher's prick when wet, and it has been raining cats and dogs.

All Wilson's ships were supplied with these leather hoses. They were made from lengths of leather rivetted with copper rivets, and were very heavy to handle when wet.

To try to make things easier for the handlers, the makers did fit beckets, (Hand holds) about every 6 feet of the length of the hose. Properly looked after, these hoses would outlast the usual canvas hoses by years. To keep them in good condition, they were never allowed to dry out. When not in use they were kept in wooden barrels full of water, so as to remain pliable at all times.

If they had been allowed to dry out they would have been as stiff as a board, and no doubt would have cracked.

I remember that part of our cargo was umteen thousands of gallons of cod liver oil for the States. This we carried in No.3 Deep Tank, situated amidships. On discharge of that commodity in New York, we the deck crowd had the job of cleaning out the tank ready for the carriage of grain back to Hull.

Before we could do anything in the way of cleaning the tank, it first had to be steamed out by the engineers. After a night of steaming it, the lids were opened to allow the tank to cool down a bit and to get rid of the high humidity before we were allowed to enter it.

When conditions were O.K., we were then given loads of cotton waste. This we used to wipe down the sides of the tank until we got the place dry enough to accept a grain cargo.

As we had several days and nights in New York, several of us went ashore each night to sample the entertainment available.

A couple of nights we went to a cinema called Billy Minsky's. It was well known for the risqué shows on the stage. Cheap thrills were to be had from the "Bump and Grind" female performers on stage. Another night we went across the harbour on the ferry to the New Jersey side of the harbour. There we went to a very well known bar, the name of which escapes me at present. This bar was noted for the fact that they provided free food to anyone having a drink in the bar. There were trays of food from which you just helped yourself as many times as you liked whilst having a beer.

All together, our stay in New York was a pleasant one, but all too evident was the poverty due to the "Depression", with people on the streets trying to sell apples at a nickel, (5 cents) a time.

This was the only way some people could earn a few cents to try and live. Things were bad in Britain, but I do not think that we were ever in a state as bad as the United States were. Having discharged and loaded our cargoes, we sailed back to Hull.

On the way back we were overtaken by the "Queen Mary" on her way to Southampton. The weather at the time was fair but with a very heavy swell running. We were doing a fair bit of rolling about in the swell, but when the "Queen Mary" rolled in the swell, we could see right across the whole width of the ship. I'll bet there were a hell of a number of seasick passengers aboard her on that passage. Incidentally, she had passed us going West and then back East whilst we were still on our outward passage to New York.

That will give you some idea of the speed of that Cunarder.

We arrived back in Albert Dock in Hull on the 10th September 1936, and paid off the next day.

I had just 8 days at home and then I got myself another ship, this time it was one of Chapman's ships, the "Grainton" of Newcastle.

She was a typical single decked tramp steamer, whose usual trade was "Coal out and grain home". When I joined her in Alexandra Dock in Hull, she loaded a full cargo of coal for Rio de Janiero. She was unusual in the fact that she was fitted with a quadruple expansion engine. In other words she had 4 cylinders to her steam driven engine. This again, was an economy measure because the steam used to drive the engine, instead of only driving three cylinders, it was used in a fourth low pressure cylinder. This meant that all the energy that could be had from the steam produced by the boilers, was extracted before being exhausted and condensed back into water. The beauty of that system was the fact that when the engine was running, you could not hear a sound from the engine. Many a time I thought we were stopped because it was so silent compared with the steady throb of a 3 cylindered engine.

She had been designed especially for grain cargoes insofar as she had extremely deep hatch coamings, which were to act as feeders for the lower holds.

These feeders had according to law, to hold not less than 2.5% and not more than 8% of the capacity of the hold that they fed. The idea being of course as the grain settles down, as it does, then grain from the feeder moves down and fills the space again.

So long as the hold is full to the brim with grain there is no danger of it shifting to one side when the ship rolls. The danger is that if the grain did move over to one side, the possibility of the ship capsizing existed.

It was for this reason that the Grain Regulations came into existence many years ago.

The "Grainton" loaded coal in Hull for Rio de Janiero, Brazil, quite a common run in the pre-war days, and it was a run favoured by crews. Even if you sailed from the U.K. in mid winter, in a few days you were down into the fine warm weather, which you would have all the way to Brazil. As the saying was, "This is the weather we signed for". Hull to Rio was about a twenty-four day run, and on arrival there the ship was anchored in the open harbour. Rio harbour is one of the finest and prettiest in the world.

It has two very well known features, the Corcovada, a high peak with an enormous statue of Christ overlooking the harbour, with His arms outstretched, The other is the Sugar Loaf, an extremely high lump of rock in the shape of the one-time sugar loaves.

I have never been up to the top of the Corcovada, but one time when I was there I did make the trip up the Sugar Loaf by the cable railway. The view from up there was magnificent. Yet another attraction is of course the Copacabana beach. The main street of Rio had the most marvellous patterned mosaic laid pavements.

In spite of all this opulence, it has of course the large "Red light" districts, these being the goal of most seamen when they got ashore for the first time.

We had about ten days discharging our coal cargo into barges, using the ships derricks and winches which made it a very dusty and dirty job. One Sunday, when there was no work being done, several of us deck crowd went for a swim overside. We set off from the foot of the gangway, the idea was that we should swim round the ship and back to the gangway. I am not and never was a fast swimmer, and I got left behind by the good swimmers. As I was nearing the stern of the ship to go round the other side back to our starting point, a huge Manta Ray fish flashed past me just below the surface of the water.

It scared the living daylights out of me, I couldn't get to the propeller fast enough. When I did reach it, I held on to it for about ten minutes to try and pluck up enough courage to swim the remaining 60 yards to the foot of the gangway. When I finally got there, I couldn't get out of the water fast enough. Needless to say, I never ever went swimming in an open harbour again anywhere in the world, no matter how inviting it may have seemed.

When the coal was discharged we sailed for the River Plate, where we were to load grain back to the U.K. or Continent. On the way down from Rio we had to sweep, clean and wash the holds down ready to load the grain. In addition we had to erect the necessary "shifting boards". They are a centre line wall made with planks of timber slotted into uprights erected from floor to the top of the hold. In those days, the boards had to be from floor to the top. In later years, it was decided by the powers that be that they need only to extend from the top to 1/3rd of the depth of the hold.

I wish they had made that decision when I was an A.B., it would have made life a lot easier for us all.

It amazes me to think that it took them all those years to realise that the grain at the bottom of the hold cannot shift. Only the top part of the grain cargo can shift.

On arrival at the Plate we sailed up river to Rosario to load part of the cargo. I went ashore there one night, but was damned glad to get back to the ship because a rebellion broke out and the army turned out to quell it. There were cavalry men on horses wielding swords and slashing at people with them, many were badly wounded from the use of those swords. I'd had enough of Rosario. With part cargo, we then went down river into Buenos Aires to complete loading. Ships cannot fully load up river because of the sand bar at Martin Garcia, over which they have to pass. Buenos Aires is a very fine city, noted in those days for what was know as the Arches. The arches were situated along one side of the Aveneda de Mayo, and were noted for all the bars and whore houses under them.

A very good time could be had at very cheap rates there, booze was cheap and so were the females. When Sr. Peron became President of Argentina, his wife Eva, closed down all the bars and whore houses, much to the chagrin of visiting foreign seamen.

Woe betide any foreign seaman who got drunk, because he was likely to be picked up by the Marineros, the Police. It was a well known gimmick, to pick up seaman returning to their ships to put them in the local lock-up, then at 4.a.m. have them out on the streets, sweeping them before releasing them. A cheap way of getting the main streets cleaned up, cunning b————s those Argentinians!

On completion of loading we sailed, and on passage we received orders that our destination was to be Antwerp. On arrival there we had a quick discharge and then sailed for Newport, South Wales.

We arrived there on the 10th December 1936, I paid off and went home. I was determined to have Christmas at home for a change. On that voyage I had made friends with the messroom steward, who came from Leeds. It was his first voyage to sea, and during our talks, he told me of his home, and showed me photos of it. To me it seems like a palace, standing in its own grounds. He said that he would invite me over for Christmas at the end of the voyage. We paid off and went our separate ways, and I thought "So much for going to his home for Christmas."

On Christmas Day, a telegram arrived early in the morning, saying that he would be pleased if I would join them for Christmas dinner. Somehow or other, he had remembered my address.

In those days there was a rail service even on Christmas Day, so I got the train to Leeds. I arrived at the station about 1 p.m. and then I had to get a bus to his home in Kirkstall Lane. The bus stopped almost at the driveway of "Oakwood", the name of the house.

I got off the bus and walked to the gateway of the drive to the house. As I walked along the half-circular drive, the house came into view. My shipboard friend had not been exaggerating when he told me about his home. It was almost a mansion, in its own grounds.

Reaching the front door, I rang the bell and waited for someone to answer it. I waited and waited, but nobody came to the door. I knew there were people in the house because I could hear sounds of merriment. I stepped to one side and glanced through a window, the interior was the dining room and around the massive mahogany dining table was my friend, his family and others.

Someone looked up and saw me outside and came to the door, they thought I was a salesman or something.

I quickly explained that I was Gordon's friend, and that he had invited me to Christmas dinner. I was then taken inside and introduced to all the members of the family, after which I was asked if I had eaten. I said that I had not, and was given a seat at the table, whereupon I was plied with a sumptuous dinner with all the trimmings. I was made very welcome by the family and asked to stay a day or two, which I did, enjoying every moment of my stay in such marvellous surroundings.

When time to leave came around, Gordon decided to come back to Hull with me to look for another ship. He stayed a few days at my home and then found himself some lodgings. We tried to find a ship together, but somehow we never managed to sail together again.

It would seem that Fate had decreed that we should never sail on the same ship again. Gordon's sea career came to a tragic end some 26 months later, but more about that in a later chapter.

Chapter 7.
Bad blood at sea

After leaving the "Grainton", I was home until the 25th Feb.1937, when I joined my next ship, the "Peterton", she was another of Chapman's ships. She also was on the coal out grain home run.

She was lying in the Alexandra extension Dock when I joined her, she had just discharged a cargo of linseed. It had been raining, and there was loose linseed lying all over the decks, it was like trying to walk on an ice rink. We the deck crowd, were soon put to work sweeping and washing down the decks, to make it safe to walk on. I fell on my arse several times when moving around the decks, so did many other crew members.

With the aid of brooms and the high pressure of the deck hoses, we finally got the decks cleared and safe to walk on.

The crew accommodation left a lot to be desired. It was down aft, under the poop. Sailors were on the Port side and the Firemen on the Starboard side. Entrance was via a scuttle on the poop, then down a steep stairway into a small space which was the messroom.

Off the messroom was the Bosun's room, and a spare room. At the after end, there was a doorway into the fo'castle. This was a fairly large space, fitted with the usual steel framed bunks. Of these there were twelve, though the ship only carried 9 deck hands.

The toilet arrangement was the most primitive I'd ever seen on any ship before or since. It consisted of a long wooden bench with three circular holes in it. Below the bench was a steel trough, with salt water constantly flowing along its length and out over the side via a scupper pipe. There was no privacy when you went to carry out a normal function. There could one, two or even three men using the facility at the same time. To save money, the whole arrangement was up off the deck level, and to use the toilet, it was necessary to mount two steps before you could get seated. The idea of this was so that when building the ship, they did not have to run the water and waste pipes below deck level. The toilet seat was in fact, 3 feet above the main deck level outside. The deck service water pipe therefore came straight in from its run along the deck, into our toilet.

It was on January 1st 1937 that the three watch system came into operation for the deck department. This meant that ships now had to carry 9 deck hands, three in a watch. Previously the deck department was on a two watch system, which meant 4 hours on and 4 hours off, making it an 84 hour working week!

The National Union of Seamen had fought for years to get the shipowners to get this concession for sailors. What a boon it was to know that you would get 8 hours off duty for a decent sleep!

The shipowner of course wanted his pound of flesh. No way was he going to let his sailors get away with a 56 hour week.

His argument was that the men would be getting the same pay for less hours of duty, and that he was having to engage another 3 men for each of his ships. He would be losing out, he cried. What he meant was that he wouldn't be making as much profit as before, when he only had to carry six men on deck.

To appease the shipowners, the Union agreed that seamen should work an extra 8 hours per week over and above their normal watch keeping hours. To this end, what was known as "Field Days", came into being. This meant that each sailor had to work extra hours during the week to make up to 65 hours a week for his pay.

How the extra hours were done varied with the ship. Some had you work 4 hours on two days of the week, others would have you work 2 hours four days a week. It all depended on the whim of the Chief Officer of the ship, the crew had little say in the matter.

Those Field Days continued even into the war years, before they were ultimately scrapped. They were aptly named, a field day means something for nothing, and that is exactly what the shipowners got. It was on the "Peterton" that I first experienced those "Field Days". They were not very popular but we had to do them. The Mate of the ship decided on 2 days of 3 hours and 1 day of 2 hours for us. This meant that if we were on the 4-8 watch, we would do our 4-8 morning watch, have our breakfast and then turn to from 9-12 a.m.

The 8-12 watch would turn out after dinner, at 1 p.m. until 4 p.m.,

The 12-4 watch would be turned out at 9 a.m. until noon, and so it went on until we had all put in our extra 8 hours per week.

Having loaded a full cargo of coal for Brazil, the ship was ordered to proceed to the Tyne for storing. This was the normal practice of Chapman's. On leaving Hull for the Tyne, we experienced a vicious storm in the North Sea. This held us up for three days on what should have been a few hours run to the Tyne.

Most of us smoked, and we had taken what we considered to be sufficient cigs or tobacco for the run, yet we went short of smokes. Being in Home Trade waters, the Master was not allowed to break the seal on the Bonded stores to sell us some gaspers. We tried, without avail, to eke out our meagre supply of smoking material, even to the extent of trying to make cigarettes out of dried tea leaves, not a very satisfactory substitute.

On arrival at the Tyne, after we had shipped the stores, the Marine Superintendent told the Chief Steward to give us all a large tot of rum. For the average Superintendent, that was very magnanimous of him, but we all appreciated the gesture. Maybe Chapmans were not such a bad outfit after all!

The laughable sequel to the tobacco shortage was the fact that while at the Tyne, some of us decided to give the fo'cstle a good clean out. Whilst I was cleaning behind the bunks nearest to the ship's side, I found a half pound satchet of Anton Justman's shag tobacco. This must have been dropped or stowed by a previous member of the crew, the pity is that we did not find it sooner, it would have allayed our cravings for a cigarette on passage. There was enough tobacco to have given us all a fair share of makings.

We had a somewhat motley crew, but we had a Bosun, one Robert Scott, who could rule any crew, he took no nonsense from anyone.

When he said jump, we jumped. Nevertheless he was one of the finest seamen I ever sailed with. Amongst the deck crowd we had one sailor who tried to be the "Cock of the fo'cstle". He thought he was the bee's knees. He tried to force his will on all of us in that fo'cstle, trying to be the tough guy. The day came when both he and I were out of work in Rio, me because of a blood poisoned hand, caused by a fine strand of manilla rope penetrating the skin. I cannot remember why Leech was off work. However, he tried giving me some order or other, I told him to get stuffed.

He got belligerent.

Undaunted, I told him that if he fancied himself so much, let's go out on deck and settle it once and for all with fisticuffs.

This was a bit stupid of me when you consider I had my right hand all bandaged up after having it lanced. Leech did not take up the challenge, but from that time onwards, neither did he try to rule the roost. I think he had realised that he might have met his match if he had taken me on.

Things went fairly well from then on until one afternoon, when I was working in the port alleyway outside the galley, painting the bulkheads. Leech, who was in my watch also, was somewhere else working on the fore deck. Sometime in the afternoon, he walked past me on his way aft. I looked up at him, and saw that he was covered in blood, his hands, shirt and even his face was spattered.

I spoke to him, but he ignored me and continued aft.

I was soon to find out what had happened. He and the Bosun had come to blows on the deck, when Leech had refused to do some work.

The Bosun, Bob Scott, who had been a middleweight boxing champ in the Navy, had floored Leech with a tremendous punch. In the melee, the Bosun had had his cap knocked from his head.

He had gone to retrieve it. As he bent down to pick it up, Leech went at him with a sheath knife. He slashed the Bosun across his throat and then across his head. So vicious was the attack that he snapped the blade of the knife on Bob's head. He had only just missed the jugular vein.

All this was witnessed by the 2nd Officer who was on watch on the bridge. It all happened so fast that he hadn't time to warn the Bosun of the attack.

The Captain, 2nd Officer and the Chief Steward dashed to aid the Bosun, who had collapsed in a pool of blood on the deck.

Fortunately, the Chief Steward had been in the Army Medical Corp and saw that before they could move the Bosun, they would have to sew up the gaping wound in his neck. The Steward did this, under the supervision of the Captain. They then got the Bosun, who was now unconscious, on to the settee in the saloon.

The Captain got the Radio Officer to send out a message, asking any ship with a doctor to come to his aid. A Union Castle liner answered the call, but according to his position, it would be at least 72 hours before he could reach us. He said that our ship was to keep in touch with him by radio every four hours, or less if the situation warranted.

Having successfully stemmed the bleeding, the Bosun showed signs of consciousness within the first 24 hours. The Doctor on the Union Castle was informed of this improvement in his condition, and he gave our Captain advice on how to look after the injured man. The Captain of the liner said that if circumstances dictated, he would rendezvous with us later and take the man aboard into their hospital.

In the meantime, our Captain had given orders that all knives used in the galley and pantry, were to be locked away when not in use.

This unusual occurrence made all on board ill at ease, none of us had ever known such a vicious attack on a fellow shipmate. Men fell out with each other from time to time, but rarely resorted to the use of a knife. At worst it was usually settled on the quay away from the ship with fisticuffs, after which the men concerned generally became the best of pals. Their differences settled in an honourable way, with nothing more than a black eye or a bleeding nose, then a shake of hands. That way the matter was resolved and forgotten. Every one of us kept a close watch on our shipmate Leech, none of us trusted him any more. However, there was no further trouble for the rest of the voyage from him. He kept his own council and thoughts to himself.

Our discharge port was to be Rotterdam, where we arrived on the 23rd May 1937. It was not the intention of Capt. Nicholson to sign us off. According to him our Articles of Agreement were endorsed

"Sign off, on the next arrival U.K. ". The "or Continent" had been struck out at the shipping office. However, they had forgotten to make the alteration on the copy of them posted in our quarters.

When told that we would not be paying off, several of us went to see the Captain. We pointed out that our copy of the agreement distinctly said, "Vessel to close Articles at the next arrival U.K. or Continent".

Capt. J. Nicholson, was not convinced, and sent the Chief Officer to check the copy posted up in our messroom. On his return, he confirmed what we had said.

Much against his wishes, the Captain had no option but to sign us all off. Those who then wished to leave the ship could now do so.

Their fare to the U.K. would be met by the shipowner, who would be far from pleased at the omission on the copy of the Articles.

It took several years for it to be proved that the crossing out of the words "or Continent" was illegal and had been so since the institution of the Articles of Agreement. The Articles were drawn up under the Merchant Shipping Acts, a legal document to which no alterations should be made by anyone.

The Captain wanted Bob Scott to prefer charges against Leech, as well he could have. The Bosun refused to so do, he said he would attend to the matter himself. He had by this time fully recovered from the effects of the attack, though he had a nasty scar on his neck from the knife wound.

Later the Bosun went ashore and came back with a vicious looking knife. In the meantime, Leech had gone ashore but returned later when the Bosun was not on board. I told Leech that he had better get out of Rotterdam as fast as he could, because the Bosun was out for his blood.

You've heard the saying that you couldn't see a persons arse for dust, well that applied to Leech. I hadn't told him of the Bosun's intentions to save Leech from harm, I'd done it to save Bob Scott from possibly being charged for murder. I have no doubts that if Bob had caught up with Leech he would have cut him to ribbons. Leech caught the night ferry from Rotterdam and got away before the Bosun could catch up with him. That was one sailor the Merchant Service could well do without. Fortunately such incidents of that nature are few and far between.

After discharge, we had several days in Rotterdam, during which we signed on a very mixed crowd. There was an Estonian sailor, who couldn't speak a word of English, but turned out to be a marvellous seaman. Then there was a Cape coloured chap, not too bad as a shipmate, but a little on the light-fingered side. There was another, who had worked in a circus, quite a comedian but a poor sailor. What I did not like was the practise of the Cape chap to carry an open razor in his back pocket. I had on one occasion to warn the Estonian, who had got into a quarrel with him. They went on the quay in London to settle their difference. As the Cape chap went down the gangway, I noticed the razor in his back pocket. I shouted to Tony, that was the name we had given the Estonian, simply because we could not pronounce his name.

"Watch it Tony, he's got a razor in his pocket". That was enough for the whole thing to be called off. Without that razor, the Cape coloured would have had no chance against the massive Tony, he would have tied him up in knots.

I stayed and did three voyages in the "Peterton", mainly because I liked the runs and I got on well with the Bosun. In that time I learned a lot about Bob Scott. He had apparently served his time as an apprentice deck officer. When the time came for him to sit for his 2nd Mate's "Ticket", he had gone on the booze, of which he was very fond, and didn't get to the examination room.

From that day onwards, he had not had the courage to go home and face his father, who he said would have beaten the living daylights out of him for being such a fool.

It was no doubt the talks that I had with Bob that got me interested in the idea of going to Nautical School and sitting for a "Ticket".

I got some instruction from Bob Scott, and more from the ship's 2nd Officer, I bought one of the necessary books, namely, Nicholls Concise Guide, part 1. This was the guide to navigation for 2nd Mates. The all-important "Rules of the Road" I learned from an old Nautical Almanack. At the end of the 3rd voyage, I left the ship to have a spot of leave. After a short leave I then got a job as Able Seaman on another of Wilson's ships, the "Thurso", and did a 2 month voyage into the Mediterranean, Wilson's usual run, and all the ports that I had seen before in one of their ships.

On arrival back in Hull, I found out that the "Peterton" was due back in the Tyne. I wrote to Chapmans and asked if there was any possibility of rejoining their ship. I had a favourable reply and went and joined her in the Tyne only six days after leaving the "Thurso".

I was to spend another nine happy months in the "Peterton", making another three voyages in her, one to Karachi for grain, one to Capetown, also for grain, and one to Galveston for more grain.

Before leaving the "Peterton" at Barry, on the 8th Sept.1938, I went to ask Captain Nicholls for a reference as to my conduct and sobriety. This I would need from each ship I now served in, if I wanted to sit exams for a "ticket".

The Marine Superintendent was present when I asked the Captain for the reference, and he said that if I got a "ticket", I was to get in touch with him and he would give me a job as an officer in one of their ships. That was nice to know even before I had got to school in that direction.

On leaving the ship, I booked in for a course on navigation and allied subjects, at the Trinity House Adult School. I did not stay long at the school, shortage of cash brought about an abrupt ending to my schooling.

I'd have to find another seagoing job to save some more cash, to enable me to stay and finish the course, which would perhaps get me through the exam for the 2nd Mate's ticket.

Chapter 8.
s.s."Llandilo", a never to be forgotten voyage.

Strange as it may seem, that short stint at the Navigation School was exactly ten years from the time that I was taken there as a boy in 1928.

A daily call at the Seaman's Union Office in Posterngate found me a ship, The "Llandilo", one of Evan, Thomas Radcliffe's ships was wanting a crew. I said I was in the market for a job, and was given a PC5 by the Union Official, which stated that I was being sent to the ship as a possible crew member as an Able seaman.

With that in my pocket, I went down to the ship, she was berthed in King George Dock at the coal hoists, which have long since gone.

Boarding the ship, I went to see the Chief Officer, I told him I had been sent down by the Union for one of the jobs as A.B.

He asked to see my Discharge Book, so I handed it to him.

After careful scrutiny of the pages, he said that he would accept me. He then signed the PC5 form and handed it back to me.

I was now provisionally a member of the crew for the forthcoming voyage. For this you got no pay until you actually signed on the ship's Articles of Agreement. It simply meant that you were promised a job, provided you were available and fit for sea service when the ship opened her Articles.

She would be opening Articles on the 20th Oct., the following Monday morning, today being the Friday.

Whilst aboard, I had a look at her crew accommodation. It was down aft at the after end of the short well-deck. I'd seen better, and worse. It was passable, there was the fo'castle, entered by passing through the messroom from the deck. To the outboard side was the toilets and so-called crew bathroom. This was the usual concrete floored space, wherein to wash yourself down. There were no such things as showers in those days. For one thing, ships didn't carry enough fresh water for that purpose. In fact, they barely carried enough for human consumption on a long sea passage.

Over the weekend, I went down to the ship to pick out a bunk for myself. Having chosen one, I then dismantled the steel frame, took it out on deck and burned all the bed bugs off it. Having done that, I asked for, and received, some green sidelight paint. With this I painted the steel frame and put it back in place.

I had learned from experience that bed bugs would not nest on anything painted green. Why, I do not know, but it is a fact.

Come Monday morning, all chosen hands assembled at the Shipping Office, sailors, firemen, catering staff, (of which there seemed very few, a Chief Steward, a Chief and only Cook, and one messroom boy).

Then there was the Radio Officer, the 2nd and 3rd Mates, Chief Engineer, 2nd, 3rd and 4th engineers. All these were Welshmen, with the exception of the 2nd Mate. He was a Liverpudlian, and for that, though he did not know it, he was to have a miserable voyage. When the Captain, J. Jones arrived at the office, we all trooped in to sign-on.

The Articles were the usual ones for a voyage not exceeding 3 years duration, and not to trade beyond the limits of 70 degrees North Latitude not 60 degrees South Latitude.

The Master was the first to sign the Articles, as the law demands, this was so that he could open the Agreement with the crew. He was followed by the 1st, 2nd and 3rd officers. Then came the Radio Officer, he was followed by the Bosun, Carpenter, and nine of us deck crew. After us it was the turn of the engineers, then the firemen, who were all Arabs. These latter were employed as firemen in most British tramp steamers in those days.

The Catering staff came last in the list of crew for the voyage.

We noticed that the Chief Steward and the Cook were both West Indians, both it turned out were really nice chaps to sail with.

The Articles having, as required by law, been read out to us all, we then started appending our signatures to the Agreement.

"Crew to report on board at one minute past midnight of the 20th of October 1938". The usual penny-pinching gaff.

By the time we reported aboard the next morning, the ship was well on the way to being loaded with "washed coal", delivered to the hoist in 20 ton railway trucks. These were hoisted up and tipped, almost end on, into the chute, down which it ran into the ship's holds. By the way, I did say washed coal. I have yet to find out why Australia wanted washed coal from Britain, when they have plenty of coal themselves. So much so, that in this day and age, the 1990s, they are exporting it to Britain by the hundreds of thousands of tons a year.

On signing the Articles, each one was asked if they wanted an Advance Note and / or an Allotment Note. Most of them took an Allotment Note, not necessarily because they had to support someone left at home, it was more as an insurance for their relatives. In the event of anything untoward happening to them on voyage, it could be held that they were supporting dependants at home. This made it easier for compensation to be claimed.

Some took an Advance Note, this was an advance on wages to be earned. This note was payable three days after the vessel sailed from her final port in the U.K. Such Notes were usually taken by seamen short of ready cash to buy seagoing gear, or to help their wives until the first Allotment became due. Allotment Notes could be drawn fortnightly or monthly. If a seaman took an Advance Note, until the time had elapsed when his wages would cover the amount he had drawn, he was said to be "flogging a dead horse".

This was seamen's jargon, and meant that he was working, until he had earned enough to cover the debt, for nothing. Not strictly true.

The Advance Note could be cashed immediately, for outside the Shipping Office would be a "Note Cracker". He/she was a necessary evil, who made their money from impoverished seamen. They would cash the note for you, less the amount of their commission for the service. The usual charge was 2/6 in the Pound, or in today's currency, 12.5p. This may not sound a lot, but considering that it was the interest on a loan for 3 days, it was a hefty 1520%, not a bad way to make a living. There was of course always the possibility that the man might miss the ship, in which case, they would not get their money from the shipowner, who paid out on the receipt of those notes. To validate the note, the seaman who had drawn it had to sign his name on the back of the note, to make it payable to the person who sent it to the shipowner for encashment.

It was not a healthy thing to try and get out of paying those "Note Crackers". Failure to pay could result in nasty things if they called out their "heavy gang".

We all reported aboard the "Llandilo" after breakfast at home the next morning, having been told at the Shipping Office, "To report on board at one minute after midnight" of the day we signed on.

Having got into our working gear, the Bosun soon had us out on deck, stores had started to arrive on the quay. Between handling stores and getting them aboard and having to shift the ship up and down along the quay to facilitate the loading, we had a full day.

We did get the usual 15 minutes break mid morning for what is known as "Smoko", and then carried on until dinner time. The dinner supplied left a lot to be desired, but we made allowances for this, putting it down to the stress of storing, in which the Cook had also to partake.

Turn to again at 1 p.m. and carry on the good work, with a mid afternoon "Smoko", finally knocking off work at 5 p.m.

After a quick lick and a promise, to get rid of the heaviest of the muck accumulated during the day, we all made for the gangway to go home for the night.

As we went down the gangway, we heard the Chief Officers voice, "Be aboard first thing in the morning, ready to turn to".

"Yes, Sir, three bags full", we were more interested in getting home and having a decent meal.

At 08.00 hrs 23rd Oct. 1938, we were all aboard, complete with our gear for the voyage, for this was to be the sailing day. Some more stores arrived, and the water man was there, piping fresh water into the domestic tank and the engineroom boiler feed tank. We, the deck crowd had to take the stores aboard, including the engineroom stores. The 2nd Engineer had not designated any of his men to handle their stuff, so we complained. We didn't mind getting the stores aboard, but bugger having to carry those for the engineroom, along there. We had enough with the deck stores, especially with 120 fathom length coils of mooring ropes and 1 Cwt. drums of paints. All had to be handled by Armstrong's patent lifting gear, namely we had to carry them all the way along the decks to the various stores.

This job was interspersed with shifting ship to finalise the loading. We managed our 15 minute Smoko break then back to work, my hearties. Come 12 noon, we were sent to dinner, and what a scratch one it was. Being fairly tolerant, we made allowances for the fact that the Cook had had to help with the catering stores.

After dinner we were turned out again, this time it was to start the battening down of the hatches as they finished the loading.

This was no mean task, there were 5 hatches to cover and batten down. This entailed lifting, by hand, some 40 wooden hatch boards. These boards were about 2 Ft by 7 Ft by 2.5 Ins. and being steel bound at each end and dowelled in three places with 0.5 In. steel dowelling, they were quite heavy.

Each hatch had to have 3 tarpaulins laid over the hatch boards, these were spread and fastened down at one end of the hatch. Then all of us would go to the other end and haul like hell, to stretch the tarpaulin tight, then fold them to fit neatly into the cleats on the sides of the hatch coaming.

The corners had to be carefully folded to make them watertight against the seas. Once the tarpaulin was in the cleats all round the hatch, the hatch bars were put in and then wedged there with wooden wedges. That part of the job was in reality the Carpenter's job, but any of the sailors would do it. Before knocking-off, the Carpenter would go right round each hatch and hammer each wedge in turn to make sure that all was well and truly secure. All this of course, was in the days before a firm called McGregors had invented their steel rolling hatches.

What a boon those hatches would have been to sailors of those days, life would have been a lot easier and a damned sight safer than they were in the 1930s.

Few people, including those who went to sea, seemed to realise that the only thing that kept a ship afloat in really heavy weather, when mountainous seas were rolling aboard, was those tarpaulins over the hatch boards.

It was not uncommon, each winter, to hear of ships in distress in the North Atlantic Ocean. The usual S.O.S. message would say that - No.1 hatch was stove in and the ship was going down by the head as the water got into the lower hold.

In fact, it was rare that the hatch boards would be stove-in. A 7 Ft. hatch board would only have an unsupported length of about 36 inches, being supported at each end and in the middle by a steel hatch beam.

What in fact happened was that when a huge sea dropped on the hatch boards, they bounced and in so doing they slipped off the end landing. The next heavy sea that came aboard, then dropped on the loose hatch board, and down it would go into the lower hold, usually tearing the tarpaulin in the process. The ship was now in a very dangerous state, replacement of the hatch board was virtually impossible in really heavy weather.

But I digress, back to the "Llandilo". Shortly after dinner the ship was ready for sailing, and it was "Stand by fore and aft" at stations. The Bosun split us into two gangs, one for forward and one for aft. Under the Master's orders, we singled up to one mooring rope and a back-spring at each end of the ship.

The Dock Pilot was already aboard, and under his instructions we made fast the two tugs, who would assist us out of the dock.

In the locks we changed Pilots, and the River Pilot took over the ship. He would navigate us down to Spurn Point, where he would be taken off by the pilot boat. Once through the locks, and into the river Humber, the tugs towed us round to face down river. Once round, the tugs left us, we were now on our way to sea.

The mooring ropes were stowed away under the fo'cstle head for the forward ropes, and in the poop lazarette for the after ropes.

The steel wire rope springs were neatly wound on their respective reels and covered up. It was now tea-time, 5 p.m., and we expected that we would be told to knock off work, get our tea and pick up our normal sea watches.

Not so in the s.s. "Landilo", the Chief Officer wanted his pound of flesh, he intended getting the 10 hours work on sailing or arrival day. This was an anomaly that existed in the 1930s. Crews had to work 10 hours on those two particular days. I have never found out why such a clause was ever allowed in the Articles of Agreement. But it was, and we had no option but to do as ordered. The Chief Officer had given the Bosun instructions that all the coal spilled on the decks during the loading, was to be swept up.

It was not to be thrown overboard, the usual practise. It had to be collected and wheeled and shovelled into the ship's bunker space, to be used to fire the boilers.

I've heard of waste not want not, but this was ridiculous. The total amount of coal that we salvaged would not have been sufficient to fire a three-fire furnace for more than 15 minutes at most.

It was dark by the time we finished the job and were sent to tea.

On our way aft to our accommodation, I called at the galley for our tea. The Cook, Chief and only Cook, was still in the galley, waiting to dish up our food for tea.

"Evening Doc, can I have the sailors' tea please?", I said to him.

"Sure, fella, I've got it here keeping warm for you".

He brought two metal "kids" out of the stove oven and handed them to me. One of them had a quantity of what was known in seamen's jargon, "Dog's Vomit", its real name according to the Nautical Cookery Book, being Minced Scallops. The other "kid" had some boiled potatoes in it, and not too many of them either.

"Is this all there is"? I asked.

" 'Fraid so fella, that's the lot".

From what I could see, there was neither quantity or quality in what we had been given for tea after a hard day's slog on deck.

I trundled aft to our messroom with the kids, and placed them on the white wooden table where some of my shipmates were waiting for the grub.

They all had a glance at what had been dished out to us, and like me, they were not amused. One of the others picked up the "growler", and said he'd go and mash the tea, "While I'm there" he said, I'll ask the Cook if there is anything else to come aft".

"You'll be wasting your time", I told him, "I've already asked the Cook, and he said this was all there is".

Off he went, and came back a little later with the growler full of hot tea.

"Well, what did the Cook say when you asked for more"?

"He said this was the lot for this meal", was his answer.

One man was at the wheel, so we shared out the contents of the two kids amongst the 8 of us. It worked out at two tablespoons of mince and three boiled potatoes per man. Not what one could call a substantial meal for a hard day's graft. That had to last us until breakfast time the next morning.

We held a hasty pow-wow and it was decided that we should go and have a word in the Chief Steward's shell like ear regarding our repast. After all he was the one responsible for the catering of the ship, or so we thought.

Two of us formed the delegation to go amidships to see the Steward, I was one of the two men.

We made our way forward to the 'midships accommodation, and arriving at the pantry alleyway door, which was closed. We knocked loudly on it, hoping that the Steward would answer it. We waited, and then knocked again and waited, still no answer.

As there was no future in standing outside in the bitterly cold wind, we opened the door and stepped over the sill into the alleyway. The pantry was just ahead of us, to the left of the saloon door. We went to the pantry door and knocked on it, even though it was open and the Steward was there, that was common courtesy on our part.

The Steward turned and asked us what we wanted.

"Well, it's like this Steward, we wondered if there was anything else for our tea, over what the Cook gave us".

"Sorry, fellas, you've had all there is for your tea".

"What, not even a bit of cold meat or something more for us"?.

"Nope, you've had what the Captain ordered you should have".

"What do you mean, the Captain ordered, you run the catering don't you"?

The Steward shook his head sadly, "No fellas, in this ship the Captain draws up the menu for the day".

We were almost speechless when we heard that, but suddenly we were brought to earth. The saloon door opened and the Captain appeared.

"What the bloody hell are you lot doing here in the Officers quarters", he demanded to know.

I was the first to find my voice, "We came to see the Chief Steward about our tea", I said.

"Well, what about it"? The Captain roared.

"Well Sir, we wondered if the Steward could give us a little of something else to top up the quantity, after all we didn't get much for our tea".

"You got all you're gonna get, and if you don't like it, you can have your "Pound and Pint".

"Now get the hell out of this accommodation, and back aft where you belong"!

That last statement had said it all, there was no point in trying to reason with a man like that. We turned and left the place.

Back down aft, we told the rest of the crew all that had been said, and after a further confab we decided that we would call the Old Man's bluff. We'd take our pound and pint, as he had suggested.

The expression "Pound and Pint" means that you take everything to which you are entitled under the Merchant Shipping Acts of 1894 and its subsequent amendments. In other words it was known as taking your whack.

Before going back amidships to tell the Steward of our decision, we went across and had a few words with the Arab firemen.

"Had they been satisfied with what they had had dished out for their tea"?

They said they were not at all happy with it.

We then told them that we had decided to go on our whack.

"Would they be agreeable to joining us", we asked them.

They held a discussion in their own language, which of course we did not savvy.

A few minutes later they said that they would also take their whack.

With that, one of the firemen and myself, went amidships and saw the Chief Steward and told him that, as of the next day, which would be our stores day, we were taking pound and pint.

The look on the Chief Steward's face said all we needed to know. There was something troubling him, and we could only guess what.

The next morning, Saturday morning, as I was off watch, it fell to me to go and draw our dry stores for the week for the nine of us deck crowd. I went amidships armed with several empty butter and marmalade tins, left by the previous crowd. These were to be used to collect our ration.

There was dry tea, coffee, sugar, butter, (If you could call the horrible stuff butter), pickles, marmalade, salt, pepper, curry powder, flour, tins of full cream condensed milk, (At the rate of one tin per man per three weeks!) As we were entitled to a 16 ounce tin, and the tins were only 14 ounce ones, we were given one extra tin to be shared out amongst the nine of us.

The only thing that I could not take, was the so called fresh meat. This was because we did not have anywhere to keep it. We had no form of icebox or refrigeration down aft. The ship didn't even have a refrigerator, all meat was stowed in an icebox, and after about ten days, when all the ice had melted, one could hardly call the meat "fresh". That commodity we had to draw each day as long as it lasted. Bread was the other item that we got each day, because the Cook had to bake it every day, when the loaves shipped in Hull ran out.

The big drawback in taking your Pound and Pint was the fact that when you did so, you were responsible for the preparation of your food for cooking. The ship was only responsible for the cooking of it. This was going to be a bit of a problem for us, but we needn't have worried. The Cook, as I said earlier was a West Indian from Jamaica, and he was not very chuffed with the fact that the Captain was running the catering instead of his pal the Steward.

When he heard that we had gone on our whack, he offered to prepare all our meals for us. All we had to do was to supply him with what he said he would need to give us three good meals a day. A friend in need, is a friend indeed, and what a friend he turned out to be.

We fed far better than the Officers of the ship, the Cook gave us all sorts of cakes, he made hot bread rolls for us, and he always managed to get us a little something extra now and then.

In return for his kindness, we, the sailors, kept his galley spotless for him. During the night watches we would scrub the place out for him, clean out the galley's fires and have them burning brightly for him when he started work at 6 a.m.

We all got on famously.

When the ship was clear of the coast, the Captain made the first issue of his "Bonded Stores", that means he was issuing cigarettes and tobacco. This can only be done legally, when the ship has left British territorial waters. It would seem that the "Old man" was not content to try and rob our bellies, but he also wanted to rob our pockets as well!

When I went along amidships to draw a ration of Anton Justman's light shag tobacco, I was told that there was none, the Officers had bought all there was. This meant that we, the ratings, would have to buy cigarettes from the bond, which was a lot more expensive than rolling your own cigs from the shag tobacco.

I asked the price per 50 for Woodbines, my favourite smoke.

The 3rd Officer, who was running the bond for the captain, told me that they were 2 Shillings per 50, (10p).

I asked him how could that be, after all these were duty free cigarettes, and ashore with duty paid, they were only 1 Shilling and 8 pence, (8p) for 20.

"These are the prices set by the captain, if you don't like them, go and see him", I was told.

After the last interlude, there was no point in going to see him about his extortionate prices. I had an idea, not the best solution, but one which would allow me my smokes and save me money at the same time.

"How much is Cornucopia plug tobacco?" I asked.

" Three Shillings and sixpence a pound" came the answer.

"Right, give me one pound of Cornucopia and twelve packets of Red Rizla papers, and one hundred Woodbines, please".

The 3rd Officer dished out my order and I signed for them.

The plug tobacco is really for pipe smokers, and isn't the nicest thing to smoke in cigarettes, being somewhat stronger then cigs.

Each and every one of us took the same from the bond. We got the Carpenter to shave the plug tobacco down finely with his plane, this he did in the ship's time when the Chief Officer was not around the decks.

This made it fine enough for us to rub and roll into cigarettes, these were going to last us until we arrived in South Africa.

The next aggravation was the locking of the fresh water pump in the galley. Not that this was unusual, it wasn't, it happened on most tramp ships on a long haul between ports.

The annoying thing was that the Officers could draw wash water from that pump but we could not. Wash water for us had to be got from the "hotwell" in the engineroom. This meant taking a two gallon bucket right down below, filling it with hot, somewhat oily water, then carrying it back all the way up the engineroom steel ladders.

If the ship was rolling, this became quite a challenge. You had to try and keep your balance on those slippery steel treads and at the same time try not to spill any water.

If you did spill it, it shot straight down the ladder onto the engineroom floor plates, and woe betide the engineer if he happened to be in the deluge.

When this happened, there would be a roar of blasphemous words, casting doubts on the legitimacy of our births!

It was all taken in good spirits by all concerned.

As seasoned seamen, we all knew the importance of fresh potable water on a long passage, and we were only allowed to draw water for drinking purposes.

I do not know who was responsible for the drawing up of the Merchant Shipping Acts, which stated that the ration of water per man per day was to be "4 quarts", = 8 Pints or 1 gallon.

Whoever they were must have been dirty old men, if they only used 1 gallon of water a day for drinking and personal ablution purposes.

Imagine trying to have a bath with only 8 pints of fresh water to use for drinking and bathing each day.

Being of an inquisitive mind and with a mechanical flair, I examined the handcuffs which were used to lock the pump.

It did not take me many minutes to see that they were the old spring loaded type of 'cuffs, they locked when you closed them.

It only took me a matter of minutes to fashion a key from a piece of wire. This I screwed down on the thread of the locking pin, then a gentle pull outwards and the 'cuffs came open.

We all knew that the Chief Officer went into the galley at 03.50 each morning, to make his cup of whatever, to take on the bridge when he went to take over his watch.

We made certain that the 'cuffs were unlocked and left dangling from the pump. When he first saw this, the Chief Officer almost went besirk, he "Would log ,flog, f*** , and fire, the perpetrator of this dastardly deed".

He never did find out who was responsible, in fact all the sailors were, with the exception of the Ordinary Seaman. We did not let him in on the act, because he was another Welshman from the same place as the Captain and Chief Officer.

In other words we did not trust him!

Before we got to Durban, the ship was in dire straits foodwise, and the Chief Steward came to see us in an effort to get us to swap some of our stocks of jam and marmalade. We could have anything we liked in exchange, were we short of sugar, or tea or milk, he asked?

We in turn asked him why he'd come aft with this offer, he told us that we had got all the ships stock of jam and marmalade down aft and the Officer's had none at all.

We told him that our hearts bled for those poor b******s amidships, but the Captain had brought this about, not us.

No, we said, we would not make any exchanges, even though we could have done with a few tins of condensed milk and some sugar and tea. The Steward went away somewhat disheartened, to tell the Captain what we had said.

A day or two later, I was coming down from my two hour stint at the wheel, and as I was passing the Chartroom door on the lower bridge, the Captain called me. I went back and he took me into the Chartroom, on the chart table was a bottle of rum and a tot glass. "How are you getting on, on Pound and Pint?" he asked.

I thought for a moment and then said, "We are feeding very well Sir, in fact better than I have ever done on any other ship".

The Captain poured out a tot of rum and offered it to me, "Here, boyo, have a tot" he said.

I took the tot and downed it in one go, even though I normally did not drink, neither beer nor spirits. The rum almost took my breath away.

"Wouldn't you like to come off Pound and Pint?" asked the Captain. When I had got my breath back, I told him that it was not for me to say.

"Why?" He wanted to know.

"Because", I said, "It was a unanimous decision amongst us all down aft, to go on the system. It will take the same unanimity to come off it".

With that he dismissed me and told me to get back to my work.

He tried this out with each of the deck crowd as they came down from the wheel. We all gave him the same answer, such was solidarity.

It wasn't long before the Steward came to see us all again.

This time it was to make it clear to us the state of the stores remaining aboard the ship. According to him, the ship would run completely out of food, unless we agreed to come off Pound and Pint. Would we think about it? We said we would hold a meeting of all concerned down aft, that meant us the sailors and the firemen, and we would let him know later.

When he had gone, we had a conference with the firemen, and told them the situation, would they agree with us to drop our demands for the time being at least. They agreed, so one fireman and myself went amidships to see the Captain.

We pointed out to him that we were not vindictive people and that we appreciated the situation regarding the food. We had therefore agreed to drop our Pound and Pint, and let the ship feed us.

"However", we said, "There is a proviso, to safeguard us".

"What's that?" asked the Captain.

"Simply this", we said, "If after storing in Durban, the food quantity or quality does not meet our approval, we shall go back on Pound and Pint, and stay on it until the end of the voyage, no matter how long it is".

The Captain promised us that we would be well fed after the stores came aboard at Durban. We accepted his assurance and went off taking our "whack".

Shortly afterwards the ship arrived at the Bluff in Durban harbour, to take on coal bunkers, fresh water and the promised stores. On the quay was a truck loaded with ship's stores. From what we took on board, it seemed as though the Old Man was keeping his promise about our feeding. I reckon the Shipowner would not be very pleased at having to meet the bills for those stores taken in Durban. That was the Old Man's worry, not ours.

I remember carrying a bag of onions aboard and pinching one of them, peeling it and eating it raw.

It was delicious, it was the first fresh vegetable I had had for nearly two weeks.

Any person who has been to Durban, particularly seamen, will know that on the Bluff there is a kiosk that sells everything a seaman could need on voyage. You name it, they sold it, whether it be a pair of socks or shoes, cigarettes, tobacco, soap, towels, pens, pencils, soft drinks, or even Andrews Liver Salts.

The usual practice was for the Captain of any ship calling at the Bluff, to allow his crew to buy from the shop by signing for anything they got. The Captain would give the shop owner a list of his crew by name and rating. He would also stipulate the amount of credit each man could have in the shop. This was so that the crew didn't go mad and spend more than they had in money in the ship.

When everybody had drawn what they wanted from the shop, the owner would present the Captain with the signed sheet, showing the total amount of credit given. Of this amount, the Captain would be given a nice percentage, tax free, to put in his own pocket.

When you consider that a Captain's salary in those days was about twenty-five Pounds a month, a backhander of say £10 from the "Bumboat shop" was a worthwhile pick up.

A seaman would obtain what he wanted from the shop and sign his name for the goods. Before the ship sails, the owner of the shop gives the Captain the signed sheet, and in return, he would receive payment for the goods. The Captain receives a handsome commission from the dealer for giving him the business, some 10-15% of the total bill.

We all took advantage of the "Bumboat", and as tobacco and cigarettes were dirt cheap in South Africa at that time, we all stocked up with these commodities. Bird's Eye shag tobacco, in sealed 1 lb. tins was only 3/- (15p) a tin. Cigarettes were about 1/6 (8p) for sealed tins of 50. At those prices we all stocked up with enough to last us for at least 3 months. The Captain may have made his commission but he wasn't going to be able to sell us any more of the "Bonded stores" he had on board. He'd still have them when the ship got back to Britain. No way was he going to get rich by robbing us of our hard earned wages with his higher than normal bond prices.

Fine Bird's Eye shag tobacco for cigarettes was only 2/6 a pound in sealed metal tins. Cigarettes were 50 for 1/-, (12.5p & 5p respectively).

At those prices we all made sure that we would never have to buy from the ship's bond again. The Captain's dream of making a small fortune out of the crew just vapourised into thin air. His commission from the shop would not be as much as he would have made from the crew by selling his bond on the ship. There was no way that he was going to get rich by robbing us of our hard earned wages with his higher than normal bond prices.

We were due to sail to Freemantle, and in common with all tramp ships, we sailed on a composite Great Circle course.

Chapter 9.
Fire down below.

Having stored, taken fresh water and coal bunkers, we sailed on the final leg of the run to Freemantle, Western Australia. The food was considerably better than before, so it seemed that we had won the day.

The First Mate was a bit of a slave driver. I remember one morning, I was down in No.1 'tween decks painting the deckhead, the hatch was open because the weather was fine and calm.

I heard the fairy footsteps of the Mate coming along the deck over my head. He stopped at the open hatch and called down.

"Is there anybody down there"?

"Yes, me Mathison", I answered.

"What are you doing"? He called back.

"I'm painting the deckhead", I replied.

"Well I can't hear any sounds of work".

I just couldn't resist my reply, "I'm putting the paint on with a brush, not with a bloody hammer"! There was no answer to that, and the next thing I heard was the footsteps receding as he walked away aft again.

Our passage across the Indian Ocean took us about 21 days, and the arrival in Freemantle was a welcome treat. The discharge of the coal took about a week, which gave us time to relax in our off duty time, in the pleasant city of Freemantle.

As tobacco and cigarettes were also very cheap in Australia, we were able to stock up again for several weeks ahead.

In port, our main job was to follow the coal down as it was discharged into trucks on the quay. This way we were able to have the holds swept down from top to bottom as the level of the cargo went down. We had already heard that we were to load grain at the port of Bunbury, which is only a few miles from Freemantle. Hence the necessity to have the holds cleaned out as quickly as possible and ready to receive cargo on arrival there. To this end, we had to work a considerable amount of overtime, but it meant that the Captain could present his "Notice of Readiness to load" as soon as we arrived at Bunbury.

This is an all important thing to the Master of a ship, because should there be any delays in the loading after his "Notice" has been accepted and the "Laytime" has started to count, if the loading goes beyond the stated "Laydays", the ship can claim "Demurrage". That is a fixed amount per day, as stated in the "Charter Party" for every hour over the "laytime" allowed for the loading of the cargo. Shipowners love it and shippers hate having to pay any demurrage to a ship, and will argue like hell against it.

Bunbury, it turned out, was a very small port, one I think was in its infancy in 1938 when we were there to load. No doubt the place will have grown since those days. I have never been back there ,so I do not know. However, we found the people very friendly. At night it was the choice of a bar, or a cinema, or the Flying Angel mission to go to for entertainment, depending on your tastes.

The local girls acted as dance hostesses at the Flying Angel, and all seamen were made very welcome, but for dancing only!

The local "Padre" from the Mission came aboard and after a talk with out Old Man, came and had a word with the crew.

"What a nice man the Captain is" he said to us, "I hear that he is going to give you all a half day off whilst you are in port".

Nice man he might appear to an outsider, but what the Padre didn't realise was that the Captain was only giving us a half day off to save having to pay overtime.

In 1938 time off in lieu of overtime worked was allowed. Personally we would sooner have had the overtime payments of 1/6 per hour, (8p) per hour, that would have been more beneficial to us hard worked, underpaid seamen. The shipowner however preferred to give time off, rather than part with any money. That is why there were so many millionaire shipowners in those days, they held onto their money in any way possible.

After several days of loading, we finally sailed from Bunbury. Our cargo, we were told, was for the U.K.

All hands were now as happy as could be, knowing that in about 8 weeks we would be back home and able to sign-off the s.s. "Llandilo", and go home, in the hopes of finding a better ship the next time.

When we were about a week out of Bunbury on passage to Durban, smoke was seen to be coming out of a small ventilator up on the boat-deck. Nothing was done about it, nobody took any notice of it, at least not until the 2nd Engineer reported that the steel bulkhead in the engineroom was too hot to touch and the paintwork on it was blistering.

It was then panic stations. That small ventilator was the one that ventilated the reserve coal bunker space!

Now it is a well known fact that coal suffers from inherent vice, that is catching fire if it is kept in a confined space for too long. This is what had happened to the coal in the reserve bunker space, it had been in there far too long and had started to smoulder.

This bunker space by the way was on the starboard side of the engineroom, extending out to the ship's side, and was in line with the main engines, and the only way into it was through a small steel plate door in the engineroom.

The engineers gingerly unbolted the steel plate and removed it.

What a sight met their eyes!

The coal was a glowing mass of red-hot coal. Economy came into action, rather than safety, and it was decided that the coal would have to be worked out of the space and used in the furnaces of the boilers.

Of course it fell to the deck crowd to do all the hard and hazardous work of digging out the glowing coals.

In those days, ships did not have to carry any form of breathing apparatus, not even a smoke helmet.

Of course when coal is baked, it gives off gas, such as is used ashore for gas cookers and can be deadly if inhaled to any great extent.

The apprentices were put at the wheel to steer the ship whilst we, the sailors worked down below for our 4 hour watch digging out the coal and wheeling it to the furnaces.

The only way we could do the job was to take a really deep breath, hold it and dash up to the glowing coal, shovel as much as we could whilst holding our breath. When we had to take another breath, we stepped back into the engineroom, and another man would do the same again. So it went on until we finally got all the burning coal out of that reserve space and into the furnaces.

In all it took us almost two days to clear the space, and not once during that time were we offered a tot of rum, which any decent Captain would have offered his men for the effort.

That hazard over, we resumed our normal watches of ship's deck work, taking the wheel, and at night, doing our look-outs.

When we were about half way across between Bunbury and Durban, an evening meal, tea-time, was served out to us at the galley.

It consisted of one meat-ball per man, plus some boiled potatoes that was it. The meat from which the balls were made, had been taken out of the ice-box that same day. Several of us sailors had watched the Cook take a couple of links of sausages from the ice-box. They were covered in green mould.

Once back in the sanctity of his galley, the Cook then washed the sausages in the usual mixture of Condy's Crystals and water.

This got rid of the mould and at the same time sterilised the meat.

We were not too pleased with this grub, but this time it was the Firemen who got belligerent. They went along to see the Chief Steward, who in turn referred them to the Old Man.

He was anything but sympathetic about their complaint. It looked as though we were back to square one.

"No can fire the boilers on one meal ball, must have more food", the firemen said. The Old man told them to get back to work, they had got all they were going to get.

"No food, no work" was the Firemen's reply, and with that they left the Old Man and went aft. On their way they called down the stokehold to the men on watch at the furnaces. We didn't know what they had said, because they spoke in Arabic to each other.

A few minutes later all the Firemen on watch appeared at the top of the stokehold ladder and on to the deck.

"We no fire the boilers " they said, and with that they all walked aft to their accommodation. If no one attends the furnaces, it doesn't take long before the boiler pressure falls. In this case it wasn't long before we could hear the engines slowing down as the boiler pressure started to fall.

There was a shouting and gnashing of teeth as the Old Man started to lay the law down. "This is mutiny on the high seas, I'll call for a British warship to come to us and have you all arrested".

"You call warship Captain, still we not fire boilers on one meat ball", answered the Firemen. The Old Man seemed to think that we, the sailors were the instigators of this incident. In actual fact, we had nothing to do with it, nevertheless, he thought we had, and he said so. That was too much for us to take, so we told him to radio for a warship, and maybe when the Commander of it had heard of the sort of grub that we were being dished up with, he might just agree that the crew had a just cause for their action.

We all knew that the nearest Naval station was at least 2,000 miles away, either Colombo or Freemantle. Even at 20 knots full speed it would mean at least 100 hours steaming for a naval vessel. Apart from that, could the ship's old spark-gap transmitter signal reach that far?

In the meantime, the engineers had tried to keep the engines going, but lack of experience at stoking a furnace soon had the ship almost at a standstill. They were unable to maintain the boiler pressure needed to turn the engines.

At this point, the Chief Engineer had a talk with the Old Man, with the result that the Old Man ordered the Chief Steward to knock up a decent meal for all hands.

Their appetites sated, the Firemen returned to their duties and soon had the ship on its way again.

That was the end of that saga.

One night, I was on look-out duty, and as usual, many things went through my mind.

Suddenly, I had a strange feeling about a friend of mine, also a seafarer. What a shock it would be to his parents if anything happened to him at sea, that was what came into my mind.

I immediately shut the thought from my mind, he'd be alright I told myself.

Little did I know that at that particular time, the s.s. "Maria de Larrinaga" was sending out S.O.s.s, she was sinking in the North Atlantic in a terrible storm, somewhere off the Grand Banks of Newfoundland.

This I was to learn, when we finally reached Birkenhead with our cargo of grain. There were letters and cuttings from the Hull Daily Mail, giving an account of the sinking, and also a list of the crew of the ship.

Gordon Abbott, my friend, was one of those listed as being lost with the ship. No wreckage was ever found, and no one survived.

What, I have often wondered, brought that feeling of disaster to mind. Was it extra-sensory perception, or the cry of a friend in terrible danger spanning two oceans to reach me? I'll never know.

As it was a weekend when we arrived in Birkenhead, I made a point of going to see the parents of my friend, to offer my condolences.

That much I owed them for the hospitality they had shown me when at their home.

His parents asked me to go and stay with them for a few days as soon as I left the "Llandilo". This I did, but only after the ship had discharged her cargo and we were forced to stay and take the ship to Barry, her bunkering port. This again, was a clause in the Articles of Agreement, so we had no option but to stay in the ship until then.

At Barry, when it came time to collect our Accounts of Wages from the Captain, he told me that he was going to give me a bad discharge.

"No way, Captain, will you give me a bad discharge", I told him.

"I'm the Master of this ship, and if I want to give any man a bad discharge, I will", he stormed at me.

This got my hackles up, "I still say you can't and won't give me a bad discharge Captain".

"And why not?" He asked.

"Because Sir, you have no entries in the Official Log Book against me, that's why.

"Oh, a bloody sea lawyer eh?"

"No Sir, just a common sailor who knows his rights", I answered.

At the pay-off table in front of the Superintendent of the Mercantile Marine Office, I received my balance of wages, and my Discharge Book. The book was endorsed Very Good and Very Good for both conduct and ability. So ended a voyage never to be forgotten.

On leaving the ship I went straight to my friend's home, and I was asked to stay for a few days. They felt that they had so much they wanted to talk about. I did all I could to try and reassure them that there was just a possibility, though remote, that their son might have survived. When I left them, they were living in hopes that they might hear of his safe return. Fifty four years on, and it has not happened.

On returning to my own home for a well earned spot of leave, I decided that if there were no better ships than the "Llandilo" for me to sail in, then it was time for me to give up the sea. To this end, I tried to find a job ashore, but jobs were scarce.

I had a short spell digging trenches for the telephone company, that only lasted about a month. Then I heard that the East Yorkshire Motor Company needed seasonal bus conductors.

I applied for one of the jobs, I was accepted, on the understanding that I would have to train, on the buses, with an experienced conductor, but with no pay.

This training took about two weeks, and when I had satisfied the Company that I was competent, they gave me my first outing as a conductor. Whilst the job lasted, I really enjoyed it, but at 1/- per hour, (5p) I had to put in long hours to earn a living wage.

One day, when I was in the canteen, I met the man who had been the Chief Officer on the s.s. "Chelsea" when I was the deck boy of the ship. He was the man who gave me a "dog's life" for six months on voyage. It gave me no end of satisfaction to meet him on equal terms. He too was just a seasonal conductor on the buses.

I greeted him with "It's a small world isn't it Mr. Bowen?"

He was far from pleased to see me. There was a man with a Master's Certificate, reduced to taking a lowly job as a bus conductor. That is how bad things were in 1938.

The jobs that the driver and myself liked to have was any private hire work with the bus. We'd pick up a party at an appointed place, take them, usually to a dance somewhere, wait for them, and then bring them back late at night. The rules said that we should drop them off at the starting point, which was generally in the town centre. As it would be late at night when we dropped them, it was usual that someone in the party would ask if we could detour and drop people off nearer to their homes.

We always agreed to this, because it meant that the person who asked, would take my cap around the bus and collect a few shillings to be shared between the driver and myself.

It was not unusual to end up with almost a week's wages from the collection, so it was well worth while to us, even if it did break the Company's rules.

That job lasted until the outbreak of the war, when all services were curtailed and the seasonal men dismissed. It had been great while it lasted.

As a registered seaman, I soon received an official notice that I was to report to the shipping federation office for assignment to seagoing duties.

I reported as ordered, and I was asked if I was willing to take a gunnery course, and become a Seaman-gunner for a merchant ship.

Full of jingoistic ideas, I naturally said I'd be only too pleased. At least it would, I hoped, give me a chance to hit back at the enemy should he attack the ship in which I sailed.

I was duly booked in at the Naval Gunnery school which had been set up in the old shut down Earl's Shipyard on Hedon Road in Hull.

As a point of interest, it is worthy of note that a ship, built, launched, tested and then dismantled and shipped out to Lake Titicaca, in Peru was, up to quite recently still in operation on the waters of the lake. That is a great tribute to Earls, as ship builders. They also built many of the ships for the Ellerman's Wilson Line of Hull.

The course that several of us were to take, was to learn the rudiments of loading, aiming and firing an old 1914-18 war relic in the shape of a 4" breech-loading gun.

The course lasted twelve days and during that time we were shown how it was loaded, ranged by the gun-layer, trained, that is swung round to the target by the trainer.

When the trainer had the target in line with the gun, we had to shout out, "On, on, on". The gunlayer would estimate the distance of the target, and elevate or depress the gun, and then fire it.

Unfortunately we could not have any real live ammunition practise. We were also put through the misfire procedure.

If all of those who attended those gunnery courses had had real live ammunition practise, the odds would have been shortened.

After all, British seamen were to face some of the finest trained gunners in the world sailing on the enemy subs and ships.

Towards the end of the course we were all given a test on our knowledge and ability to man and use the gun. If successful, we were given a certificate stating that we had satisfactorily completed the training course, and that we were acceptable as Seaman-gunners for the defence of a Merchant ship.

Having received my certificate, I was told to report back to the Shipping Federation Office for appointment as such, to a ship.

It was 5 p.m. when I reported into the office, and I was amazed to be told that I was to be sent to a ship called the "Stangrant", lying in Barry Docks, South Wales.

I was to travel, the next evening on the 8 p.m. train out of Hull for Cardiff. I was given a rail voucher and a small amount of cash for meals en route.

I had not expected to be shipped out so fast, but the Ministry of War was desperate. They needed every seaman they could lay their hands on to man the ships. My war service was about to start.

Chapter 10.
South America, and sickness

It was now late October, and the evening I went to the station to catch my train to Barry, South Wales, it was snowing. My parents went along with me to the station, hoping to see me off on the train. However, when we arrived at the station, we were informed by the armed guard that only those actually travelling were allowed on the station. This, no doubt to thwart saboteurs. I said my farewells at the station gates, and humped my luggage to the platform and boarded the train. It was a very crowded train, packed with service men reporting for duty, all the services being represented; the Army, Navy, Royal Air Force, and not forgetting the Merchant Navy. All of whom were going away to serve their country now at war with Germany. The train left Hull at 8 p.m. and it was a long tedious journey down to South Wales. Though we had many stops on the way down, it was almost impossible to get a drink of tea, or of anything for that matter. I tried at several stations to get a bite to eat and a drink of tea, but the canteens were so full of Service personnel that we did not have the time to wait to be served by the overworked canteen staff.

I think it was at Crewe, that there was a Salvation Army trolley, and they thankfully provided me with a bun and a cup of tea.

It was like manna from heaven, for I was hungry and parched.

We finally arrived in Cardiff at 8 a.m. the following morning. There I changed trains for the one to Barry Docks, where I arrived about half an hour later - Journey's end. My first thoughts were to go and find a cafe and have me some breakfast. Having done that I then made my way down to the Docks to join the ship. At the gate I was stopped and challenged by an armed guard, and was only allowed to pass through the gate after he was satisfied that I was who I said I was.

The ship I found, was lying on the far side of the dock, under a coal hoist, so lugging my two suitcases, I made my way there.

On boarding the ship, I went and reported to the Chief Officer.

"Ah", he said, "You're just the man we are waiting for".

That was in response to my statement to him that I had been sent down from Hull to join the ship as Seaman Gunner.

He then told me to go aft and settle myself in the crew accommodation. He would, he said, inform the Master that I had arrived.

I went aft and found that the accommodation was for three men in a room. I found an empty room, choose a bunk and made myself at home there. We signed on a couple of days later, the usual Articles for "a voyage not exceeding 3 years duration" etc.

The only difference being, so far as I was concerned, was that I would receive 6d, (Two and a half pence) per day as a supplement to my normal wages. This was for having a gunnery certificate.

Any illusions I had, of being rated as a Seaman gunner, were soon to be shattered when we got to sea on voyage.

Despite all the warning signs posted up all over the place saying "Careless talk costs lives", the dockers were able to tell us that our cargo of coal was for Santos, Brazil, South America. In other words the Germans would know our sailing date and destination in advance, so much for the hush hush approach.

The ship, now named the "Stangrant", owned by Bilmiers of Cardiff, had originally been built in 1912 for the Port Line as the "Port Macquarrie". Several years later she had been sold to the Clan Line, who named her the "Clan Grant", and when she was about 25 years old, she was sold to Bilmiers, who simply changed the name to "Stangrant". Though she was a finely built ship, she was of course 27 years old when I joined her. At that age, a ship is well past its sell-by date. In other words she was well past her prime, as I was to find out when we sailed out of Barry.

We had only just dropped the Pilot and steamed away at full speed for Milford Haven, where we were to have joined an outward bound convoy, when the engineers reported a serious fault in the engines. We turned around and went back to Barry for repairs.

A couple of days later we sailed again, but once more had to be towed back into Barry for more repairs in the engineroom.

One would have thought that that would have been enough for someone in authority to say enough's enough, hold that ship, she is not fit to send on a 5,000 mile sea passage through a sub infested Atlantic Ocean.

No such luck, after a few more days of repairing we sailed for the 3rd time. Strangely enough, I had made friends in Barry and the last thing I said to them was that I had a feeling that I would not return to Britain in that ship. That was to come true, but not in the way I had expected.

We finally made it to Milford Haven, and teamed up with the West bound ocean convoy, and sailed with two destroyers as escorts.

When the convoy had sorted itself out and ships had got into their allotted stations, the Commodore ship signalled that the speed of the convoy would be 9 knots, flags K-9.

At first all went well, we were able to keep our station, then disaster crept in, we started to fall back, we couldn't keep the speed of 9 knots. We quickly became the "Tail-end Charlie", despite the Commodores signals for us to get back into station.

Try as they might, the engineers could not keep the engines going.

The rule in convoy was that you could not jeopardise a whole convoy of ships for the sake of one slow ship. To this end, the Commodore sent one of the destroyers back to tell our Captain that he would have to leave us, and that we should make our way to the appointed rendezvous, somewhere out in the middle of the Atlantic. That of course was known only to the Master of the ship and contained in his confidential papers issued by the Admiralty.

There we where, stopped, a sitting duck for any marauding German submarine, and all we could do was to watch helplessly, as the convoy slowly became hull-down to the West of our ship.

We were alone now, and very lonely.

In any case, at this stage of the war, ships were only given cover by escorts for a distance of 1,000 miles out into the Atlantic Ocean. The Navy was too short of ships to be able to protect Merchant ships any further than that.

The engineers finally got our ship moving again, much to the relief of all on board the ship. Our speed left a lot to be desired, at best we made about 8 knots in a flat calm sea, as I said earlier, the ship was clapped out and fit only for scrap. One very dark night, with the moon just about touching the Western horizon, I was at the wheel doing my two hour stint.

There, silhouetted again the moon was a warship, she would be some 15 miles to the West of us. By the little time it took her to pass across the Moon's face, she was travelling at great speed.

We learned later, that the ship was the "Graf Spee" heading South.

Fortunately she did not sight us as we were against the dark Easterly horizon.

Some 28 days after sailing from Barry and with stops too numerous to remember, we finally made it into Santos. When the Agent boarded the ship he told us that he had given up all hope of the ship arriving. In fact he said that had we not arrived by the next day, he was going to report us as missing, presumed lost by enemy action!

During our stay in the port of Santos, we met quite a few German seamen in our visits ashore. There were no signs of enmity amongst us, they like us had not wanted to be at war. The engineers took advantage of our fairly long stay in port to try and rectify some of the faults that had plagued us from the time we left Barry.

One of them, it appeared, was the fact that the boilers needed cleaning out. They were scaled up with lime scale, and this made it all the more difficult to maintain steam pressure. One of the boilers was "blown down", that is, allowed to cool down by withdrawing the fires and blowing off the steam pressure.

This procedure can take at least 48 hours before the boiler manhole covers can be removed for access to the inside.

Our 2nd Engineer was dead keen to get inside and examine the boiler, and he did not give it sufficient time. All steam pressure had gone from the boiler and he had the manholes unbolted and removed. He should have then let all the remaining heat and humidity dissipate, by leaving the doors off for several hours.

This he failed to do, thinking that it was cool enough for him to enter the boiler. He climbed through the manhole into the boiler, and as soon as he was inside, he collapsed. It was far too hot and humid inside.

There was of course, another engineer stationed at the manhole in case of emergency. Seeing the 2nd collapse, he immediately raised the alarm for help. With great difficulty they managed to get to the boiler, but not before his body had swollen a great deal through the high temperature and humidity.

He was immediately rushed into hospital, his condition serious.

I have no idea whether he survived his ordeal, as we left him in hospital when we sailed for the River Plate to load grain for home.

On sailing from Santos, there was the usual panic stations to get the holds cleaned out and washed down ready to load grain in the River Plate. Shifting boards had of course to be erected in all the holds on the way down the coast of South America.

In conformity with Admiralty rules, we put into Montevideo, this was to land all the ship's confidential documents and code books for safe-keeping, with the British Naval Attache stationed there.

On steaming up the River Plate to Montevideo there was a sight that none of us will ever forget, for there in the middle of the river just outside the harbour, was the smouldering remains of the infamous "Graf Spee". She had been scuttled only a matter of hours before our arrival.

The famous battle of the River Plate had taken place and the "Graf Spee", along with the British Naval ships which had taken part in the battle, had all put into Montevideo to land the dead and the wounded.

Captain Langdorf, Commander of the "Graf Spee", had wanted to go out sea again and fight the British ships. Hitler over-rode Langdorff's request to proceed out to sea, he didn't want the "Graf Spee" to fall into British Naval hands.

Hence his order for the "Graf Spee" to be scuttled in the Plate.

This proved too much for a proud German Imperial Naval Commander, he could not face the ignominy of such an action. He shot himself in his room at an hotel in Buenos Aires, where he and his crew were being housed after the sinking of the "Graf Spee".

To me, the sight of that once proud ship, lying there pouring out smoke and flames, was tragic. There was one of the finest battle ships of all time, albeit a pocket battle ship, destroyed to fulfil a madman's desire.

In writing, I must express the deepest admiration for Captain Langdorff, he may have been the enemy, but he abided by all the rules and conventions of war. He did not sink a ship without giving all members of the crew time to get clear of the ship.

He also made sure that any person who needed medical attention, got it. He also made sure that the people in the lifeboats had sufficient food and water to last them until they were rescued. In addition he supplied them with spirits and cigarettes. To cap it all, he even radioed the British Admiralty and gave them the name of the ship and the position at which he had sunk it.

Such actions as these were in the best traditions of the sea, and the acts of a truly humane Officer of the German Imperial Navy. Despite whatever anyone else may think of him, I have the greatest admiration of the man. It is a great pity that his humanity was not shared by the Officers commanding the German submarines during the Battle of the Atlantic.

Leaving Montevideo, we sailed up river to Rosario to load part of our cargo and then we came down to finish off in Buenos Aires.

On completion of loading we sailed for Montevideo again, and it was there that we had to

land our first-tripper Ordinary seaman. He had suddenly been taken ill, and was running a very high temperature, a Doctor ordered that he be landed and put into hospital. After we sailed from Montevideo, I was at the wheel between 0200 hours and 0400 hours, and half way through my stint at the wheel I felt strangely ill. How I managed to steer the ship, I shall never know, but come 04.00 hours when I was relieved, I was just about out on my feet. I made my way aft to my room and got straight into my bunk and fell asleep. I was called at 07.20, seven bells, by the watch-keeper but I was in no state to get out of my bed. I told the caller to go and tell the Chief Officer that I was ill and would not be turning out for duty. He did so, and at 08.00 hours, the Chief Officer came aft to see me.
His words to me were, "What's matter Mathison, got a belly ache?"
I told him it took more than a belly ache to keep me from doing my duty. He then left my room.

After breakfast, the Captain and the Chief Steward came to see me. The Steward took my temperature, it was 104, he told the Captain that I was too ill to do any work. The Captain then said that I was to stay in my bed until I felt better. I didn't get any better, I got worse. The next thing was that I heard that one of the catering staff had gone down with a very high temperature. Two days later two more men fell ill, again with high temperatures.
In the meantime the "Stangrant" was steaming Northwards along the coast, heading for Pernamboco, a port in Northern Brazil.
From there, ships turned on an almost due Easterly course for Freetown in West Africa. The distance between those two ports is the shortest crossing of the Atlantic Ocean. Freetown was the port at which ships bound for Britain congregated for convoys with Naval escorts.
In the days that passed, the other sick men and me were still running high temperatures, and one of them became delirious.
The ship would not normally have called at Pernambuco, it was merely the turning point en route for Britain.
The worry of the failing health of that crew member forced the Captain to proceed into the port for medical assistance.
On berthing, two Doctors came on board to examine the sick men.
They came to my room, accompanied by the Captain. Fortunately one of them spoke good English, and he was told that I was the first one to go down with whatever the malady was. He asked me various questions, then gave me a thorough examination, part of which entailed prodding my stomach. He touched one spot and I immediately cringed with pain. He then turned to the other Doctor and conferred in Portuguese, after which he called he Captain outside my room. I could hear the conversation, after which the Captain came back into the room and told me to get my gear packed, as I was to be hospitalised.
The same applied to the other sick men. My shipmates packed my gear for me, and two hours later a boat arrived to take us four men to the hospital.
When the boat got to the quayside, and we had been landed, there was the Agent to see us to the hospital with the ambulance that was waiting for us. At the Dock gates, the local Customs officials stopped the ambulance, they wanted to see what we had in our suitcases. An argument went on between the Agent and these officers, until he told them that we were bound for the Hospitale Isolamenti, (The isolation hospital). They couldn't get away from that ambulance fast enough, they dashed away from us, waving to the driver to get the hell out of it. I think they must have gone and fumigated themselves as soon as we were out of sight.
At the hospital we were each put in a separate room, and it was several days before I learned what was wrong with us all.
We had Typhoid Fever, the Doctor said, and in those days there was no Penicillin, not even M&B tablets for the treatment.
Nevertheless, whatever medication they gave us, it eventually did the trick, and we survived. Not so our first-tripper, landed in Montevideo. I learned later from the Agent that the lad had died in hospital from the fever.

I spent two months in the hospital, the Real Benifico Hospitale, which was run by nuns, and they were kindness itself.

They did everything possible to help us get well. In the latter part of our stay in hospital, we had visitors from the English community, who said they had only just heard that there were British seamen in the hospital. When two of us were well enough to go outside the hospital, the wife of the Manager of Cable and Wireless invited us to their home for a meal.

She had to get the permission of the Matron of the hospital to have us taken to her house. I remember the Matron telling the lady what we must not eat or drink at that stage. Any form of alcohol was strictly forbidden. I know only too well why that was.

I had reached the stage in my treatment where my temperature had stayed normal for several days, and I was told that I was now cured of the disease, and that subject to clinical tests, it would not be long before I would be able to travel home.

Unbeknown to the hospital staff, I had a bottle of Cherry Brandy in my suitcase, and I partook of a wee dram in celebration.

That was my undoing, my temperature shot up, and the Matron wanted to know why.

She decided to search my cases, and she found the bottle. She drew her own conclusions, but nevertheless asked me if I had touched the spirit. I had to admit that I had, whereon I got a severe dressing down. I had, she said, made the fever flare up again, and this would keep me in hospital for some time to come. It did. I was there another three weeks before I was passed fit to travel.

Getting back to Britain was going to be a bit of a problem, so few British ships were calling at Pernambuco now the war was on, so we had to wait for homeward bound ships arriving. We were of course to be shipped home as D.B.S.'s, that means we were classed as Distressed British Seamen, and under British maritime rules, we could be put aboard any British ship, homeward bound, provided they had accommodation available and fit for us.

Two homeward bound ships arrived the same day, one was the "Saint Merriel", the other was the "Crispin", a Booth Amazon Line ship.

Myself and a lad from Wales were put aboard the "Crispin" and the other two men were put on the "Saint Merriel". As it turned out, I would have been better off on the Saint ship, she went to my home port of Hull. The" Crispin", on the other hand was destined for Liverpool. The crew members of the ship made us very welcome, even though we were total strangers to them. We did not of course have to do any work on the ship, in fact neither of us was in any condition to do any after being in hospital for so long.

The "Crispin" was flying the Blue Ensign, which meant that she had a Captain and Officers who were Royal Navy Reserve men. This was apparent from the efficient way the ship was run. There was a lifeboat drill every day, and the Captain and his Officers inspected the ship on numerous occasions, more than would have been the case in a ship under the Red Ensign.

We had a fine pleasant run across to Freetown, where we joined a North bound convoy for Britain. I noticed that we had the "Jervis Bay" as our escort. Little did we know then, that the "Jervis Bay" would sail into the annals of history five months later, when she was escorting a 38 ship convoy which was attacked by the German battleship "Admiral Scheer". After giving the convoy orders to scatter, the "Jervis Bay" took up the challenge with the battleship. The odds against them were too great, and the "Jervis Bay" was hit several times and set on fire.

Despite terrible damage done to his ship, Captain E.S. Fogarty Fegen, Commander of the "Jervis Bay" tried to ram the German ship.

Captain Fegen died, along with 191 members of his crew in that gallant defence of the convoy.

By the time the "Admiral Scheer" had dispatched the "Jervis Bay", the convoy had so scattered that only five out of the 38 ships were sunk. In recognition of his bravery, in the face of such overwhelming odds, Captain Fogarty Fegen was posthumously awarded the Victoria Cross. His name will live forever more in the annals of history of the British Merchant Service.

About seven days after sailing from Freetown, we arrived at Liverpool, having had two or three calls to action stations after submarines had been detected. These it would appear, had been driven off by depth charges from the destroyers who were also part of our escort. For us two D.B.S.s, our arrival in Liverpool was to be a bit of an anticlimax, not quite what we had expected would happen to two British Merchant Seamen returning home to serve our country again.

Chapter 11
"Welcome home sailor!"

The "Crispin" docked about 10 a.m. in Huskisson Dock, Liverpool, and when she was all secured in berth, all of the crew went home for the weekend. They were all Liverpool men, so it was natural that they would want to get home quickly, and for as long as possible.
However, we two D.B.S.s had to be taken to the Immigration Dept. in Liverpool to see if we qualified for entry into Britain.
They had to be certain that we were not enemy agents!
The "Crispin's" 3rd Officer took us ashore in a taxi.
We were allowed out of the docks after being stopped by the Policeman at the gates, when the 3rd Officer had explained that we were on our way to the Immigration Office.
On the way there the 3rd Officer told us that as the ship would be "dead" for the weekend, we had been booked in at the Sailors' Home. He went on to say that once we had passed through the Immigration Office, he would then drop us off at the Sailor's Home.
All we had to do, he said, was to go in and report at Reception, tell them who we were, and they would fix us up with a room and board for the weekend. Come Monday, we should then be at the Mercantile Marine Office at 10 a.m. There we would be paid our balance of wages from the "Stangrant", and given a voucher for the rail journey back to our respective homes.
At the Immigration Office, I had no trouble proving who I was, I had my National Identity Card with me, this was proof positive.
The Welsh lad, Taff, did not have his Identity Card with him.
This momentarily posed a problem for him, then the Immigration Officer spoke to him in Welsh, asking him to describe the town he came from. The lad answered instantly in Welsh, and the Officer was satisfied as to his identity. The Officer came from the same area as this lad, and the answers he got satisfied him that the lad was indeed a bona fida Welshman.
Coming out of the office, the 3rd Officer had the taxi take us to the Sailor's Home, where he dropped us off, and off he went for his weekend at home, unaware that he had left us stranded.

Going inside the Home we asked to see the Superintendent, and when he came, we told him who we were and that we understood that we had been booked in for the weekend. He consulted the register, and then told us that as there was no mention of us, he could not therefore give us any accommodation or meals.
This was a fine state of affairs, here we were, landed in Liverpool, not a penny piece between us, and nowhere to stay.
The Superintendent suggested that we try the Salvation Army. We did, but they did not have any accommodation. However, they showed some compassion about our situation. They made up a package of sandwiches and gave them to us, so that we would not be hungry.
It seemed that we had no alternative but to go back to the ship.
It was a hell of a long walk back for us, and by the time we reached the dock gates we were both knackered. This was the longest walk we had had for at least three months, and it told.
More aggro at the gates - the Policeman on duty wanted to see our Dock Passes before he would let us on to the docks.

We explained to him that we did not have passes, as we had just been taken out an hour earlier by the 3rd Officer of the "Crispin". His answer, was that as he was not on duty then, he was unable to allow us on the docks.
He suggested that we go to the offices of the Booth Line and get a pass issued by them. Booth Line being the owners of the ship. By this time it was past noon, and all the offices would be closed for the weekend, so what to do now?
Not feeling too good, my temper was by now being stretched to the limits. I told the Policeman that if he did not let us go back to the ship, I would report him to the highest authority possible.

I pointed out that we had been let off the dock without passes, and that we were going to get back without passes.

My threat of taking the matter to high authorities seemed to do the trick. After a few minutes rumination, he decided to let us go back to the ship.

If he had not, I would have taken the matter even to the Prime Minister if need be.

Had we have been German prisoners of war, we would have been given food and accommodation when we arrived. Here we were, two British seamen returned to this country to serve again in British merchant ships, and we are treated like pariahs. I told the copper so, and I think it must have finally got through his thick skull that we were genuine seamen on our uppers.

He let us through the gate to get back to the ship.

Arriving back, we made our way down to the accommodation where we had our room. Much to our surprise, there was one of the crew still on board, packing his gear to take home with him.

He asked how we had got on when we went ashore. I told him the whole sordid story of the shabby treatment we had received.

I was pleasantly surprised and very grateful when he put his hand in his pocket and took out 5/-.

"Here, take this, maybe it will help you over the weekend, sorry I can't make it any more than five bob, but that's all I can spare".

I expressed my thanks, and with that he was away ashore to go home.

There was only a watchman left aboard now, and we managed to scrounge a cup of tea from him to help boost our spirits.

It struck me that five Shillings wouldn't get us very far. I suggested to my mate that we go ashore to the Post Office and telegram to my mother and ask her to telegraph some money to me. The General Post Office was open 24 hours a day early in the war.

We made our way back to the Dock Gate and explained to the Policeman what we were going to do, and that we would be back very shortly. We didn't want to have all the hassle again about getting into the dock without a pass. He said that as he would be on duty when we got back there would be no problem.

I think it cost me two shillings to send the telegram. I asked for some money to be telegraphed to me care of the Post Office, Liverpool. All we could do now was to wait until an answer came from my mother.

To fill in time we found a cafe, where we had something to eat and a cup of tea. We still had some change left even after that. With that we were able to buy a quarter pound of tea, some sugar and a tin of milk. We had the sandwiches on board that the Salvation Army had given us, so now, at least we could survive until that money arrived. So it was back to the ship again, for a bit of a rest before going to the Post Office for funds.

Some five hours later we went back to the Post Office, where I was delighted to find that the money had arrived. Our troubles were over for the time being.

On Sunday morning we went ashore to the cafe we'd been in before and we were able to have our breakfast, after which we bought some newspapers and returned to the ship to pass the time away until dinner time.

On the Monday morning, the ship came alive again, the personnel had returned after their weekend at home. The Chief Steward came aft and told us that we were to be at the Mercantile Marine Office at 10 a.m., when we would receive our balance of wages and a rail voucher to get us to our homes. A taxi had been ordered to take us and our gear to the office and we were soon on our way there.

When we got into the office, I asked if I could have a word with the Superintendent. He came to the counter and asked what he could do for us.

I explained the circumstances of our arrival in Liverpool, and the lack of attention we had had. I told him about not being taken in at the Sailor's Home, and the hardship this had caused as neither of us had a penny between us. We had just been dumped ashore without any means of support, and this was not good enough. I wanted something done about the situation, I told him I was making a formal complaint about our treatment.

He was most sympathetic and promised us that he would take the case up with the shipmaster. He did when the Master of the "Crispin" arrived at the office, he gave him a right dressing down. He pointed out that you cannot just bring D.B.S.s home and dump them on the quay, as it would appear they had done with us two. He pointed out in no uncertain terms, that the law demands that D.B.S.s must either be sent straight to their homes or be properly accommodated until such time as they can be.

I fancy that the 3rd Officer of the "Crispin" would be in for a roasting when the Master next saw him. After all, he was the one who should have seen to it that we were put up for the weekend at the Sailor's Home. He was all too interested in getting to his own home to be bothered with two lower deck ratings such as us.

That was the illustrious homecoming that we two had got on arrival in Britain after two months in hospital abroad. It summed up the general attitude of the public to Merchant Seamen, even in war.

When I got home, my mother told me that the "Stangrant", the ship from which I had been put ashore, had returned to Hull, and she had gone down to the ship to see the Captain. All she wanted to know was how was I when put in hospital. The Captain, she said, was most abusive and said he couldn't have cared less, so she was no wiser.

I note from the entry in my Discharge Book, which was deposited by the Captain of the "Stangrant" in the Shipping Office in Hull, it is dated the 20th March 1940. Having been put ashore on the 21st Feb.1940, it must have taken the ship a month to reach Hull.

If that was the best speed she could do there is no wonder that she was lost in the North Atlantic on the 13th Oct.1940. No doubt she was straggling again and could not keep up with the convoy.

She was sunk to the North-West of the island of St. Kilda by the submarine U-37, whilst bringing a cargo of steel from the United States to Britain. Sadly, eight of her crew were lost in that attack.

After arrival home, I was taken ill again and it was to be several months before I was fit enough to go back to sea. I utilised the time at home to continue my studies for 2nd Mate's certificate.

By the October of 1940, I was able to take the examination for the certificate, and I am pleased to say that I passed with flying colours. I used my last 20/- to pay the exam fee.

I was now broke.

It is worthy of note that during my forced stay ashore, the National Union of Seamen, of which I was a member, took up my case about the stoppage of wages when landed ashore in hospital in Brazil. They took the case up with what is now known as the Ministry of Social Security, but at that time was the Ministry of Health. They did this because seamen were not entitled to any sick benefit for the time they were out of this country. They pointed out that I had no choice in the matter, and that had I not had been in a fever infested country, I would not have contacted the disease. They won the case, and in so doing, made legal history.

I was awarded the sum of fifteen Pounds, which was the equivalent of 20 weeks sick benefit of 15 shillings per week, the going rate at that time. It also meant that in the future, any seaman put ashore in hospital abroad, would be entitled to the payment of his sick benefit for the weeks spent out of Britain.

This was a great deal of money to me at the time, considering that I had nothing other than my meagre pay from the "Stangrant", and that had ended in February 1940.

In the early afternoon of July 25th 1940, the door bell rang at home. I answered it, and when I opened the door, the person who had called was the Superintendent of the Ellerman's Wilson Line in Hull. I knew him by sight. Before he has a chance to say anything, I asked him to tell me the worst.

I wanted to know what had happened to my brother, who was serving on the s.s. "Leo" at the time.

His question to me was, "How did I know that he had bad news"?

To which I said I knew he was Wilson's Superintendent, and he would not have been calling unless something disastrous had happened.

He then explained that they had just received news that the "Leo" was bombed and sunk just off Dover Harbour a few hours earlier.

He also said that it was known that there were some survivors, but they did not know who at that time.

I told him I would break the news to my mother, for which he thanked me. It saved him a harrowing task, after all he had the job of informing the relatives of all the crew members of the ship. Needless to say, there was a' weeping and a' wailing and gnashing of teeth when I broke the news to mother.

After this, I pointed out to her that there was hope, as there were some survivors, and Laurie could be one of them.

With the aid of a cup of tea and a few well chosen words, I got mother to dry her tears. Save them, they could be tears of joy, I told her.

That's how it turned out, for at teatime we received a telegram from Dover stating that my brother had been picked up from the water, unhurt, by a Norwegian Air-Sea rescue vessel, and had been landed at Dover.

He would be home in a few hours it said.

My brother arrived home the next morning, clad in the clothes he had been wearing when the first bomb from the German aircraft, which hit the after gun position and killed the gun crew.

A second bomb had penetrated one of the holds and the ship started sinking. As the main deck came level with the water, my brother and the 3rd Officer of the ship, dived overboard and swam away from the sinking vessel.

Talking to my brother later, he said it was worse in the water when a bomb exploded, than it was when they hit the ship. He said the concussive effects on the body were terrific when in the water.

At the time of his homecoming, Hull was having hell knocked out of it by German air-raids. I remember one night when he and I were going around the houses near to us, putting out fires started by incendiary bombs. We did this using buckets of water and a stirrup-pump. We carried on until it became too dangerous. One night, a bomb blew all our windows and the front door out.

The bomb that had done the damage had fallen into the lawn in front of the house in Trinity Square, I well remember the strange silence after it exploded, for I was almost deafened by the blast. As my hearing returned, I could hear a hissing sound coming from the front room of our house. This puzzled me, but I just had to find out what it was making the noise.

My first thought was that it must be some new devilish device the Germans were using. I finally located the source of the hissing.

It was gas coming from a pipe buried in the wall above the fireplace. A piece of shrapnel from the bomb had cut through the gaspipe. I immediately turned the gas off at the meter, and then dug a few inches of the pipe out of the wall and folded it over several times and then hammered it flat. This effectively sealed the pipe until permanent repairs could be carried our by the gas authorities, and enabled us to make a welcome cuppa.

Later in the year 1940, I put my application in to sit the B.O.T. examination for 2nd Mate's Certificate, and I am pleased to be able to say that I passed with flying colours.

Within hours of being told that I had passed my examination for my "ticket" I had a telegram from a Hong Kong shipping company, Jardine Mathesons, offering me a job as 2nd Officer. This was followed by another offer from a British company. It seemed that there was a great shortage of certificated officers for ships. I explained over the 'phone, (reversed charges), that I had no sextant and Log tables, or money to buy the necessary gear.

In both cases, they said they would provide me with a sextant!

When I went to the Board of Trade office, to pick up my certificate, the examiner asked me if I had had offers from any shipping companies. I told him I had. I named one of them. He hoped that I hadn't accepted their offer. I said I had not. He then told me that they were a hard outfit to work for and that they only carried two deck officers. That would have meant doing four hours on and fours hours off duty in their ship, and in war time that was not an acceptable condition to work under.

During my enforced stay ashore, I heard almost every day of the losses of British Ships sunk by German U-Boats. The news was grim and the losses of ships and men were heartbreaking. It was only natural that I wanted to devise an easy method to help ships to be protected against subs.

Eventually I came up with the idea of wire nets being strung overside, held well clear of the ship's side by means of steel booms. Having formulated the idea, I sent if off personally to the Prime Minister, Winston Churchill.

I pointed out that I was not a qualified ship designer, but that I did realise that such an arrangement would slow a ship down owing to frictional resistance.

My original suggestion was that the ships ordinary derricks could be lowered so as to rest in crutches fitted to the bulwarks on either side.

This I explained would speed up the installation of the anti-torpedo nets on Merchant ships. The Prime Ministers secretary answered my letter, conveying Mr.Churchill's thanks, and also stating that the suggestion had been passed on to the appropriate department of the Navy.

After that I heard no more, but was hopeful that it might have been the means of saving one or more ships from destruction.

About a year later, I saw a ship fitted with my idea, and I was able to ask the personnel about it. They said that the system had been tried out by the Navy, using a scrap vessel. Torpedoes had been fired at the target and the net idea worked, thus saving the ship.

Over the years that have passed since then, I have often wondered who got recognition for the idea to protect our Merchant ships.

No doubt it was some back-room boy. If so, the honour went to the wrong person.

My first job as navigational officer came with joining one of Associated Humber Lines ships, the s.s. "Selby". I was to join her at Birkenhead I was told. On the appointed date, I travelled to Birkenhead and put up in a hotel for the night to await the arrival of the ship. She did not arrive the next day as expected, no one seemed to know when she would arrive. The following day I went across into Liverpool to the Sea Transport Office, this was a Naval establishment. I had some difficulty in getting into the place, such was the security. Eventually they imparted the information that the ship was due to arrive from the Bristol Channel the next morning.

When she arrived, I reported aboard to the Master, Capt. Westerdale.

I pointed out to him that I had only just got my "ticket" but he didn't seem to mind, as he said "I'd soon learn, the hard way".

On discharge of her cargo of cotton for Manchester, we sailed for the Clyde. There we were to load sugar from an ocean going ship by the name of "Peterston", at first I thought it was my old ship the "Peterton", but it was another company's ship.

We tied up alongside the "Peterston", lying at anchor in Holy Loch, just off Dunoon, and there we loaded our cargo of sugar for Hull.

It couldn't have been better, going back to my home port with sugar. It was then that I learned that Hull was one of the premier ports for sugar cargoes. We had several days loading, and I was able to see the sights of Dunoon, not that there was much to see. On sailing, we proceeded through the Minches and up round Cape Wrath to the Pentland Firth, and it was there that we came across very dense fog. The Pentland Firth is not the best of places in which to encounter fog. I remember it was a trying time for me, on watch on the bridge for the first time, but of course the Captain was up there on the bridge with me. As he had said, I would soon learn. It was a case that I had to learn, and fast.

Having cleared the Pentland Firth safely, we then headed down the coast for Methil, that was where we would join a South-bound convoy for Hull and beyond.

It turned out that we would have a couple of days in Methil, and we found that the Dock Gate Policemen were very obliging in letting us out with parcels of sugar. They of course got a share of the ill-gotten gains. I think most of the crew sent a parcel of sugar home from Methyl. Had we have been caught purloining the sugar no doubt we would have been classed as 5th columnists, and severely dealt with.

To us, the sugar was the legitimate perks of the game.

A couple of days later we arrived in Hull and I was paid off to be sent to another one of the company's ships, the s.s. "Alt", which had just completed repairs at Goole.

We left Goole just after high water, and made our way down river, out of the Ouse and into the Humber. With the tide starting to ebb, and the ship at full speed, we were doing about 14 knots.

Before too long we were approaching the boom gate, the steel nets stretched across the river to deter enemy submarines getting in and creating mayhem with ships in the river.

We had signalled the boom gate vessel, so that he would open the gate for us to pass through. As we approached, we could see the gate being opened, and just as we were about to pass through it, the ebb tide caught us and bore us down onto the boom gate vessel.

We contacted the vessel with our Starboard side, hitting his stern. There was an almighty flash as the impact cut through our De-Gaussing cables strung around the ship on the outside of the plating. As we swept through the gate we could see the boom gate ship heeling over and it seemed as though he would capsize.

Our Captain, Capt. Earnshaw, stopped our ship and then turned her to stem the tide. The purpose was twofold, first to render aid to the boom gate vessel if need be, and secondly to find out what damage had been sustained by our ship.

He instructed me to go down along the foredeck and see what damage had been done. I didn't have to go very far along the deck to find the damage, the foredeck had been buckled upwards by the force of the impact. In addition, the shell plating of No.2 hold had been severely indented.

Continuance of the voyage was now impossible, as we had no protection from Jerry's magnetic mines, and it would have been suicidal to even dream of proceeding out into the North Sea in such a state. We therefore proceeded back up the river to anchor off Sammy's Point and await orders from the owners. They soon came, we were to proceed back to Goole for repairs.

My voyage as 2nd Officer of the "Alt" had lasted just 15 days!

Next, a few days later, I was sent to join the s.s. "Harrogate" at Glasgow, she had a load of cotton destined for Manchester. She had picked this cargo up from an ocean-going ship. On sailing from the Clyde, it was found that the cargo was on fire in No.2 hold, and the fire was a very fierce one. This was reported to the Admiralty, who ordered us to make for Troon, where they said they would have a fire-fighting tug waiting for us.

We entered Troon harbour and tied up alongside the jetty. By this time, the deck coatings inside the accommodation were starting to melt owing to the heat from the fire.

Looking over the side of the ship you could see the water bubbling owing to the heat of the ship's side plates.

The promised tug and fire-fighters arrived, and to assess the extent of the fire they gingerly opened a hatch. As they did so, there was a whoosh, and flames shot out of the hatch.

They quickly closed the hatch again and said that they would steam the cargo for several hours. This they did by injecting steam through hoses, into the holds. They carried on with this treatment for some twelve hours, then decided to have another look at the situation. Again, when they opened the hatch, and some air got in, the cargo immediately burst into flames again.

At this stage, the Officer in charge of the operation said that the only thing they could do now was to pump the holds full of sea water, as it would be the only thing that would douse the fire.

This they did, and the Harrogate ended up sat on the bottom of Troon harbour. A severe form of treatment, but at least it had the desired results, for the fire went out.

The next thing was that the cargo had to be unloaded, and there were no stevedores available in Troon. This was where the crew stepped in and earned a few welcome quid to do the job. I was hoping to be part of the operation and make a little extra money myself, my wages only being about £7 a week.

All thoughts of getting rich were quickly dispersed when I got orders from the Head Office to proceed on leave, as I was wanted for another of the Company's ships.

After a few days at home, I got orders to proceed to Scapa Flow where I was to join the s.s. "Aire" She was, I was told, under the Admiralty as a Fleet Ammunition Supply Vessel, and permanently moored at the buoys in Scapa Flow for that purpose.

I was given my rail ticket from Hull to Thurso, and told what train I had to take so as to arrive at Thurso at a certain time.

It was a long tedious journey, with a change of trains at York for Edinburgh. There, a change for the train to Perth, where there was a wait for the departure of the train at 8 p.m. prompt. It appears that the train only did the journey North during the hours of darkness, this was to try and protect it from German air attacks. I noticed that the drivers cab was well blacked-out so that the glow from the fires was not visible from the air.

It was a single track line from Perth to Thurso, and a slow run overnight. At 6 a.m., the Salvation Army catering staff brought breakfast around, which we could buy for 1/-. It consisted of two "bangers" and mash, a slice of bread and butter, and a cup of tea.

God Bless the Army, it was like manna from heaven after all night without a drink or a bite to eat.

The train arrived at Thurso at about 8 a.m., where a bus then took us to Scrabster, the port for Thurso.

There, I had to undergo thorough interrogation before I was allowed to board the ferry to Scapa Flow. The military were very efficient, as you would expect when people were travelling to a place where a great part of the British Navy was stationed.

A saboteur would have had a whale of a time let loose there.

After a short sea trip across the Pentland Firth in the ferry "St. Ninian", we anchored off Liness, where a leave boat took each of us to our respective ships.

In joining the "Aire", I had been demoted slightly, I was now 3rd Officer, I didn't mind that. I had a nice large room and the ship's personnel were great shipmates. Every evening we had our supper in the Engineer's messroom.

The Captain, Capt. Aaron, the Chief Officer, Chief and 2nd Engineer and myself would meet for a natter and a bite to eat. The Chief Cook, Mr. Depledge, used to lay on nice suppers for us.

For some reason, the 2nd Officer never joined us, he was a loner.

I can't remember exactly how we all filled in our time there, but life seemed quite rosy. There we were, snug in harbour, no worries about submarines, only the occasional German air raids to contend with, and these were ably handled by the anti-aircraft armaments both shore based and ship based.

When they all opened up at the marauding aircraft, you needed your tin hat to defend you from the snow-like fall of shrapnel from the bursting shells.

Weather permitting, there was a ship called the "Autocarrier", which in peacetime was a cross Channel car ferry, but had been altered and her lower hold made into a cinema auditorium.

She would come along and moor up alongside us, and we could attend the cinema show for the evening. There was also a bar on board her so that Officers and ratings could enjoy a few drinks.

After the show was over, and the men returned to their various ships, we would be allowed to stay on board for further light liquid refreshment if we so desired.

There was also the N.A.A.F.I. boat, a converted trawler, which came once a week, from this we were able to buy our cigarettes and whatever, at the cheap rates available to the Service personnel.

Once a week, there was a leave boat laid on to take us ashore to Kirkwall. The Chief Cook used to travel on this boat to buy the food stores needed for the week for all the Officers. As we were being paid weekly rates of pay, we had to pay for our own food.

Each week, the Cook would tell us what our share of the cost would be. It varied slightly week by week, according to what the Cook had had to pay for the goods he bought ashore. As I remember it, what he charged us was good value for our money, he fed us extremely well. In inclement weather, his job was not a pleasant one. Of course we all mucked in to help him load the stuff onto the leave boat, and to get it aboard when we got alongside our ship.

I used to go ashore each week in the boat, initially for a break, but I always had a load of stuff to take back for those who preferred to stay aboard. I used to enjoy a nice meal in a cafe right opposite St. Magnus Cathedral. The food and service were excellent, and prices were very reasonable, considering it was wartime.

Mind you, there were days when it was hard to hold on to your stomach, the Scapa Flow can be very nasty in some weather conditions. The smell from the hold of the converted trawler did not help matters, and once or twice I had to get out on deck to get a breath of fresh air. The alternative would have been to bring my dinner up, and that would have been a waste of money!

Despite the welcome break ashore, it was always nice to get back.

Chapter 12

Floating mines and falling shells.

We had on board the "Aire" just about every type of shell from the 15" armour piercing shells for the battleship guns, down to the smallest, .303 bullets. In addition there was a stock of German small arms bullets, and a load of French 75 m/m. shells.

When any of this stuff was needed for any ship, we, the crew and Officers would have to load or unload the stuff. For this, we were paid extra money by the Admiralty, so we always welcomed the work when it came along.

On board we also had a space set aside as a laboratory, in which three munitions experts used to work. Their job was to make safe for transit any faulty ammunition which was returned to us.

Periodically a ship called the "Sinclair", would come alongside and load up with the faulty ammunitions. These she would take back to the factory at Fort William, via the Caledonian Canal.

Sadly the "Sinclair" was lost at sea, off the coast of Scotland, on her way to Fort William during a very bad storm.

One afternoon, on a nice calm day, an armed trawler was seen to be approaching us very slowly. Several of us stood and watched what she was going to do. Very gingerly she came alongside us.

We of course dropped a line down so that she could moor alongside.

At first we thought that she had come to replenish her munitions supply, but not so. She had brought something for us, a floating mine which she had in tow astern of her, being carefully kept clear of contact with the trawler by members of her crew.

A floating mine is a sinister looking object when it is bobbing up and down in the water.

Contrary to popular belief, sea mines are not bristling with horns. They have 5 horns on the entire surface, but when one of those horns strikes the hull of a vessel, seconds later a charge of 300 lbs. of Amatol explodes.

Woe betide anyone or anything in the near vicinity. The loss of dozens of ships during the war due to mines, tell of its deadly effect when they are detonated. So it was understandable that the crew of the trawler were treating this one with great respect, their lives depended on handling it so.

As soon as the trawler was moored, one of our technicians boarded her and went to the stern of the vessel and weighed the position up. He then got into a "jolly boat", a small rowing boat, and got close to the mine, then carefully turned it over in the water, so as to reach the bottom of the mine.

I watched this procedure. Once he had the mine bottom up, you could then see the mooring shackle protruding from a bracket.

With the aid of a 2lb. hammer, he hammered away at the shackle. As he did so, the shackle was slowly knocked into the bracket.

When it was as far in as it would go, he then pushed a 4" nail through the aligned holes in the bracket and the shackle. This done he then bent the nail over so that it could not slip out.

"She's safe now, take her aboard", he called up to us, whereon we lowered a runner from our winch to lift the mine on board.

We laid two planks of wood for it to rest on when we landed it on No.2 hatch. The idea of the timber was to keep the horns from contacting the ship, and also to stop it rolling off the hatch.

When we had it down on the hatch cover, the Technician then got to work removing the 5 deadly horns, handing them to me as he did so. Next he got on removing the base plate, with the aid of spanners and of course, the 2lb. hammer! So many of life's little problems are solved by a judicious blow from a 2lb.hammer, ask any Engineer. Once he had removed all the nuts from the dozen or so bolts holding the base plate on, and of course making it waterproof, he loosened the cover plate with hammer and chisel.

With the coverplate off, I was able to see the inside of the mine, it all looked so brand new. The Technician lay on the hatch and crawled inside the mine to remove the primers. These were the smaller charges that detonated the 300 lbs. of high explosive.

With those out, the mine was now perfectly safe to handle, and we stowed it away to await transport to Fort William.

The thing that intrigued me most was the fact that when the Technician cleaned around the flange which held the base plate, there was the date of when the mine was manufactured, stamped into the metal.

The date was 1918, and that mine had been moored on the sea bottom for 24 years and had just broken loose, and it was still as deadly as the day it was laid. Even today, 42 years after the end of WWII, mines are from time to time found floating around the seas.

It will be an awful long time before the seas are truly safe for ships at sea anywhere in the World.

I was up at Scapa Flow in the mackerel season, when they simply swarm the waters around Scotland. One evening the whole of the waters of the Flow were alive with thousands of mackerel flashing about in the water. Several of the ships lowered their motor boats into the waters to make a catch of nice fresh fish.

Unfortunately we did not have a motor boat, but nevertheless we lowered our small rowing boat in an effort to catch some fish.

No bait was needed, all we had to do was to tow hooked lines, several hooks on each line wrapped with the silver paper out of cigarette packets. The fish simply snapped at the silver paper, and they were hooked. With a supply of about thirty fish, we went back aboard, the Chief Cook turned out and gutted and cleaned the fish, and then fried us some for supper. They were delicious. It was things such as this that helped to get rid of boredom of being stationed at Scapa.

After about 4 months, I was given home leave, a most welcome break indeed. The only thing was the length of time it took from leaving the ship to arriving in Hull.

I left the ship on the liberty boat at 10 a.m., and was taken to the "Baltiki", which was acting as a headquarters ships for the Navy. Once on board there, we were cleared for exit from Scapa Flow, our passes and rail warrants were issued on board that ship.

At about 3 p.m. the ferry boat for crossing the Pentland Firth to Scrabster, would come alongside.

All shore leave men would then board the "St.Ninian" for the trip across the Firth. In fine weather it was pleasant, but on the other hand the seas could be really rough. Landing at Scrabster, we Officer types, and I was one of them even though I was the 3rd Officer, were taken by bus to the hotel, were for a very reasonable price, we could have our evening meal.

We boarded the train at 7.45 p.m. for the run to Perth. The train left promptly 8 p.m., and travelled through the night. Having left the ship at 10 a.m. one day, I arrived at Hull Paragon Station at 8 a.m. the next morning, feeling as though I had been dragged through a hedge backwards. I used to feel really sorry for those chaps headed for the South of England on leave, it must have taken them more than 24 hours to complete their journey.

A week at home soon passed and I was on my way back for another stint on the s.s. "Aire". One afternoon, we had to supply some French 75m/m ammunition to a ship which came alongside. Those 75 m/m shells were packed in pairs, two in each wooden case. The cases had rope carrying handles at each end. To lift them out of our holds, we used clip hooks, so as to lift twelve cases at a time. I was the Hatchman, that is I gave instructions to the winch driver when to lift or lower a load. I gave him the signal to heave away and bring the stuff up on deck, so he set the winch in motion.

The dozen cases were just coming up out of the hold to deck level when the ends dropped out of two of the cases, and the shells went hurtling down below. I was horrified, but I managed to shout the age-old call of "Under below". This is the standard call used at sea to warn anyone working below, to get out of the way.

There was a mad scamper for whatever shelter there might have been in a hold loaded with munitions.

My heart stood still as I heard the shells strike on top of a stock of 6" shells. I waited for the big bang, but thank God it did not come. The shells had landed in a manner that had not exposed the percussion cap in their base. Being fixed ammunition, that is the shell and charge are all in the one brass case, they are fired from the gun by a pin which strikes the percussion cap, in the same manner as the bullets in a rifle or hand gun.

I can only say that had those shells exploded, the men down in the hold would have had no chance of survival.

Needless to say, we never ever lifted them that way again, we loaded them into cargo. You live and learn, but some might not have lived for us to learn.

Having had my leave, I returned to the "Aire" and did another 5 months service on her, then came orders that she was to go down to Leith for what the Navy calls a re-fit.

In reality, it was a drydocking and general overhaul. On arrival at Leith, I had orders to leave the ship as I was wanted on another of the company's ship. Mind you, this wasn't too bad because it meant that I got some more home leave before joining the other ship.

I joined the s.s. "Rother", at Goole, the company's home port, on 11th May 1942, and after one coastal voyage I was promoted to 2nd Officer. I was to be in the "Rother" for 10 months during which time I did a number of voyages down the East Coast of Britain from Leith to London, carrying frozen meat as we were a "fridge ship". If it wasn't meat it would be butter, which we off loaded at Hay's Wharf in the Pool of London.

Occasionally the cargo would be apples and fruit, these we took into West Indies Dock in Poplar. Our short stay in that dock could be quite pleasant as there was a theatre, known as the "Sod's Opera" close by, and we could have a nice evening watching the burlesque shows they put on. Of course each voyage South or North meant passing through the famous, or should I say infamous "E Boat Ally", which was the buoyed channel between Sherringham Shoal and Harwich. It was along this buoyed channel that the German E Boats used to lie in wait for the convoys to pass through. They would tie up to a buoy and wait, for they knew exactly when a convoy was due to enter the channel. As we had passenger accommodation on the "Rother", we were always the Commodore Ship.

In other words, we had on board the Naval Commodore and his staff and we were the leading ship which all others followed. This was very much to our advantage, the Germans were wily enough not to attack the leading ship of a convoy. That would have given the game away. They invariably made their attacks on the rear end of the convoy.

If there was an air attack, it could be on any ship in the convoy.

The Luftewaffen were not so choosy as the E Boat commanders.

Our protection against them was the Lewis guns and the Holman projectors. These abortions were supposed to fire a grenade into the air, after the style of a mortar. However, the powers that be thought that they could be launched by using steam pressure.

What they had not considered was the fact that steam in a pipe condenses to water when it gets cool. In the event of an air attack it took too long to blow out the water from the pipes before you got the steam.

By which time, Gerry had made his attack and was away to hell and gone. We used to have a test for this apparatus, using "spuds" as the ammunition, and when it was fired, it usually just plopped out of the barrel of the projector and rolled onto the deck.

Just imagine what would have happened had if that spud had been a real live round! So much for the Holman projector, the idea was good, but it should have had high pressure compressed air bottles to make it an efficient weapon of defence.

Another slightly better means of defence against enemy air attacks, was the P.A.C. rockets. These were rockets fired into the air and they had a length of thin wire cable attached to the parachute that opened when the rocket exploded at a given height.

The idea was to wait until the enemy plane was coming in on his bomb run, and then fire the rocket so that it would be right on his flight path, and woe betide the plane if she hit the dangling cables. As I say, the idea was good, but I never saw or heard of any plane being brought down by one of these rockets. Nevertheless, they acted as a good deterrent against planes.

My final voyage in the "Rother" was an interesting one. We loaded stores for our Service men stationed in Iceland, our port of discharge was to be Reykjavik.
We joined a North bound convoy at Leith and had a very pleasant passage North. The weather was glorious as it was mid summer. The sea was like a sheet of glass, and it seemed that we would have no problems with the enemy. Then one afternoon, we saw the black flag being hoisted on the Commodore ship.
For once, we were not Commodore ship, he had preferred to have a much larger ocean-going vessel under his feet and command. The black flag indicated submarine activity, and it was action stations.
Suddenly, an American ship opened fire at something in the water.
It turned out to be a floating mine, recently released by a sub. As this mine drifted down past us, the American opened fire again. Fortunately for us he missed it.
It would have blown our stern off. Talk about trigger-happy!
That was the sum total of enemy action on that passage, but not all passages were like that one.
The Captain of our ship, knowing that Iceland was a "dry" country, and that a bottle of whiskey could bring a high reward, made a point of selling each of us officers, a bottle of spirits.
These were to sell on our arrival in Iceland if approached by a potential buyer.
I managed to get hold of a clean empty whiskey bottle, I then halved the contents of my full bottle. Half in one bottle, and the other in the second bottle, this done I then topped the bottles up with cold, strained tea, so as to maintain the colour.
When finally asked if I had any liquor to sell, I sold the two bottles and raked in the sum of 20 Pounds Sterling!
Not a bad return for an outlay of 10 Shillings, (50p), I just wish I had had more bottles to sell at that rate of profit!.
The currency received was of course Icelandic, but there was no hassle changing it for a British Postal Order, which I could bank or cash on arrival back in the U.K.
Going ashore in Reykjavick, was like entering another world. There were no black-outs, nothing was rationed, all the shops were full of all the things that were missing in Britain.
The only thing was, that the Icelandic people just tolerated us.
They hated the Americans stationed in their country, but at least they would be pleasant to any Britisher.
The thing I found most awkward to put up with was the Sun, it shone all night through.
You could watch it get to its lowest point above the horizon, it never set during the time we were up there. In other words it was daytime all night, and this sort of upset our sleeping habits.
Leaving Reykjavick, we went to a small port in the Westman Islands, there we loaded a full cargo of frozen fish for Britain.
Seeing the waters of the harbour teeming with haddocks, no wonder the Icelandic Government were keen to protect their fishing waters from all the British trawlers after the war.
After all, fish were just about the only viable asset that the country had, and without jurisdiction those waters would have finally have been fished out.

By April 1943, I had the necessary sea time in to allow me to go ashore to sit my next B.O.T. exam for Mates certificate.
I requested leave to do just that. It was granted by the Company's Superintendent, but he

insisted that I should go on the "Pool", (The Shipping pool) whilst I was ashore. This way, he said, I would be paid by the Merchant Navy Officer's Pool, thus saving Associated Humber Lines money.

Shipowners' penny pinching again! I reported to the "Pool" and was granted study leave and pay, but that action was to lose me my job in the Associated Humber Lines ships.

I had about 7 or 8 weeks back at Trinity House Adult Navigation school, after which I was fit to sit the Board of Trade, sorry, Ministry of War Transport, exam. I am pleased to say that I passed it with flying colours, and looked forward to going back to sea as a 2nd or even 1st Mate in A.H.L. ships.

Miss Hoodless, who was in charge of the Hull "Pool", had other ideas. She maintained that as the "Pool" had paid me, then they had the right to send me to any ship of their choice needing an officer. That is exactly what happened, for at first they were going to send me to a ship going to Murmansk in a Russian convoy.

Then, owing to a machinery breakdown she was going to be delayed for some time, so my appointment to her was cancelled.

A day or two later I was told that I was being sent to a ship called the "Fort Livingstone" lying in King George Dock in Hull.

I duly joined her, she was loading Army and Navy stores and loads of ammunition for North Africa.

We had ammunition stored on the bottom of the holds and this was overstowed with Bren Gun carriers and vehicles, and finally, on the decks we had light tanks.

We sailed from Hull about the 23rd of September 1943, and by the time we got down river, just off Spurn Point, fog descended on us.

That fog was to last for almost a week, all of which time we laid at anchor. I have never known fog so dense to last as long as that spell did, but to have tried to put out into the North Sea in that pea-souper would have been madness. We did not have Radar in those days.

After seven days at anchor, we were able to get under way and made it out into the North Sea. Somehow we got lost! We actually ended up inside one of our own declared minefields, but by the Grace of God we came out of it unscathed and proceeded to Methyl, where we got orders to proceed to Loch Ewe to form up in a North Africa bound convoy. Prior to sailing, I had had a tooth filled at the dentists, and on the way round to Loch Ewe it was giving me hell.

I was taken ashore in Loch Ewe to see the Naval dentist there.

He refused to attend to me. His excuse was that he was there to attend to Naval personnel, not Merchant Seamen!

The Naval Officer who had accompanied me ashore, pointed out that I was also a human being, as well as a Merchant Seaman, and that as the ship was sailing for North Africa in an hour or two, he the dentist, must attend to me. He did, in bad grace, I couldn't feel my face for several hours after the treatment. He must have used enough anaesthetic to stun an elephant.

Shortly after I got back to the ship, we sailed in convoy for North Africa. By the time we had passed through the Minches, and got down off the Northern coast of Ireland, it was a dark and stormy night, with the wind howling in from the Nor'west with a rising sea.

At 2000 hrs, I had laid down on my bunk to have a sleep before my watch at midnight. Before so doing, I had laid out my emergency things. That is my lifejacket, a small flask of Brandy, my oilskin, and seaboots. All handy in case I had to vacate the ship in a hurry, should the worst happen.

I laid down, almost fully dressed, and had fallen off to sleep.

Suddenly, my sweet dreams were shattered by the strident clamour of the alarm bells. They were sounding the "submarine attack" signal.

I shot off my bunk and grabbed my jacket and oilskin coat, then I slipped my feet into my seaboots and donned the lifejacket.

All this took just a few seconds, and as I got the lifejacket on, there was the most unholy crash, and the ship seemed to come to a standstill.

As I made my way to the door of my room, I could feel the ship going down by the head. "That's it, I thought, we've been torpedoed".

I dashed along the alleyway to get out on deck, and as I got on deck, I saw several of the crew, mostly Firemen, trying to launch the port lifeboat. The thing that amazed me was the fact that they were up there on the boat deck dressed only in their short underpants and singlets. My first thought was that they would freeze to death on a night like this in a lifeboat. I shouted to them to hold on while I found out what had happened.

I made my way up to the bridge, and now that my eyes had adjusted to the darkness, I could see a large tanker embedded in our No.1 hold.

This tanker, it turned out, was fully loaded with high octane spirit, bound inwards for the U.K..

Some maniac in the routing office, had an inward bound convoy routed on the same course as the outward bound one.

In the darkness, ships had passed one another on opposite courses, and some of them thought they had missed a signal to alter course. They therefore tried to join in with the ships they saw going the opposite way.

This tanker had not been able to see us clearly in the murky weather and had turned to join us, in so doing he ended up in our hold. He had struck us just forward of the bulkhead between No.1 and 2 holds. The hold instantly filled with water and we went down by the head to a critical stage, our foredeck was awash in the heavy seas that were running. As the tanker went astern to free herself, we sank even further in the water and it seemed that we would sink.

It was a Godsend that she had hit us with her stem, I dread to think what the consequences would have been had we struck her in one of her main tanks. I reckon there would have been an almighty flash and explosion, with umpteen millions of gallons of high octane spirit and a ship load of munitions going up.

In the meantime, our Captain, Capt. Weatherall, had asked the Commodore to send an escort to stand-by us in case we had to abandon ship. They sent us the only one they could spare, an armed trawler. Well at least we had someone there to pick us up if need be. We were told to try and make it back to Londonderry if possible. Possible it was, with the escort close by us, we made it into Loch Foyle, where we anchored to await further instructions. As we lay there at anchor, salvage tugs brought in other ships that had been victims of similar collisions. One ship they towed in had had her back broken by the force of the collision, and she was write-off.

Eventually they put us alongside the quay in Londonderry to carry out temporary repairs, sufficient to get us back to Glasgow to off load our cargo.

It was interesting to watch the way they fitted plates of steel over the huge gash in our starboard side. They lowered the plates into position and then using a special gun, they fired case-hardened bolts through both the new plates and the original steel of the hull.

I actually went down into the hold and watched as a bolt was fired, I could see it cut its own thread as it penetrated through the plates. When the hole had been completely covered, divers then went around the edges of the plates, driving soft wooden wedges in.

These I was told would swell, and in so doing would keep the water out enough to allow us to proceed to Glasgow. All this work took about a week to complete, so we the crew had a pleasant break there, and we were made very welcome by the people ashore.

Leaving Londonderry, we made it across to Glasgow, and moored up near the Custom House to discharge our heterogeneous cargo of war goods.

As there was a great shortage of stevedores for the job, the Army brought in a gang of American coloured soldiers to do the job.

By the way they went on, I doubt if any of them had ever been on a ship other then the one that had brought them over from America.

We had been told that they were inexperienced men, and had made all necessary arrangements for the safe handling of the heavy goods, such as tanks and Bren gun carriers. We had rigged double purchase gear on the derricks for the purpose, and instructed the men that only the light items were to be lifted with the single purchase runner. All other items had to be lifted with the doubling gear.

They took not the slightest bit of notice, and just went ahead no matter what the weight was, they picked it up on a single wire runner. I remember going for a cup of tea and coming back to see a tank weighing about 5 tons suspended over the hold on that single wire. I almost shit a brick when I saw it, but they got it ashore safely, more by good luck than good management.

Finally, when all the cargo was out, we sailed for Mount Stewart Dry docks in Cardiff, where they were going to build a new bow section on to the ship. Though I could have stayed in the ship, I decided that I would leave her and find another ship.

For some reason or other, the owners of the ship were not pleased when I said I was leaving her. Anyhow, I left and returned to Hull, and reported back to the pool.

I was still having a lot of trouble with my teeth, and on seeing the Shipping Federation Doctor, he ordered that I should have all my top teeth out, as they were in such a bad state. I followed his instructions and had them out, after which I was given sick leave, as the rules were that a seaman had to have teeth sufficient for him to be able to eat the hard tack in a lifeboat if necessary. A person without top teeth could not possibly chew the hard emergency biscuits carried in lifeboats.

Many a seaman had died from starvation through the lack of teeth, whilst in a lifeboat after his ship had been lost at sea.

I could return to sea as soon as I had an upper denture fitted, I was told. In the meantime, as there was a shortage of Officers, I could be of use as a relief Officer for a ship needing one such person, teeth were not necessary for that job in port!

Chapter 13.
Normandy Beachhead, D Day + Five.

The Pool office requested me to go down to a ship called the "Rembrandt", lying in King George Dock, Hull. I was to see the Marine Superintendent regarding the job as relief 2nd Officer. This was to allow the permanent 2nd Officer to take some leave before the next voyage.

I reported on board the ship and met the Super, a Mr. George Lockley. He explained to me that I would be required for about three weeks. He then went on to say that the company did not pay any overtime, but they did pay the wartime "danger money" to all men working aboard in port.

The usual custom of shipowners was to stop the danger money payment as soon as a ship arrived in port. Most shipowners thought danger only existed at sea. I wonder if they still thought that after the s.s. "Malakand" was bombed in Liverpool Docks, when she was almost fully loaded with munitions. She caught fire and blew up taking most of a dock and several ships with her.

Anyhow, I was quite chuffed at the idea of receiving the Ten Pounds a month "danger money" on top of the £23 a month pay for the job. This was my first encounter with a Bolton's ship since I saw the s.s. "Romney" in Poti, 10 years earlier. When the time came for the permanent man to return to the ship, George Lockley asked me if I would be good enough to join another of their ships which was due in Hull after a very long voyage. He wanted me to act as a stand-by 2nd Officer for the duration of her stay in Hull. According to him, she would be at least 6 to 8 weeks in Hull.

What could be better as far as I was concerned. She had docked in Albert Dock, and that was only a ten minutes walk from were I lived. I was glad to have the job.

The ship that I went to join in Albert Dock turned out to be the s.s. "Romney"! Little did I realise when I joined her as relief 2nd Mate, that she would play a major part in my life at sea. The idea of being in my home port of Hull for several weeks appealed to me. It meant that I was able to see my fiancé almost every day, if she was not on duty as a telephonist in the National Fire Service.

On going down to the ship, I was surprised to see the state she was in. She looked as though she was a candidate for the scrap yard. A far cry from the smart looking tramp steamer I had seen 10 years earlier loading at Poti for Baltimore.

Lying on her after deck was the severed remains of what had once been the "jolly boat", (a small rowing boat used for general purposes).

Her paintwork had seen better days, in all she was a decrepit apology of a ship.

Things began to fit when I learned that she had just come home after a voyage of 27 months away from the U.K.. No wonder she was in a bit of a mess, It was easy to understand why all the crew, Officers and ratings had left her.

I would have done the same after all that time away from home.

There were bags and bags of mail for the members of the crew who had left the ship, and for several days I had the job of re-addressing mail to their home addresses. This was mail that they would have dearly loved to have received whilst on voyage.

Whilst re-addressing them, I often wondered how many of them contained good cheering news or not so good news for the recipients. Many of them would no doubt bring joy, others possibly tragedy in those uncertain days of the war.

Part of my duties was to sort out all the old charts and Sailing Directions, they were the ones issued to the ship when she first left the shipyard of her birth.

The Admiralty Sailing Directions consisted of some 50 volumes, giving directions for the approaches to almost every port and island in the World. I spent a lot of time looking through them, and found that in the 1929 editions, they were full of most interesting things about the flora and fauna of the places dealt with. All these books were to be destroyed and a new, up to date collection was to be delivered to the ship.

I have often wished that I had kept a few of those books, they were most enlightening to read.

Then all charts had to be renewed, and I was given the task of compiling a complete list of the charts needed for world-wide coverage, all had to be folioed and catalogued. So by and large I was kept busy during my duty hours.

The repairers came aboard and started squaring things up and more or less modernising the ship.

The "Romney" was a three island ship, that is, she had a short well deck forward and the same aft. From No.2 hatch through to No.4 hatch, was a long 'tween deck. In this 'tween deck in the way of No.4 hatch was the D.E.M.S. accommodation. D.E.M.S. were Naval ratings put aboard Merchant ships for their defence, they were all gun's crews. The "Romney" was fitted out for 20 such men.

On the opposite side of the 'tween deck, was the catering staff's accommodation. The crew's accommodation, which had originally been, as usual, under the forecastle head, had for the war been shifted to the poop space.

The Sailors had the Port side and the Firemen the Starboard side of the poop.

The Captain's room was on the lower bridge and had a small bedroom attached. His toilet and bathroom were down the stairs on the saloon deck, where the Chief Officer, 2nd Officer, 3rd Officer, and two apprentices were accommodated.

The wireless room and Sparks's accommodation were on the lower bridge abaft the Captain's quarters, and what poky little rooms they were. Of course being wartime, the ship carried a second wireless operator, and he too was roomed amidships.

The Officer's toilet and bathroom meant a walk along the deck to the Engineer's quarters, quite a distance if you were caught short! As time went by, the shipyard workmen got things back into shipshape fashion. All the necessary jobs that needed doing, were done, and the ship painted up.

In a very short time she was starting to look pretty good. After a while, the Superintendent asked me if I was prepared to sail in the ship when she was ready for sea again. I gave the matter a moments thought, and then said I might just as well sail in the ship. After all, if I did not join that one, I'd have to take one that the Pool sent me to.

I had at least got to know the ship and the people in her, and some of the office staff, so what had I to lose?

As time went on, the "Romney" was shifted from Albert Dock down to King George Dock, where she was to start loading for her next voyage. In the meantime she had been fitted with extra gun positions and a lot more guns for her protection. An anti-aircraft gun was fitted on the forecastle head, 4 Oerlikon guns were fitted, one each side of the navigation bridge and one each side of the boat deck. Monkey Island was fitted with a machine gun, and of course there was the 4" gun on the poop, and also an Oerlikon gun fitted each side on the fore end of the poop.

It soon became obvious that we were to form part of the invasion force for the Normandy beaches. Hence our number D + 5. We were to arrive at the invasion area 5 days after the start of the invasion.

I was sent on a small arms shooting course, the purpose of this was that I was to be the Gunnery Officer of the ship, and would be armed with a revolver. This, I was told was to be used if any member of the crew refused to obey orders under fire.

I became a crackshot with a Service revolver whilst on that course. I am pleased to say that I did not need the revolver.

It was the 27th May 1944 when I signed on Articles for Special Operations, as the venture to Normandy Beaches was called.

All the ships which took part in supplying the invasion forces were given a definite day on which they were to arrive off the beaches. Also every ship was given a specific area in which they had to anchor and as close as safely possible.

Our area, I was to find out later, was the Sword area. That area was the closest to the German positions at Le Havre.

When fully loaded and ready to sail, we were provided with a North Sea Pilot, who would stay with the ship until we were off the coast of the Isle of Weight, there he left us and we turned on our course South for the French coast.

Under instructions from the Beach Master, a Naval Officer, we dropped anchor to await further instructions. This was the 5th day after the initial landings by the Allied forces.

I remember that our position was off shore in line with the light-house at Point de Ver. I used to use a bearing of that and a church steeple at Courselles to ascertain the position of our ship, to be sure we maintained our station.

Almost alongside the lighthouse was a German concrete pillbox, which had withstood the pounding with 11" shells from a British warship. We heard that the Germans finally gave themselves up, because they could not stand the noise and concussion any longer from the battering. The pillbox was still intact.

It appeared that we were in range of the German guns, and to thwart them from getting our exact range, there were Motor Torpedo boats engaged 24 hours a day laying a smoke screen between them and all the British ships anchored nearby with us.

Not infrequently, there would be a running battle between German "E" boats and our own torpedo boats. On several occasions we saw the explosions as one or the other were hit by torpedoes.

Early one evening, for some reason or other, the smoke screen failed. All us ships were there for the German gunners to see.

I must give them credit for the speed at which they reacted.

With uncanny accuracy, they had our range in a matter of seconds.

They opened fire on us with their 11" guns at Le Havre. The first two shells straddled us, one either side of the ship, and only a few feet short of the mark. They exploded almost alongside us.

Our Captain, Captain Copping, decided that it was time to get to hell out of that anchorage, and asked permission to shift.

The Beach Master wasn't too keen on the idea, and suggested that we stay where we were. With that, another shell landed perilously close and the Beach Master heard the explosion over the radio.

He immediately gave permission to move the ship. As the engines were on standby all the time, we lost very little time in getting under way and steamed to the West out of the range of those guns.

As soon as the other ships saw us moving they asked us what was going on. We told them, get the hell out of this anchorage. They did, each of them following us to a new anchorage. One of the ships which followed us to the new position was the "Iddesleigh", the very next mooring we saw her break her back as the Germans torpedoed her, using their one-man subs, of which they made good use.

Another morning, at about 6 a.m., I was keeping my watch on the bridge, I looked out ahead, and where there should have been a ship, the "Fort Lac La Laronge", there seemed to be a space.

I suddenly realised that what I could see, was a descending column of water. As the water went down, I saw the ship, she too had been torpedoed, again by the one man subs. Sadly there was a large loss of lives on her as the soldiers who formed the unloading parties, had been asleep in her 'tween decks when she was hit.

The soldiers who worked the cargo out of our ship, did not sleep aboard us, they all went ashore or slept on the landing craft tied up alongside us. One morning at 6 a.m., the Engineer on one of the landing craft, started up her generator, to get things ready for work. As soon as the generator roared into action, there was a most unholy explosion under our ship. I saw our stern being lifted out of the water by the force of it.

The Germans had planted an acoustic mine under us during the night, again using their one-man submarines.

Fortunately the "Romney" survived the explosion and came to no harm.

When all our cargo was out we sailed back to Hull for a second load. I remember the look on the faces of the Dock staff when we arrived at the pierhead at King George Dock. They wanted to know how we had got there, according to them, the "Romney" had been sunk at the beaches by the Germans. I also remember the look on my fiancé's face when I called for her that same night. She too, had heard that our ship had been lost.

We loaded a second cargo and sailed again for the same anchorage, but this time we had to proceed to anchorage at Southend to await our turn to sail for the beaches.

It was whilst we were at anchor there, I saw my first "duddlebug". It was 2 a.m. of my anchor watch, and I heard what I thought was a high powered motor launch. I looked out of the wheelhouse and saw this thing with its arse on fire travelling at a hell of a speed, just about 20 feet above the water. It passed us and when it was about 500 yards further ahead, the engine cut out.

That I knew, was the sign that it was about to detonate, and detonate it did with a huge flash. Fortunately no-one and nothing was harmed. It had fallen short of its intended target, possibly the centre of London and district.

We saw many more of those fiendish flying bombs as we made our way through the Dover Straits. I was all for opening fire on them with an Oerlikon, but we were advised by the Naval escort to leave them to the R.A.F., in case we brought any of them down on the convoy of ships.

At the beachhead for the second time we saw the Liberty ship, I think it was the "Samlong", break in two as she was torpedoed as she was making her way back to Britain, and the same day a Tank landing craft struck a mine. As it exploded her fore end was virtually lifted out of the water. Fortunately she remained afloat and made it to safety without any loss of life.

It was whilst we were at the beachhead for the second time that the Allied Air Forces made their 1,000 bomber raid on the German stronghold of Caen. The Germans had dug their heels in there and were holding the advancing British troops.

The day the raid took place was a fine and almost calm day.

Over the coast of Britain there was a belt of beautiful snowy white Cumulus clouds, that had all the appearances of large balls of cotton wool. The forerunners of the raid were the Pathfinders, they hopped over the balls of cotton wool and headed for the target area, where they dropped their marker flares.

As the last of them cleared the area, the first squadron of heavy bombers appeared over the clouds. In a short time they were over the target area and as they approached we could see them peeling-off one by one to make their bombing run.

It wasn't long before clouds of dust and smoke was rising from Caen. For hour after hour, squadron after squadron of bombers hopped over those clouds in a seemingly never ending stream.

By the time the raid was finally over I cannot imagine there was very much left of the town of Caen.

As we watched, we saw only two aircraft shot down by the enemy, and as the aircraft was plunging towards Earth, we saw the crews bailing out.

As their parachutes billowed out, we counted the number. When we had counted them all out safely, we all gave a hearty cheer.

One unfortunately landed in the sea, not far from where we were anchored. By this time a fairly stiff breeze had sprung up, and it filled his parachute. The result was that he was being blown out to sea at the rate of knots, and he was unable to do a thing about it. He had been towed for about a mile when an Air-sea rescue craft grabbed him and hauled him out of the drink.

When all our cargo had been landed, we received orders to proceed back to London, where we docked in the Royal Docks. Our crew was signed off, our Normandy landings run was over.

We had a couple of weeks in London with no crew on board other than the Officers, Engineers and Naval Ratings, and a skeleton catering staff.

We had on board shipyard workers doing various repairs and our Superintendent wanted some chipping, scraping and painting done in the rusty 'tween decks. He asked me to ask the Naval Ratings if they would like to earn some cash. He'd allow them 10/- a day each for the job. I went to their accommodation and put the proposition to them. In view of the meagre Naval pay they nearly snapped my hand off at the chance to earn a bit of spending money.

They all donned their blue overalls and reported for work, all 20 of them. I armed them with chipping hammers, scrapers and wire brushes, then showed them the rusty areas to be cleaned up and painted, and then left them to it.

They worked like Trojans, and had the area scaled down to clean bare metal in next to no time. They worked better than any ordinary crew would have done. I then gave them pots of red lead paint and brushes to complete the job.

As they started the painting, a shipyard Shop Steward saw them doing the job. He immediately came to me and said that I would have to stop my men painting, otherwise he'd call the workers out on strike. A strike in wartime, I ask you!

I stopped the painting, but I was not going to be beaten by some jumped up Shop Steward. I asked him if he had any objections to my men applying oil with wads of cotton waste instead of brushes.

After a few moments thought, he said he could see no objection to that. I thanked him and away he went. I took the paint pots and thinned the paint down a bit with boiled oil. I then asked the men if they minded applying the mixture with wads of waste, so long as they had no open cuts or sores on their hands.

None of them had any such defects, so they painted the steel plates using that method, we got the job done and we hadn't broken any of the Unions rules.

Applying paint with a cloth is not painting according to their rules, painting is when you use a brush!

Chapter 14

Cuban sugar and American 'planes.

After about two weeks in London we got our next voyage orders, we were to proceed in convoy, to Cuba for a cargo of sugar for Britain. I cannot remember whether we sailed through the English Channel or round the North coast of Scotland to join a West bound convoy for the States. I do however remember that we were escorted most of the way across the Atlantic Ocean. We parted company with the convoy when we reached a certain point off the American coast, and then made our way through the Florida Straits for Cuba. En route, we called in at Guantanamo, on the South coast of Cuba, being used as an American Naval base. There we landed all our codebooks and confidential papers into the safe keeping of the Naval Authorities, before proceeding to our load port.

Our port of lading turned out to be a place called Manzanillo, on the Southern coast of Cuba. As we had several hundreds of tons of rock ballast in the bottom of our holds, put in when the ship had previously been carrying heavy Forces equipment, we had to get rid of it before we could load our sugar cargo.

The Port Authorities instructed out Captain as to where he could safely discharge the stuff overboard. We went and anchored in the designated position well off the port approach, and spent several days getting rid of the ballast. We must have left a small mountain on the sea bed after dumping several hundred tons of rock down there.

The loading was to be done out at an anchorage about two miles off shore from the town of Manzanillo. The cargo being brought out to us on barges first thing every morning, along with the dozens of labourers to handle the bags into the ship.

Whilst there, the 3rd Mate and myself went ashore one evening to sample the delights of the place, and not unnaturally, we ended up in a brothel for the night.

It had been our intention to catch the labourers boat back to the ship at 7 o'clock in the morning, but having wined but not dined, and satisfied our sexual desires during the night, we overslept. We missed the launch by a few minutes. That meant that we had to find someone with a boat to take us back to the ship.

We finally found such a person, but he wanted his pound of flesh for the journey, he cleaned us out of what Dollars we had for the trip back. Arriving at the gangway we made our way to the top, and who should be waiting for us, the Chief Officer. He gave us a right dressing down for being such reprobates staying ashore to sow our wild oats. I wonder if he had ever been young before.

That was the one and only trip ashore I made whilst we were at Manzanillo. We sailed about ten days later, calling again at Guantanamo for orders regarding convoys etc.

We were to be routed through the Florida Straits and sail up to Boston, Mass., where we were to load a cargo of 'planes on deck.

We were only a few hours in Boston loading the cargo, and off we went again, this time for Halifax, Nova Scotia, the major convoy assembly port for the North Atlantic crossing.

Our stay in that port was only a matter of 24 hours, but we found the people most friendly towards the British seamen. They brought loads of parcels, one for each member of the crew of the ship, containing many things in short supply at home.

All these were handed over to the care of the Chief Officer, to be given out later. This however was a grave mistake. Before handing them out, he went through each parcel and removed some of the articles, which he kept for himself, not a matey thing to do.

This was our holier than thou Chief Officer who dared to chide us for answering our basic call of nature. He later turned out to be a piss artist of the first water.

We sailed from Halifax in a convoy of about 30 ships of various nationalities bound for Britain. Escorting us were several Naval units, mostly destroyers. On passage, the weather deteriorated at an alarming rate, developing into a full North Atlantic storm.

Nature in the raw is seldom mild. A storm in the North Atlantic is proof of that old saying.

The "Romney" was the best "seaboat" I have ever sailed in. The huge flair of her bows made it possible for her to ride out the worst that Nature could throw at her.

In the huge seas that were running she just descended on them, sending out a tremendous bow wave, having ridden over the top of the heavy sea.

We had several American ships in the convoy, in particular one on our starboard beam in the next column of ships. One night, at the height of the storm, the Romney rose to meet a sea, and as it passed, her bow crashing down, creating a tremendous bow wave.

A few seconds later one of the American ships opened fire on us.

In the pitch blackness of the night, he had mistakenly thought we were a submarine surfacing. Several of his shells pierced our funnel, others raked the bridge, and one of them hit the shell plating in the way of the Firemen's for'castle. The large indent it made shed some of the insulation off the plate, cutting the face of a sleeping man. With friends like that, who needed enemies.

Trigger happy Americans again!

Though we were having an uncomfortable passage, my heart went out to the crews of the destroyers they were really taking a pounding from those awesome breakers. There were times when it seemed that they could not possibly survive the hammerings they were getting. For most of the time they were awash from stem to stern, and access to the decks would have been impossible in an emergency.

Slowly the storm passed away ahead of us, it was travelling at a far greater speed than the convoy. As the seas died down, life returned to normal as we made our way East. We saw no enemy action, Britain had finally beaten the U-boat hazards to shipping.

Approaching the Western Approaches to Britain, the convoy started to disperse, and ships made their way to their destinations.

Ours was to be Hull, my home town, where we arrived on Boxing Day 1944, a nice Christmas present indeed.

I had nearly three weeks at home before signing on for the next voyage. The 15th of January 1945, saw me signing on for a voyage that would last 8 months. We sailed from Hull for Swansea, where we were to load a cargo of stores and munitions for the British troops in the Far East. Among that cargo was thousands of bags of mail for them.

I remember seeing two Post Office railway vans arriving alongside carrying all the sacks of parcels and letters, these unfortunately we loaded in the after hold, No.5, close to the crew's accommodation. That turned out to be a big mistake, as some of the crew broached those bags and stole things from the parcels intended for the beleaguered troops out there fighting the Japanese. Our cargo was destined for Bombay, where it would be transhipped further East. In Bombay, I sent ashore to see the parcels that had been tampered with. I found it a rather saddening sight. Some of the parcels contained things like a worn towel and a small tablet of soap sent by some woman for her husband or son stationed out there and short of such luxuries.

It was a dastardly deed that I have never forgotten. How could anyone be so paltry as to rob another under such circumstances?

During our stay in Bombay, I went ashore to have a look at the place. I'd never been there before. I was appalled by the amount of poverty and poverty stricken people begging in the streets.

Going back to the ship in the early evening, it was a case of stepping over people bedded down on a grass mat or an old blanket for the night. They had no homes, the street pavement was their only place of abode. There were young women with babes in arms, laid on the ground, begging alms from any foreign passer-by. The sight of all that misery brought home to me how lucky we were and are in Britain. Admittedly we do have people sleeping in the streets in Britain, but a lot of them are there by choice not of necessity.

On completion of discharge we sailed for South America, via Cape of Good Hope. The war in the Far East was still in progress, and there was just the possibility of meeting a Japanese man of war or submarine on passage, so we had doubled lookouts all the time.

Fortunately we saw only one vessel at a great distance, smoke from its funnel was spotted and we immediately altered course away from it. The other ship must have at the same time spotted our smoking funnel, because he also took evasive action, turning away from us.

It was whilst we were on passage between Capetown and South America that we received the news that the war in Europe had finally come to an end. Loud cheers rang through the ship at the news. Our Captain spliced the mainbrace, a drink for every member of the crew. That same night, for the first time for five years we were able to have the deck lights on and not have to black out all ports and doors. It was great to be able to breathe fresh air in the rooms instead of foul, stuffy air, due to having to keep doors and portholes tightly closed during the black-out hours of the night.

On passage we experienced some trouble with the boilers, and on arrival in the bay at Rio de Janeiro, ship repairers were called in. They found that the fire tubes of our old Scottish boilers were in need of replacement. As a result we had a lovely three weeks laid at anchor whilst the repairs were carried out.

Captain Copping, our Captain, laid on a liberty boat for the use of members of the crew during our stay. During our trips ashore, we made many friends with members of the British community there.

Those people did their utmost to make our stay in port a worthwhile one.

We were made most welcome to their homes for meals and entertainment, they even sent their cars down to the quay to pick us up when we landed from the liberty boats. After a pleasant evening they would then drive us back to the quay.

I personally had a very pleasant time in Rio, I was taken for the trip up the Sugar Loaf mountain by cable car. It was my first time ever ride in a cable car, and the view on the way up was a sight never to be forgotten. You could see the whole of the city of Rio and miles and miles of the Copacabana beach as far as the eye could see.

In spite of all the pleasure afforded me in Rio, my heart was still with my fiancé back in England. I had to buy something for her whilst in Rio. To this end I went and asked Captain Copping for a sub. He willingly agreed to give me one, but the only money he had on hand were large denomination Brazilian notes.

The smallest he had was a 1,000 Cruzero note, I could have that if I wanted it. It was actually more than I wanted at the time, being worth about a half month's pay to me. Anyway, I took the note, got ready and went ashore to see what gift I could find suitable to take home for my lady love.

I visited one of the big departmental stores in the city, and decided on a nice leather handbag. Having chosen the one I thought ideal, I told the shop assistant that I would have it.

She wrapped it up and handed it to me, I in return handed her the 1,000 Cruzero note in payment. She then gave me my change, but when I checked it, I found that I had been very much short-changed.

I called her back and tried to explain to her the size of the note I had given her. She acted dumb, "No comprehendi" was her ploy. I kept on at her, but was getting nowhere very fast. I asked to see the Manager. By now she could see that I was determined, and she called for the Manager. He came over to me and asked me, in perfect English, what was the problem.

I explained to him that I had paid for my purchase with a 1,000 Cruzero note, but I had been given change only for a 500 Cr. note.

The Manager then asked the assistant about this. She of course denied I had given her a 1,000 Cr. note. The Manager then asked me if I was sure of this, to which I was able to tell him the colour of that particular note. I told him I had given the assistant an orange coloured note. Thereon the Manager told the girl to empty out her cash bag. All the shop assistants wore a leather cash bag slung from their shoulders by a strap.

She tipped out the contents of the bag, then handed the bag to the Manager. He carefully examined it. Tucked away, in one corner of the bag was my Cr. 1,000 note, carefully folded and hidden!

I got my full change, I had proved my case. The Manager apologised to me for the unfortunate incident.

The next evening I was in the Flying Angel Missions to Seamen, and I mentioned to the Padre, the incident in the shop. He said that he had heard about it from the Manager, who was a friend of his.

The shop assistant had been sacked on the spot after I left the shop, for trying to feather her nest with customer's change. I am glad that I made a mental note of the colour of a 1,000 Cr. note.

When all our repairs were completed, it was time to say goodbye to the hospitable people of Rio, we were to go down the coast to a place called Paranagua. There we were to load a full cargo of general for Britain. That consisted of bales of rubber, 1,000s of sheets of plywood, bales of leather, cases of tinned products and hosts of other commodities desperately needed in Britain.

Our otherwise pleasant stay in the port was marred by a tragedy.

One afternoon, our Donkeyman, an elderly man, had gone ashore for whatever reason. On his way back to the ship, in fact only 100 yards from the ship, he was run down by a hit and run driver who left him to die on the roadside. He was found by another of the crew returning from a trip ashore. He was buried the next day, all of the crew being present at cemetery. That incident saddened us all. There was a man, close to his retirement, his life cut short and his mortal remains buried in a foreign land.

Standing at the grave side listening to the sermon given by the Padre of the Seamen's Mission, I glanced at the shallow grave in the stony earth and the words of part of Rupert Brooke's poem came to mind.

"If I should die, think only this of me,

That there's some corner of a foreign field that is forever England".

Our old shipmate had gone, and he would soon be forgotten, and none of his relatives could grieve at his graveside. Sad indeed.

Shortly after this, we sailed for home, our deceased shipmate's home port, Liverpool.

After arrival we were all paid off and sent on leave. I had about four weeks at home because after discharge the ship went for an overhaul in drydock over at Birkenhead. After my leave I reported back to her, and on leaving the drydock we proceeded up the Manchester Ship Canal, we were to load a full cargo of general there. Whilst there, I heard that my fiancé had been in hospital for a minor operation, and I was anxious to go home and see her before we sailed on voyage.

I asked our Captain if I could have 24 hours off. I gave the reason for my request. He refused to let me go, so that same afternoon I caught the train to Hull, and saw my girl friend. I stayed at home for the night and caught the first train back next morning. When I arrived, the Captain went beserk because I had disobeyed his order. A stupid argument ensued and in the end I told him he'd better get another 2nd Officer as I was quitting. The Company's Marine Superintendent came and saw me and wanted to know what all the fuss was about.

I told him. His answer was that as it was so close to sailing time that he would have a job getting a replacement Officer, would I not reconsider. I said I would, so long as the Master would not hold it against me for the voyage. Mr. Lockley, the Super, took me up to see the Captain and explained that I was willing to stay in the ship if he, the Captain, would let the matter drop.

The Captain readily agreed and said the matter was closed and forgotten. I went down to my room and unpacked my gear, which I had already made ready for leaving the ship.

It was now early December 1945, and the ship had had a job getting any crew at all. All the really good seamen were going to have their Christmas at home.

The "Pool" Office in Salford did the best they could to round up a crew for the "Romney", but unfortunately they got us the bottom of the barrel men, as we were to find out on voyage. There were some fairly decent men among them, but there was also a vicious and evil element in some of them.

Our Superintendent said not to worry, his words were "You'll only be away on voyage for about six weeks". Our cargo was for discharge in Beirut and Haifa, so I figured we could put up with this crowd for six weeks.

We sailed from Manchester about the 19th December, so we were going to have our Christmas at sea. My estimate was somewhere in the Mediterranean, weather permitting. On passage, somewhere off Cape St. Bincent, we met terrible weather, the seas were mountainous to say the least. During my watch below, 8 p.m. to midnight, I was awakened by an almighty crash outside my room.
I wondered what the hell had happened, then all went nice and quiet. The ship was sailing along as though in a comparatively calm sea so I dozed off to sleep again until I was called at 20 minutes to midnight by the watch on deck.
When I got onto the bridge to relieve the 3rd Officer, I asked him what the hell happened earlier. He told me that he had brought the ship round so as to have her "hove to" as the weather was so bad and she had been shipping very heavy seas.
I asked him why he hadn't called the "Old Man" out. The answer was simply enough, he couldn't wake him up. He'd been on the whisky bottle again. In which case I said he should have called the Chief Officer. I then asked him if he had reduced speed whilst he brought the ship round head into those mountainous seas.
He hadn't and that was the reason for the tremendous sea coming aboard. It could have had disastrous results.
However, during my watch, I noticed that the ship seemed down by the head, and she was steering very poorly. At first I thought it was the helmsman's fault, poor steering, so I took the wheel for a few minutes. The "Romney" had always been a very good steering ship, even in the worst of weather. I soon found out that it wasn't the helmsman's poor steering. She was well down by the head, hence the poor course keeping.

When the Chief Officer relieved me at 4 a.m. I told him he had better have the Carpenter sound the fore peak and forward holds for water, as the ship was badly down by the head. At first he ridiculed the idea, but I persuaded him that I was right. After all, I had been in the ship well over a year and I knew what she was like in any weather.
After breakfast and during a lull in the storm, he had "Chippy" go forward and sound the fore peak tank. It was half full!
That meant that there was about 150 tons of water right in the fore end of the ship that should not have been there.
That was why she was down by the head. It turned out that she had started some of the rivetted plates in the fore peak due to the heavy pounding she had taken before the 3rd Officer hove her to.
On entering the Medi, we proceeded to Algiers to get repairs done.
The ship repairers brought down a heavy duty pump to get rid of the water, then they put in a "cement box". That means they poured in 10 tons of cement to a height that was above the leaking plates.
We stayed in port long enough to allow the cement to set before sailing on the final leg of the run to Beirut.
Our first taste of vicious behaviour came whilst we were in Beirut. One evening the Chief Officer, the 3rd Officer and myself, were sat in the saloon playing cards, when two of the firemen came in. One of them have his face slashed from his mouth to his ear, blood was pouring down his face. We called the Captain, who strapped the wound together whilst I went and phoned for an ambulance to get the man to hospital.
In the meantime, the injured man had said what happened down aft in their quarters. According to him they had been skylarking and it had happened then. The Captain told the Chief Officer and I to go aft and bring the man responsible for the injury back to him.
We went and found the Fireman concerned, and told him he was wanted by the Captain. His remarks about the Captain were most derogatory, but he went out of the forecastle

ahead of us.

We were halfway along the deck when the Chief Officer said to me,

"Go down on the quay and find the knife he's has just thrown over the side".

I hadn't seen him throw anything away, but nevertheless I went on to the quay. After a close search I found an ordinary table knife wedged in between the railway lines. I picked it up and found that it had been sharpened like a razor. That was the weapon that had inflicted that facial wound. An ordinary knife could not have cut so cleanly.

Our injured man was taken to the British Military Hospital for treatment. British troops were still stationed in Lebanon at the time. The next thing was that we had the M.P.s down wanting to know how this had occurred. They had questioned the injured man, and he had said that it was an accident. They didn't believe him, and neither did we. We later learned that the man was so scared of the miscreant that he dare not say any different.

One of the real baddies was one sailor who was his bosom pal. A right pair of bastards they were too, as I was to find out later in the voyage.

After that incident, things seemed to go along alright, for we discharged what cargo we had for Beirut and then sailed for Haifa in the hopes that we would soon be on our way back to the U.K., having been away about 6 weeks.

Chapter 15.
"A six weeks voyage, they said."

Our stay in Haifa was short and sweet, and though I did not see much of the biblical parts of the place, I found it interesting enough. As we completed our discharge of the remains of the cargo, our orders came through for our next employment.

We were to load phosphates at a port in the Red Sea called Quosier. This is an Egyptian port. We left Haifa for Port Said and Suez Canal transit into the Red Sea. As usual we were pestered with the persistent Arab "Bumboat" men trying to sell the "Ver good Spanish Fly, it make girl want you".

"It make you ver good for jig-a-jig".

"You like feelthy postcard yes? I have ver dirtee cards for you."

Whatever your tastes, those men had what you wanted, if they hadn't, they would try damned hard to get it for you, at a price.

Nothing had altered in Port Said over the years, the same junk, the same boatmen, each giving themselves fancy names, like Jock McKay.

They seemed to favour Scottish sounding names.

We tied up at the buoys to take on some bunker coal, stores and fresh water. We also shipped a man to replace the fireman who was slashed in Beirut. It had been decided that it was in his best interests to leave him in hospital where he could have any necessary treatment for the gash on his face.

The man we shipped at Port Said was a Maltese chap, and at first he seemed to get along well with the rest of the firemen, who were all U.K. white seamen.

Having stored, bunkered and watered, we sailed for Quosier, about 300 miles South of Suez, and what a hole of a place it turned out to be. There was no port as such, all there was, was a loading chute sticking out from the sands of the Sahara Desert, and about a half a mile inland was the phosphate works, beyond that was only miles of sand and more sands of the desert.

The habitation of the place consisted of a few houses for the workers, one bar come shop and a football ground. It was very obvious that our crew were not going to have a gay time in Quosier. During our stay, we did manage to rake us a team to play against the Arabs at football. They ran our fellows ragged, and it goes without saying, they won the match.

Where, we wondered, was the cargo of phosphates destined to be discharged? It wasn't long before we knew, Melbourne, Australia.

That news put paid to any hopes of a six weeks voyage.

It would take the "Romney" almost that length of time to reach Melbourne. In view of the sequence of events after leaving Quosier, it took us a lot longer than six weeks.

On completion of loading the phosphate, we sailed down the Red Sea and through Hell's Gates, as the Straits of Beb el Mandeb were known, and out into the Gulf of Aden, into the cooler weather.

After the temperatures approaching 100 degrees in the Red Sea the nice cooling breezes were very welcome by all.

We put into Aden, to fill up our coal bunkers to capacity for the 5,000 mile run across the Indian Ocean to Freemantle.

When the coaling and taking of the all important fresh water was completed, we sailed, heading on a South Easterly course for Aussie.

The weather and the seas were as calm as anyone could wish for, and we had all accepted that we could load a cargo of grain for home after discharging the phosphates.

Hope springs eternal in the human breast. If we did that, the voyage would not be too long after all. Fate had other ideas.

On passage we saw very little of our Captain, he kept himself very much to himself, with bottles of whiskey for company.

I remember one night, when I was going up to the bridge to relieve the 3rd Officer, he called

out to me watch out, "The Old Man" had just emptied his piss-pot outside the door".
Charming, to say the least.

As 2nd Officer, it was my job each day, to give the Chief Engineer a chit stating our position, and the distance we had run from the previous noon. From this information, the Chief was supposed to work out the bunkers used and the slip of the propeller.

Well one particular noon, as I came back from his room, I looked down the bunker space, which was open because of the tropical heat. Surprise, surprise, I could not see any coal. I went across the deck and looked down the other side pocket, no coal in sight there either. We were by this time almost 2,300 miles out of Aden, with the same distance still to go. We're short of bunkers, was the thought that came to mind, but who am I to say such a thing?

I went along to have words with the 2nd Engineer, a man who had been years in the company. I explained to him what I had seen in the bunker space, and that I felt that we were short of coal.

He heartily agreed with me. Well my duty was clear, I had to inform the Captain, which I did. He at first ridiculed the idea, "We filled up with 1,200 tons at Aden, so how the hell can we be short of coal? "

I went on to tell him that it wasn't only my opinion, but also that of the 2nd Engineer. I also pointed out that before noon next day, we would be at the point of no return. That is that we would be at the halfway mark of the crossing.

That galvanised the Captain into action, "Get me the Chief Officer and the Chief Engineer". I did so, and whilst they went away to measure up the bunkers, I went into the chartroom, plotted our position and then the course and distance to the nearest port.

The nearest port was Colombo, Ceylon, (Sri Lanka), and the distance was 1,200 miles. About an hour later, a very dirty, coal dust covered Captain made his appearance on the bridge.

"What's the nearest bunker port and distance"? he asked me.

I had the answer off pat, "Colombo Sir, and the distance is 1,200 miles as of now".

"Turn her round and head for there", he commanded.

"Yes Sir, I'll bring her round onto North 10 West", I answered as I went into the wheelhouse to give the helmsman the new course to steer.

I stayed in the wheelhouse until the helmsman had brought the ship round the 145 degrees of the compass, and finally steadied her on the new course.

I then blew my mouth whistle, an Acme Thunderer, for the standby man to go and read the log down aft and bring it to me.

I needed that information to enter in the log book.

Going back into the chartroom, I noted down the time of the alteration of course, and the log reading at the time, also entering the new course being steered.

The Captain left the bridge to go and clean himself up, and no doubt fortify himself with a tumbler of the golden liquid he was so fond of. Can't say I blame him for that, I reckon I might have done the same thing if I had been in his shoes.

Our aged Chief Engineer must have fallen for the age old con trick with the bunkers at Aden. If you did not carefully check each barge for contents of coal, the unscrupulous supplier would put upturned coal baskets in the bottom of the hold of the barge.

This in effect reduced the cubic capacity of the coal. By that I mean that by measuring the length and breadth and depth of the coal, you could then work out what tonnage there was in the barge.

Several baskets, placed in each barge, considerably reduced the cubic capacity, which in turn meant that the ship did not get the amount that she appeared to get.

All very crafty business!

Those Chiefs who had visited Aden before, knew of this trick, and they would take an iron rod and poke it down through the coal to see if there where any jiggery-pokery going on. Our Chief Engineer was uninitiated in this lark, hence our bunkers being short shipped.

Five and a half days later we arrived at the port of Colombo, with only one more day's stock of coal on board. Had we not turned back when we did, we would have been a towage job in the middle of the ocean. The overnight stay in Colombo was a welcome treat for us all after 20 odd days at sea. We sailed the next morning fully replenished with fuel, stores and water, for the 4,600 mile run to Australia.

With having to back-track, this added considerable distance to the run from Aden to Freemantle. In fact what started as a 5,000 odd mile passage, ended up being nearly an 8,000 mile one. This had added another 11 days for the passage. Well the old saying is "More days, more Dollars", this may be true, but sloshing about on the ocean isn't the best of pastimes.

It was on this passage from Colombo to Freemantle that I had an occasion to reprimand the man at the wheel about his erratic steering. I asked him if he had gone back to dot the "Is". The ship's wake was like a dog's hind leg, and the use of excess helm to correct the course takes speed off the ship.

The man concerned happened to be one of the "baddies", and if looks could have killed, I'd have been a goner for sure.

I got a lot of caustic comments from him, in seamen's vernacular.

I suppose I could have had him logged for insubordination, but with the Captain we had, I saw no point in it. I let the matter drop and thought no more about it.

A couple of nights later, when the watchkeeper called me at 20 minutes to midnight for my watch, I asked him to mash my mug of tea for me.

It was normal practise for the caller to make the tea if asked.

In response, I heard a voice say "Make your own effing tea, I'm not doing it for you"!

I recognised the voice and immediately became fully awake, "Why not?" I demanded to know.

"Because of the other morning in the wheelhouse", came the answer.

I asked the man a second time to make my tea, but he still refused.

"OK, I'll remember this", I told him as he left my room.

When I went on the bridge to relieve the 3rd Mate, I told him of the incident. He suggested that from now on that he made that man the standby man, to have to spend that part of his watch on the bridge where he could be watched by the 3rd Officer.

Normal practise is that the standby man can spend his time in his accommodation, doing whatever is his thing. Seamen hate to have to do their watch on the bridge, unable to have a smoke or a cuppa.

For several evenings after that, he did his watch on the bridge.

Now as I mentioned earlier, the Officer's toilet was a long way from our accommodation, and this particular night I went along to it prior to going on watch.

As I was on my way back, the man was standing by the starboard side pocket bunker hatch. He stepped out in front of me and said,

"You and me are for it, nobody gets away with making me do my standby on the bridge".

This got my hackles up, here he was wanting to have a go at me, all because I'd pulled him up with a round turn.

Now I was not a particularly pugilistic person, but if needs be, I was able to take care of myself.

"Don't start something you may not be able to finish", I told him.

He said something else, I can't remember exactly what but I knew that he was hell bent on revenge. I readied myself for his attack, when I heard a movement in the far dark corner of the deck, someone else was waiting there!

They say discretion is the better part of valour, and my senses told me this was one of those times. I turned and made my way straight to the bridge, there at least I'd also have a pal to help me if necessary. The cunning bastard had ganged up with his pal the firemen to waylay me and duff me up, or even worse.

After all, we were in the middle of the ocean, the night was dark, and the deck was unlit.
It might have been a case of missing, presumed lost overboard, had I taken him on. Two to one, I had no chance. One to one I'd have had a go.
That incident showed me just how rotten those two men were, and one day maybe I hoped I could sort them out, separately of course.
That day was to come sometime in the future.

A day or so before we arrived in Freemantle, an argument took place in the firemen's quarters, between "Slasher" and the Maltese we'd shipped at Port Said. I don't know who attacked who or how many were involved, all I know is that they kicked the man's eye out. We had to land him on arrival in port, having radioed for an ambulance to be waiting on the quay.
This had been the work of our two pals again, something was going to have to be done about them. We'd have to get rid of those two, they were a menace.
After the usual coaling, storing and taking water, we sailed for Melbourne, where we were to have quite a long stay discharging the phosphates.
Part of my job as 2nd Mate was to collect in the sub lists from all members of the crew, and calculate how much cash they could draw each Saturday without going into debt to the ship.
As I knew that we were likely to be on the coast for some considerable time, I devised a quick method for these accounts. I could tell at a glance how much credit a man had, and no matter what, I would not sanction cash to him if he was in or very near debt. For one thing, I would not consider the money owing them as leave pay. Leave pay was only earned when the voyage ended.
Many's the time a man has said "But I've got several days leave pay due me." I then had to explain that that was not so, much to their disgust.
During our discharge in Melbourne, we got our next Charter orders.
We had been Chartered by the Westralian Farmers Association, to shift over fifty thousand tons of grain from Sydney, New South Wales, to Auckland, New Zealand.
This meant that we would have to do at least five trips from Sydney to Auckland to shift that amount of grain. Little did we realise that we would be engaged on that charter for ten months.
The only thing I can say in its favour was the fact that the Charterers agreed to pay us, the Officers, overtime at the then Australian rates, a most welcome addition to our meagre income.
My monthly salary at that time was £33 a month!

As the cargo was to be shipped in bags, loading in Sydney was very slow. In fact it took two weeks to load us because of the construction of the ship, for she had three decks. Most ships usually have holds and one 'tween deck. We had two 'tween decks, this made loading a slow process. The long stays in port were welcome, but it was disastrous from a money side, after all, nobody wanted to stay aboard when they could go ashore. The constant calls for subs kept me very busy trying to keep men out of debt.
The run across the Tasman Sea to Auckland only took us five days, and then we would have at least two weeks in Auckland discharging the bagged cargo. Then there were times when loading would be held up by dockers, or wharfies as they are called down under, went on strike. I got to know Sydney and Auckland like the back of my hand as we'd spent so long in both of those ports.
To save cash, many of my visits ashore were to the Merchant Navy Officers Club, which held dances and the like, and all for free.
We were still out in Australia come the Christmas after we sailed from Britain. This was the second one away from home, and still no signs of us going home. After the one year had passed, time seemed to have little meaning, and somehow home seemed as though it didn't exist. In all this time away, I had kept in constant touch with my girl friend by letter, but of course that was no substitute for her cheerful company.

It had been our intention to get married at the end of that six weeks voyage, and here I was, out in Australia thirteen months later, with no prospects of going home. Unbeknown to me, this long separation had played havoc with my girl's health, but she had said nothing in her letters to me.

She didn't want me to worry whilst on voyage, very caring indeed. If she had informed me, there was little or nothing I could do.

Coming back to the subject of issuing cash subs to the crew, I knew that sooner or later I'd have some awkward cuss, and I did.

When one day our slasher friend came along for a sub of several pounds, I had to tell him that he could not have any money that week as he was in debt.

An argument ensued, he wanted to know who had said he could not have money.

"The Captain", I told him.

"Oh, fuck the Captain, I want a sub" was the answer I got.

Well, one thing led to another, and he got really belligerent with me. He was, as he put it, "Going to duff me up".

By this time I had had enough. I got up from my desk, went over to the door and locked it, pocketing the key.

"Look, so and so, I've had it up to here", indicating with my hand, and I haven't forgotten you waiting in the background that night out at sea to give your mate a hand."

There was a hushed silence from him.

"Now", I said," If you think you are a better man than me, have a go at me now that you are alone." I could see that he was staggered that I knew he had been hiding in that dark corner of the deck. I tried to goad him into a fight, I wanted to have a go at him, but as an Officer, I could not make the first move.

He started to make some excuses, I told him I did not want to hear them. I then went on to tell him that if he started anything, there would only be one of us walk out of that room. The other would be carried, and I did not intend it to be me.

To make it more plain to him, I produced a knife and said, "If you have any ideas of using a knife on me, beware, I too have a knife and I'll use it if necessary".

There was no more to be said, all he wanted to do was to get out of my room as fast as possible. Needless to say I had no more trouble from him for the rest of his stay in the ship.

His stay in the ship was somewhat foreshortened, because he and his pal were later jailed for breaking into the Captain's quarters to do a robbery. That got rid of our two trouble makers, we could now enjoy, if possible, the rest of the voyage.

With those two leaving the ship, we thought we had heard the last of them, not so however. A short time after we had sailed and they came out of clink, another of our company's ships was in and needed two men. She got our two cast-offs.

Apparently they were not very long in the ship before they were up to their tricks again. They went along one evening and beat up the Chief Engineer. As I remember, he was a small good natured little man, and against those two he would have no chance.

The Captain of that ship was the very one I had first sailed with when I joined the company, and he was a tough man in all respects.

As the ship was going to be in port for some considerable time, he arranged with the Chief to swap sleeping accommodation each evening for a while.

The ploy worked, the two thugs, not knowing about this change of arrangements, went along a second time to harass the Chief.

The Captain waited until the pair were in the room, then leapt out of the bunk and locked the cabin door, pocketing the key. It was so sudden that they were taken aback.

Before they recovered the Captain laid into the pair of them with great gusto. In a matter of minutes, the pair of them were hors de combat flat on the deck of the Chief's cabin.

The pair needed hospital treatment, and from what we heard, one of them had suffered broken ribs from the hammering that he received. No doubt he would have the cheek to try

and claim against that Captain.
We never heard any more of them, I only hope that they learned a lesson by that experience.
It would have been worth a month's wages to have watched that encounter.
I remember that Captain once telling me that he was frightened of nothing on two feet.
I can well believe it.

Chapter 16.
Home - eventually!

The total time the "Romney" spent on that Sydney to Auckland grain run amounted to ten months, most of which was spent in port, as the run between the two ports was only five days each way.

After the final run to Auckland we returned to Sydney, where the ship was to be handed back to the owners, after an off hire survey.

Such surveys being done to ascertain whether any damages had been sustained during the hire period and can be charged to the Charterers. In our case, none had been occasioned, and we were now free for further employment.

We lay at anchor just off Taronga Park, the World famous zoological gardens in Sydney, to await orders from the owners in London.

After several nail biting days, the Agent came out one evening with our latest orders. Everybody was on tenterhooks waiting for the Captain to make it known what they were. When we eventually heard what they were, there was doom and gloom all over the ship.

We were to bunker and store in Sydney for a light ship passage to Antofogasta, Chile, to load a cargo of nitrates for Egypt.

Well, considering that Antafogasta is 6,000 miles across the Pacific Ocean, and Egypt is about another 7,000 miles from there, the voyage was going to turn out far longer than any of us had expected.

However, problems for the ship were not over.

The Australian miners had gone on strike, and when our Captain told the Agents that he needed 2,000 tons of bunker coal to get the ship to Chile they made an application for that amount of coal.

We could not have anything near that amount, in fact the authorities said that they could only allow us sufficient bunkers to enable us to get to West Port, New Zealand, where we could get all we needed. Somehow or other, the local miners heard of this and they contacted the New Zealand miners, who in turn stated that they would "black" our ship if we sailed to New Zealand.

In their eyes we would be breaking the strike, and they were dead against any strike breakers. Solidarity boys, that was the cry.

This turn of events no doubt gave the Bolton S.S. Co. a bit of a headache. They had to look around for some other charter to get the "Romney" on the move again.

The next news we got was that we were to load a full cargo in Sydney for Antwerp and Avonmouth. The cargo was to consist of 4,000 tons of concentrates, (that is, concentrated iron ore), and several hundred bales of wool. It was hoped by the owners that the strike would possibly be over by the time we had finished our loading.

It took us about two weeks to load the cargo alongside the Circular quay, and the strike had ended by the time we were ready for sea. We got our quota of bunker coal to get us round to Albany, Western Australia, where we would bunker again for the ocean crossing to Capetown.

Things were starting to look well for us now. We'd soon be on the long haul home, only 12,000 miles to go, when we got away.

Come sailing time, with all hands at stations for leaving port, I was aft on the poop, my station as 2nd Officer. As I got orders from the Captain to cast off our moorings, three of our firemen jumped ashore and chased the rope handlers on-shore. They would not let them drop the last wire rope off the bollard. By this time the ship was slowly steaming ahead.

I phoned the bridge and told them to stop the engines as we were still moored to the quay by a wire rope, which by this time was twanging like a guitar string.

The Chief Officer was sent aft to find out what was going on.

He soon weighed the situation up. The three men ashore were sat on the bollard, the Chief

Officer went and got a fire axe, and telling us to stand clear, he brought it down on the wire with amighty blow. The wire parted, and the longer end to the shore snaked away like greased lightning. The three men saw it coming, and you couldn't see their arses for dust. I reckon they broke the 4 minute mile long before Chris Chataway, or whoever it was who did it!

More delays, as the men disappeared ashore and apparently got into trouble and strife and ended up in the local lock-up. They went to court and were sentenced to jail, after the magistrate had asked our Captain if he urgently needed them. He said he didn't, so to jail they went and we found crew substitutes, three Aussies to take their places. We finally sailed from Sydney, praise the Lord, for Albany, Capetown, St.Vincent, Cape Verde Islands, Madeira, and our first discharge port, Antwerp.

We only had a few hours in Antwerp getting the bales of wool out and then we sailed for Avonmouth with the balance of the cargo.

Our six weeks voyage had lasted 72 weeks, 1 year, 4 months and 12 days from leaving Salford Docks to arriving back in Britain.

Whilst I had been away, there had been some changes, both in wages and working conditions for Officers. Companies could now offer two year contracts of employment to Officers serving in the companies.

When I asked Boltons about this scheme, I was told that they were only going to offer it to the senior Officers. I raised a bit of a stink about this, after all I had served in the "Romney" for just over three years, and as far as I knew I was respected by the Captains I'd sailed with, as a good and reliable Officer.

So why the discrimination? In view of the fact that I was going to get married, I needed a secure job, not to be on the dole and looking for one. Bolton S.S.Co. had a rethink, and said that they would consider me for a two year contract so I got married, safe in the knowledge that I had a job to go to after the honeymoon.

Our honeymoon was in London for a week, and I was able to go to the company's office to sign the contract, and to have a dressing down for my somewhat forthright letter to them about the matter.

I was ashore for several weeks, and then I was appointed 2nd Officer of another of their ships, the "Ocean Wanderer", and she did turn out to be a wanderer. We sailed from Hull to the Tyne for a cargo of coal for Port Said and spent a couple of weeks there discharging the coal. From Port Said we sailed to Aden to load a full cargo of salt. The salt being destined for Japan.

Great importers of salt the Japanese. I often wondered what they did with all the salt!

We had a good time in Kobe, our discharge port, and at that time cigarettes were good currency.

I remember buying a beautiful coffee set in gilded china, using cigs to raise the cash to buy it. Unfortunately that set never came home with me. After discharging at Kobe, we then sailed for Nauru, a small island in the Pacific Ocean. There we were to load phosphates for Australia. When we first arrived off the island, there was one ship at the loading berth, and another waiting its turn to load.

We therefore were told that we would have to wait our turn, which as it turned out was to be about two weeks later.

There is no anchorage at Nauru, half a mile off shore, the depth of the water is 3,000 fathoms deep! The harbour Master instructed us to just stop engines and drift, the current always taking us away from the land. This we did and let the ship drift. In the meantime our Captain had sent a radio message to the Owners, telling them that we were drifting off Nauru.

Within hours a message came from Lloyds of London asking if we needed assistance.

They obviously monitor all radio messages from ships, and they thought that were in trouble, broken down or something like that.

We had to send a message to them clarifying the position.

As we had been unable to obtain any supplies of vegetables and potatoes in Japan, we were desperately short of these items. We sent a message ashore asking if it was possible for them to supply us with any. The answer was that they too, were short of these items too. Nauru depends on the ships from Australia to bring them supplies of all foodstuffs, and at that time they were awaiting the arrival of that ship.

The other ship waiting came to our rescue, their radio officer had read our message to the shore. Their Captain sent a message to us saying that he could supply us with the necessary items.

Payment for them was to be made by our owners to his owners on production of a note from our Captain acknowledging receipt of them on board.

They sent their motor lifeboat over to us with several bags of potatoes, carrots and cabbages, with some lettuce and tomatoes thrown in as well. They were most welcome by our crew, who had been denied the pleasure of these items with our meals.

Eventually our turn to load came, and we steamed in and moored to the buoy which was to be our moorings.

What puzzled me was how did they anchor that huge steel buoy, when there was 3,000 fathoms of water underneath it.

I asked the port authorities, and they explained to me that the island was shaped like a mushroom under water. It was a coral reef standing on a leg of coral from the ocean bed.

To anchor the buoy a cable laying ship had steamed in with a mushroom anchor suspended from her bow several hundred feet below the water. The ship steamed in as close as she safely could, by which time the mushroom anchor had caught under the protruding edge of the reef, and a cable from the shore was then attached to the buoy along with the cable on the anchor. The buoy was then dropped over into the water, and remained, permanently anchored in position.

It was whilst we were loading that the so-called Harbour Master, I say so-called because there is no harbour at Nauru, came aboard and asked if anyone had a tea or coffee set to sell.

Knowing we had just come from Japan, it was a foregone conclusion that somebody would have bought such a thing. Our Chief Officer told him to ask me. Apparently, he wanted a set to give as a wedding present to his daughter.

There are no shops on Nauru where such things can be bought, there is only the store run by the British Phosphate Commission, and what they stock is mostly provisions and the everyday needs of the people on the island. Luxuries are not catered for.

He came and asked me if I had a set to sell. Well, it had not been my intention when I bought the set to sell it, it was for home use. However, in view of the circumstances, I decided to let him have it. Having obtained it with the barter of cigarettes, it was a bit awkward to name a price. We agreed on a price and he paid me in Australian Pounds.

Our cargo was partly for Brisbane, Queensland, and the balance for Adelaide. Whilst we were in Brisbane, I saw a Rolex Oyster wrist watch in a jewellers shop. The price on it was what I'd got for the coffee set, and so I went in and bought it. It was the first really good watch I'd ever had.

That was 47 years ago, I still have that same watch and it is as good a timekeeper as it was on the day that I bought it. They don't make watches like that any more.

From Adelaide we went to Port Lincoln to load a full cargo of bagged wheat for London. It was during the long stay in Port Lincoln that I made friends with a family with whom I still keep in touch with all these years later, though I have only seen them twice in the ensuing 45 years.

Incidentally, the name of the ship "Ocean Wanderer", was changed just before we sailed from Britain on that voyage. Boltons had bought her from the Ministry of Transport and re-named her the "Ruysdael". All Bolton's ships were named after famous painters, Ruysdael being a famous Dutch painter.

I signed off the "Ruysdael" in Victoria Docks in London on the 10th of December 1948.

We had been away 10 months, quite a long separation when you have only been married a few weeks.

That's a sailor's life for you!

The company let me have a fairly long leave before I joined my next ship as 2nd officer. She was the "Reynolds", an ex Liberty ship.

During that long leave I went back to Nautical College and was able to sit the exam for my Master's certificate. I am pleased to say that I passed the exam this second time of trying.

The day I went in the exam room for the oral part of the exam, it turned out that I was the only candidate in that afternoon.

The examiner, a Captain Crosby Fox, had a field day with me.

I remember one of the questions he asked me, "What did I know about trimming tariffs".

"What do you want, full trim or easy trim?" I asked.

"We'll skip that one", he answered, "You obviously know about them".

Personally, I hadn't a clue about them, but I'd done one voyage on an East Coast collier, and the foreman loader had asked me what trim we wanted. As I didn't know what he was talking about, he told me the difference. Easy trim was when the trimmers simply hauled the coal down from the hatch space, full trim was when they shovelled the coal right out to the ends and sides of the hold, thus completely filling the hold space.

The difference was the cost of the two methods of trimming.

Shipowners always went for the easy trim, the less costly of the two methods.

The "Reynolds" had been the "Samcebu", before she was re-named by Bolton's.

She was the first Liberty ship I'd been on, and her accommodation surprised me.

In comparison with what I'd been used to, it was palatial. Each room fitted with a wash basin with running hot and cold water, a nice settee, an arm chair, a desk and a good wardrobe space.

In the alleyway outside my room was the bathroom, beautifully fitted out, with three shower spaces. It was a pleasure to sail on her.

To make things even better, the Captain was the one I'd been with at the Normandy Beachhead, and I got on very well with him, so things could not have been better from my point of view.

We sailed from North Shields on the 6th July 1949, one day before our second wedding anniversary, and my wife was pregnant. The result, no doubt of my long spell ashore between ships!

I had been told when the child could be expected, and I was hoping that I would be back home before that event.

It was not to be so, my daughter was born six weeks before I got back to Britain.

Our voyage on the "Reynolds" was to load a full cargo of salt, at a place called Cape de Gata. Cape de Gata is actually the name of the cape on the South Eastern coast of Spain. There is or was no actual port, just a jetty sticking out from the shore where barges loaded the salt from the salt pans to bring out to the ship at the anchorage.

As it took us about ten days to load the cargo, could we get ashore in our lifeboat to sample the delights of the place? There was a very small village complete with the sailors heaven, a bar, there may have been other attractions, but I didn't look for them.

I was a married man now!

I only went ashore the once, and had a drink in the smoke filled small bar. It was a dingy little place, but will I always remember that it was the custom for seamen visiting the place to make little cups out of the silver foil from cig packets. They then wet the base of them with spittle and throw them up to the ceiling of the bar, where they would stick, if your aim was good.

There were hundreds of those little cups stuck on that ceiling. By the tarnished colour of some of them, they must have been up there for years.

The games seamen play!

Leaving Cape de Gata, we sailed for, where else but Japan, via the Suez Canal, Red Sea, Aden, Singapore and finally to Japan to a place called Otaru.

I remember our Captain telling me to get the charts out for Otaru, and I mistakenly thought that Otaru was a New Zealand port.

I searched through our chart folios for such charts of New Zealand, to no avail. Imagine how foolish I felt when I told the Captain I could find no such place amongst the New Zealand charts. He had a good belly laugh and then told me Otaru was in Japan. Some navigator I turned out to be!

Otaru was another nondescript sort of place, and I was pleased when we sailed from it after our discharge. Our next port of call was to be Nauru for my second visit there.

As Nauru is just 30 miles South of the Equator, it was decided, on the suggestion of our Captain, that we should hold a Crossing the Line ceremony to initiate all those who had never crossed the line. Everybody aboard joined in with the preparations for the event. A swimming pool was constructed using old hatch boards for the sides, and a tarpaulin to line it with. A length of rope was teased out to make Queen Amphitritie's long flowing hair, and also used for King Neptune hair.

Various costumes were fashioned out of old flags, helmets made from old charts. Our Carpenter fashioned a large wooden razor for the shaving ceremony, and the Cook mixed up the foul shaving mixture.

The ceremony was held the day before we actually crossed the Equator, because we would have been arriving off the port within a couple of hours of the crossing.

It was held at No.4 hatch, I was on watch on the bridge when it started, but our Captain came up and said he would take the watch, and that I could go and take photographs of the event.

I was very keen on photography at that time and I had all the necessary gear with me to develop, print and enlarge photos.

In all, I took 72 photographs from start to finish. I developed them and then made small prints of them, which I posted up in the Notice board frame, so that all could see them.

The next thing was that I had enquiries about selling sets of them to the crew. I agreed to do this.

In all, I printed nearly two and half thousand pictures, every one of the crew wanted a full set of them.

I was heartily sick of the sight of them by the time I finished.

The plus side of the deal was that what I received in remuneration paid for my camera.

The only sad thing is that my own set of prints and the negatives were lost when my wife and I moved house. They disappeared and I have never been able to find them. I would have liked to have kept them as a memento of a very happy voyage.

Sailing from Nauru we proceeded to Melbourne to discharge, and there we made a lot of friends during our stay in port, but all good things have to come to an end, as ours did when we completed discharge of the cargo.

Our next port of call was to be a very long way off, we had been Chartered to load a full cargo of Canadian wheat at Prince Rupert, on the Pacific coast of Canada, a distance of some 7,000 miles from Melbourne.

Fully bunkered with fuel oil and stores and water, we sailed. With the agreement of the Captain, I laid off the courses so that we sighted several of the many Pacific islands on the way across the ocean. As I and the Radio Officer were running a weekly magazine aboard the ship, I wrote about each of the islands we passed.

I got the details from the Admiralty Sailing Directions books we had in the chartroom. My efforts were appreciated by the crew, and it helped to relieve the tedium of the long passage.

One island, I remember in particular, was McLean Island.

Our Captain approached as close as he dare, the soundings being somewhat unknown around the island.

I was keeping a very close watch on the echo sounding machine, ready to give a warning if the depth of water showed any appreciable drop. If it did it was time to get the hell out to sea again. The island was only about half a mile square, and only a few feet above sea level, situated in the middle was the remains of a small brick building, which might have been a house.

That was all there was on McLean Island. I have often wondered who had built that shack, and when, in such a lonely and very isolated spot in the ocean. Ships would not normally pass anywhere near the place on the route across the Pacific Ocean.

We made a brief call into Pearl Harbour for more oil bunkers, but no one was allowed ashore because it was a naval base. In any case we were only there three hours taking oil, and then on our way to the loading port.

Before we arrived at Prince Rupert, we received instructions to proceed to Vancouver, as there was a 'flu epidemic in Rupert and in consequence there were no people available to load the ship.

Consequently our orders were changed, we would load at Vancouver.

This was welcomed by all of us.

Vancouver is a large and lively city, with plenty of places of entertainment to suit all tastes. Seeing we had had our Christmas at sea, we were all looking forward to having the New Year's Eve in port.

The Captain and several officers were invited to a party ashore on New Year's Eve. At the appointed time, taxis were ordered to take us to the house. Our Captain intended it to be a good party.

He was taking a stock of spirits and wine with us. However, we were stopped at the Dock gates by the policemen on duty, they searched the taxis and saw the bottles of liquor. Their first reaction was to confiscate them. We were breaking the law.

Our Captain explained to them that we had just arrived, after spending our Christmas at sea, and that we had been invited to this party, and we did not want to go empty handed.

I know a few Dollars changed hands, and the police let us go, complete with our hoard of bottles. I must admit that a great time was had by all of us at that party, and it was all good clean fun!

I was still awaiting news from home, and each morning in port I used to get "Sparks" our radio officer up to listen in to Portishead Radio, in case there was a message for us.

No such news came whilst we were in port, but Sparks had taken it all in good humour.

About three days after we sailed from Vancouver, the Captain sent for me. I had no idea what he wanted.

When I got to his room he called me inside.

"Congratulations Second Mate, you are now a father", he told me as he handed me the radiogram sent to him by the shipowners, requesting him to inform me of the birth of my daughter.

The cable read "Daughter born 13th, both mother and child well".

Tears of relief and joy rolled down my face at the news. My daughter had been born on Friday the 13th January 1950.

Captain Copping invited me to sit down and have a drink with him to "wet the baby's head". I did.

Whilst having the drink, he was pulling my leg about walking the plank at night, with the baby in my arms, trying to get her off to sleep. As he said, I'd soon learn to be a father.

The ship couldn't get home fast enough for me now, all I wanted was to see, and hold my daughter in my arms.

We finally arrived and docked in Victoria Docks, London on the 25th February, and I got home the next day.

My daughter was then 45 days old, and when I saw her, I knew that I was looking at a gift far more precious than all the gold in the World.

Hitherto, I had been sailing as a 2nd Officer with a Master's certificate, and Captain Copping suggested to the owners that they promote me to Chief Officer. As he had put it, I learned later, if they didn't, some other company would.

The company gave me the maximum amount of leave they could, then I rejoined the "Reynolds" as Chief Officer with Captain Copping in command for the next voyage. The ship was to load a full cargo of bagged cement at Gray's Wharf near Tilbury, for discharge at two ports in Malaya. A small part of the cargo was for Penang, and the balance was for discharge at Port Swettenham, (Aptly named).

I think it took about four days to load the bags of cement, it was interesting to note that the cement was loaded hot as it came out of the works. Sailing from Grays it was the Medi route out again, only this passage through the Medi proved to be a stormy one. It was the first time I had seen bad weather in the Medi, and I was surprised at the ferocity of it. It smashed our starboard gangway, which was in its stowed position at sea.

Then it was on to Port Said again to be pestered by the Arab bumboat men with all the usual junk, postcards, Spanish Fly, etc. as we passed through the port.

Next stop, Aden for bunkers and then on to Penang and all the mystery of the Far East. Our stay in Penang was short and sweet before we moved on to Port Swettenham, where we moored up with what was almost jungle on either side of us.

The discharge of the cargo there took several days and nights, and I did not bother about going ashore. It was too hot and sticky for my liking.

It was as we were nearing completion of discharge, that the Captain asked me if the Boss of the stevedoring firm had made any offer of "perks" to me.

I said he hadn't. Had I asked him? No I hadn't, I didn't have the nerve to broach the subject. "O.K. Mate" replied Captain Copping "I'll have a word with him for you".

He apparently did, because shortly afterwards, Charlie, the Chinese boss of the stevedoring firm came to see me.

He asked me what I would like for a gift from him. Well, I knew that they made some marvellous linen chests out there, so I said I would like one of those to take home to my wife.

Charlie said he would see to it, and see to it he did.

The most beautifully carved teak chest arrived onboard for me.

It was carved almost in 3-D carving, and it was lined with Camphor wood. That chest is in constant use in my home all these years later as a linen chest. Every time it is opened to put in or take our linen, the room is filled with the perfume of the Camphor. It is something that I shall always treasure, and hopefully, will become a family heirloom, to go on to my daughter and then in due course of time, to my grand-daughter.

To get the chest home safely, and undamaged, I had the ship's Carpenter make me a wooden crate large enough to contain it. The chest was then wrapped in a couple of old Army blankets and put in the crate, the lid then being put on.

Initially, that linen chest stood on the landing in our old house, and when my daughter, whom we had affectionately nicknamed Sprout, was old enough, she used to like playing by the chest, for she was intrigued by the carvings on it.

One day she came and told my wife and I that there was a mouse on the box. Horrified, we both went upstairs to look for the mouse. Sprout, of course had followed us upstairs.

We found no signs of a mouse, and told Sprout there was no mouse there. Sprout went over to the chest, bent down and with a cry of triumph, pointed to the side of the chest, "Here is", she said.

We both had a close look at the place she had pointed at, and sure enough, there was a beautifully carved small mouse on the chest.

Something we had never noticed in the time we had had it.

Chapter 17.
Copra bugs and margarine

Before sailing from Port Swettenham, our Captain and several of the Officers were invited to a traditional Chinese meal by the owner of the stevedoring company. At the appointed time he sent down transport to get us to the restaurant for the meal.

This turned out to be at a very plush hotel with all the trimmings. The meal consisted mainly of sea foods, and though they all tasted fine, somehow they disagreed with me, and I ended up by the time we got back to the ship, feeling green about the gills. As a result, I spent a good part of the night sat out on the boat deck feeling very sick indeed.

That put me off sea food from tropical waters for evermore.

On sailing from Malaya, we headed for Indonesia, where we were to take a cargo of Tapioca root and Copra for Holland.

Our first port of call in Indonesia, was Jakarta, and this was at the time when the Dutch were pulling out of the East Indies.

To a certain extent, law and order had broken down somewhat, and thieving seemed to be the order of the day.

We even caught some of the native dockers cutting our hatch tarpaulins into strips to take away ashore. They were slitting the canvas at the seams and then rolling their ill-gotten gains up as small as they could to pass them ashore to pals on the quay. Nothing was safe. Anything that was not fastened down was easy prey to their paddy paws.

It was here we loaded the Tapioca root, it reminded me of parsnips, because that is what it looked like in its natural state. I understand that in its natural state, as dug out of the ground, it is deadly poisonous to humans. Only after it has been processed is it fit to eat.

As we were also to load Copra, the dried meat of coconuts, which is used for crushing, and the oil obtained in the process is used to make margarine. We put the Copra in the forward deep tank and secured the lid on it, to keep it well out of the way.

With the Copra came millions of Copra bugs, they live only on the stuff, nothing else.

They got everywhere, even into our bunks. I used to lift my pillow each time I got into bed, and there would be hundreds of the little black sods.

Copra is a hazardous cargo to carry, it is prone to spontaneous combustion, and it will invariably take fire if its temperature rises above 130°F. In order to reduce the risk of it getting too hot, vertical wooden ventilators are fitted, several of them to each hold. These reached from the bottom of the cargo to the top of the hold.

After leaving Jakarta, we then went to Sourabaya to complete the full cargo. As we were piloted into the harbour, I as Chief Officer, was on the forecastle head, when I got the order to drop the starboard anchor, I gave the Carpenter the signal, and he released the windlass brake, and away went the anchor.

With about 1 shackle out, that is 90 feet of cable, I was told to hold on.

I shouted to Chippy to hold on. He screwed up the brake, in the meantime the ship was going astern at the rate of knots.

The brake would not hold, and the cable started to run out again.

More calls from the Pilot to hold on, we screwed the brake to its limit, but the cable still kept going. Not only that, but the friction between the steel drum of the gipsy and the brake block linings, was so great that they caught fire.

Nobody could understand why the anchor had held so firm on the bottom of the harbour, which was supposed to be mud and clay.

It turned out that we had hooked the remains of a Japanese craft, sunk during the war, and nobody had been aware that it existed, until we hooked it.

There were to be consequences to that incident. When we got to Holland, we went into dry dock after the discharge, and they found that we had buckled some of the bottom plates, due to the tremendous strain of that anchor holding the ship the way it did.

Sailing from Sourabaya, we came home via the Sundra Straits, and I was able to see for first and only time the still smouldering remains of the island of Krakatao. It had in the past produced the greatest explosion the World had ever experienced, when it blew more than half the island away. For months after the event most gorgeous sunsets were experienced around the World, due to the fine dust in the atmosphere.

Homeward bound, our next port of call was to be Aden for oil bunkers.

On passage across the Indian Ocean, Capt. Copping received news that one of his daughters had contracted polio, and on top of that, our cargo of Copra had started to heat up. We had to take the temperature several times a day, by lowering thermometers down the ventilation shafts.

We were getting temperatures up to 126 degrees, too close to the limit for comfort.

Then the Engineers reported that the steel bulkhead between No.3 hold and the stokehold was getting too hot to touch.

The Captain and I held a confab, and I suggested that we should open No.3 hatch lids, and if there were any signs of fire, we could deal with it immediately.

This we did, and though the cargo was hot, there was no signs of it having taken fire. We left the hatch open for several hours, and to our relief, the temperatures started to drop.

Problem solved and a great weight off the Captain's mind, and all went well until we were in the Mediterranean, for our Chief Engineer had an accident whilst in the engineroom.

He had been checking the bottom end temperatures of the engine, by touching them as they revolved. This was the old method of doing it, and called for a good nerve and a very steady hand.

The idea was to slide the fingers in between the connecting rod and the crankshaft as it came round. The hand had to be held vertical so that the fingers could get between the two. Somehow or other, the Chief slipped up, and in consequence lost a good deal of his fingers. Captain Copping treated the injuries. I am not certain, but I believe it was done by diving the finger ends into flour to seal them, and stop the bleeding.

As we were not far from Malta, we headed there with all possible speed to land the man for hospital treatment. In the meantime a cable was sent to the owners, who flew out a replacement Chief Engineer.

On arrival in Rotterdam, where our cargo was destined, we tied up alongside the margarine factory to discharge. I asked the people there what did they do about all the Copra bugs in the cargo.

The answer I got was that they simply crushed them as well as the Copra, because they too were full of oil!

Remember that the next time you enjoy your toast and margarine!

As the ship was due for her six monthly drydocking, the owners decided to have it done in Rotterdam.

This enabled me to get home for a couple of weeks, which was a welcome break.

CHAPTER 18.
The ship that died at noon

I re-joined the s.s. "Reynolds" in Rotterdam on the 18th August 1950, for my third voyage in her. This time I was to be with a different Captain, one Captain Grugan, who I got on with fairly well once we got to know one another.

We had been chartered by the Shaw Savill Line to carry a general cargo from Liverpool to New Zealand and Australia.

We were to proceed to Liverpool, where we would be "loading on berth", that means accepting cargo up to a certain date, so long as there was space for it. A good deal of cargo had already been booked for us to start loading on arrival in berth.

It could not have been better for the Captain, he lived in Birkenhead, so he was almost in his home port for the duration of the loading, and he was good enough to invite me to his home for tea one evening.

On sailing, we found our first ports of call were in New Zealand, so of course we made for the Panama Canal, to make the shortest sea passage there.

Having passed through the Canal and headed out into the Pacific Ocean on the 6,000 mile run to Auckland, I have never forgotten the day we crossed the Equator. It was so cold that on the bridge we found it necessary to wear a heavy woollen jumper, this I learned was due to the ocean current that flows Northwards up the South American coastline from the more or less Antarctic waters off the Southern extremities of the continent.

It sounds laughable to say that we were cold on the Equator, but it is nevertheless true.

I remember that as soon as we arrived in Auckland, we had people coming aboard asking if we had their new cars on board.

We were carrying new cars, and the would be recipients of them must have been told that theirs were being shipped out on our ship. As Chief Officer, I was pestered with people asking if I knew about their car. I had to tell them that I had no idea if any particular car was for them.

All cars were consigned to the car dealers in New Zealand, and they would have to contact the dealer with whom they had placed their order for a new British car.

After all, they would have to undergo a pre-delivery check before the customer received them.

We discharged part of the cargo in Auckland and then went down to Wellington and Lyttleton to complete the discharge of the remaining cargo for New Zealand. Sailing from there we went across to Sydney, Australia to land their portion of our cargo.

Our next employment was to load bagged grain in South Australia for the U.K.

This bagged cargo was to be loaded at several different ports in the Spencer Gulf, some of it was taken at Port Augusta, a place right up at the top end of the Spencer Gulf. As it was summer down in Australia, I experienced some of the hottest weather I've had anywhere in the World. It was so hot that our cargo stacked on the quayside actually caught fire.

For us on the ship, the only relief we could get from the heat was each evening. The town had two cinemas, and the programmes changed every other day, so the Captain, Chief Engineer and myself used to go to the cinemas each night. They were air-conditioned and we were able to enjoy the cool until late evening when we returned to the ship.

By alternating between the two cinemas we never saw the same picture twice. The next port was Port Pirie, another stinking hot spot, but we were not there long, then down to Wallaroo for more bags of grain, and finally to Port Lincoln, where we were to spend Christmas and the New Year.

This suited me fine, as I had friends in Port Lincoln, and I was made welcome to their home every day whilst we were in port. It was whilst we were there, that something went wrong with my right hand, for no reason that I know of. It swelled up and I was unable to use it. My friends insisted on taking me to the hospital, to see a friend of theirs, a Doctor at the hospital, by the name of Longbone!

When he saw my hand he asked me who I had hit, I told him I hadn't hit anybody or anything. He treated the swollen hand and then put it in a plaster cast. Being right-handed, this made certain functions rather difficult to carry out, particularly when going to the toilet.

We had a long stay in Port Lincoln loading the cargo, owing to the difficulty of stowing all the bags, many of which had to go down in the deep tank to enable us to take a full deadweight cargo.

In all, I think we spent three weeks there, and then it was time for me to say farewell to my friends. I have never been back to Port Lincoln since then, I am sorry to say.

However, I did see my friends once more on a later voyage, as they had shifted house to Adelaide and I docked there for just one night, and so was able to make a flying visit.

On sailing from Port Lincoln we headed for Britain via Freemantle, Aden, Port Said, Gibraltar and then to Avonmouth.

On arrival in Avonmouth, we were told that the ship had been sold to some Greek shipowner. All our crew, with the exception of the Captain, Chief Engineer, 3rd Engineer, and myself, had to stay to see to the handing over of the ship to the Greeks when our cargo was out.

I had to hand over a complete list of all stores remaining in the ship, appertaining to the deck stores, show the new Greek Chief Officer around the ship, and give him all the information he required about her. The new Greek crew swarmed all over the place.

Our owners had had stone ballast filling the bilge spaces to give the ship more stability when she was empty. The Greeks knew about this and couldn't get it out fast enough. They said what a waste of good cargo carrying capacity. They took out about 250 tons of that stone ballast.

As time got close to the hand over, which was to be noon, I asked when should I take down our ensign, the Red Duster.

"Take it down at noon prompt, that is when the "Reynolds" dies", I was told by our Superintendent Mr. D. Grierson.

It was a sad thought, that the ship I had sailed many thousands of miles in, was to die at noon. At that time she would no longer exist as the "Reynolds", she would be just a memory.

Chapter 19.
Cuba for sugar again

After my leave, I was sent to join the s.s. "Ribera", lying at Middlesborough. This was one of the ships that I had not sailed in before. I was also to be with a Captain I did not know, but unfortunately was to get to know.

For this voyage, we were also to carry a passenger, a retired Army Colonel, a relative of the owner.

This person had been given the exalted position as Catering Superintendent. He had been in charge of stores in the Army.

The Captain, a hard-bitten South Welshman, had little or no time for the "Pongo" as he referred to our Colonel.

Besides, when our Captain had had a few drinks, he had no time for anyone, and that included me, his Chief Office for the voyage.

The old Colonel was a decent bod, and he spent a lot of time talking to me on voyage, trying to find out as much as he could about ships and the storing thereof.

He had some very good ideas on many things and ways to improve them. For instance, he noted the milled-up state of most of the officers woollen blankets.

He talked to me about them, "Why", he asked, "were they so milled up?

I gave him the answer, "Because they are washed at the laundry, and rinsed in cold water, wool must always be rinsed in warm water."

He made a note of this for future reference. All he learned went down in his note book.

Though there were times when I could have done without his presence, I found him to be a good companion at sea, more so because of the Captain's attitude towards him.

When we arrived in Cuba, we berthed in Havana to load the sugar.

What better place could we have had than that.

Our Colonel went ashore to enjoy the sights of the place, and came back very impressed.

However, from his conversation, I gathered that he wished to see the seamier side of Havana. To this end he invited the 2nd Officer and myself to dine with him at a posh restaurant he had visited.

So the following evening the three of us went ashore, suitably attired for the occasion. It was indeed a posh restaurant, not the kind that we on our own would have dined at.

The meal and the wine were superb, as was the service.

During the meal, the Colonel said we would know our way around these sort of ports, and he was willing to join us in any place we went to.

I don't know whether he had in mind the houses of ill repute, but he wanted to see something out of the ordinary.

After the meal, we left the restaurant and headed for the seamier side of Havana, guided by numerous young boys, who vied one another for the job of showing you all the low down joints. They were well versed and streetwise. One dollar was all they asked to act as your guide to the "good times".

We ended up being accosted by lots of Cuban maidens, of varying ages, size and shapes. These we shrugged off, despite their offers of a " very good time for very little monies."

We finally settled for the stage show at some theatre, which turned out to be all bump and grind stuff.

Judging by the actions of the audience, mainly males of course, the actions of those on stage made them half hard and playful.

Some of the "girls" came down amongst the audience, handing out sweets, and ended up being touched-up by straying hands.

Not mine I would add, even though I was tempted!

By and large, I think our host really enjoyed his night ashore with us. To finish it off we went back for a nightcap at the bar of the restaurant, before making it back to the ship.

As the loading came to an end, it was the beginning of a period of trouble for me.

I'd been checked the loadline, to see how much more cargo we could take, when the Captain sent for me. He wanted to know how much cargo we had loaded. I gave him the figures, and told him that we could only take another 150 tons, and we would be down to our marks, having made due allowance for the density of the water.

The Captain had been at the bottle, and was in an aggressive mood.

"I want some more cargo in than that!" he stormed at me.

"Sorry Sir," I said, "But we are nearly down to our marks now, and 150 tons more is the limit".

"You'll take more cargo!" he stormed at me.

"No way Sir, you've got what we can take and still be on our marks".

"Are you defying my orders".

"No Sir, I'm sticking to the loadline rules, and I will not knowingly overload any ship of which I am Chief Officer".

I left his room and went and gave the stevedores the final orders for the cargo. When that was aboard, the ship was fully loaded as far as I was concerned.

Captain or no Captain, I was not going to overload the ship.

Even when we sailed he was as drunk as a skunk, and it was we three officers who kept him out of trouble on the bridge.

Once well out at sea, he sent for me again, by this time he was sober, and his manners were a bit better towards me.

I think what really got his goat was the fact that I would not go and have a drink with him. Times out of number I refused to go to his room and sit and drink with him. He just could not understand that I was to all intents and purposes, a teetotaller, which is a rare species at sea.

Our cargo was for discharge in Hull, my home town. It could not have been better, we paid off there and I had a fortnight's leave before re-joining the ship. What at the time I was not aware of, was the fact that that Captain had put in a damning report about me to the owners. This was later to have disastrous effects on my career with the Bolton S.S. Co.

I had orders to rejoin the "Ribera" in Hull after the cargo was out. There was a new Captain when I reported aboard, and much to my relief, one with whom I had sailed before and got on well with. Our voyage was from Hull to Conakry, West Africa for a cargo of iron ore for Greenock. I do not remember much about Conakry, except for the run ashore with the Agent, and seeing for the first time, native women walking the streets naked to the waist. It was good for the eyes, and other parts too!

The night before we sailed the Agent took the Captain and me ashore for a meal at the port's posh hotel, the Hotel Conakry.

It was there that for the first time, I tasted baked ice-cream as the sweet. I had never heard of it before, and it puzzled me how you could bake ice cream, but they did.

On arrival in Greenock, I was relieved and sent home on leave.

After a spell of three months ashore, I was ordered to join the s.s. "Rembrandt" at the drydocks in North Shields. I was to be with a Captain Kyne, who I had never met before. He turned out to be a really kind and gentle man, far removed from the one I had recently sailed under.

Our voyage was to be another short one, down to Pepel, West Africa to load a cargo of iron ore for Middlesborough.

Pepel is a small loading station up river from Freetown. There is nothing there except the loading quay and a few houses, so I did not see the sights of Pepel.

The ore mines were owned by a British company, Mungo Campbells of Newcastle on Tyne. They had an age old custom, dating back to the days of sailing ships, whereby they gave a gratuity to the Master and the Chief Officer of a ship loading at Pepel.

It was the sum of one guinea, a lot of money in the days of sail.

That is what they gave me, not much, but better than nothing at all.

It was on this voyage that we got a distress call "On fire", from a Finnish ship bound from the Argentine to Europe with a cargo of Sunflower seed expellers, I am not sure what this is but I understand that it is some form of dust from sunflower seeds. It is a very volatile cargo and can easily catch fire.

This is what had happened on this particular ship. Her Captain radioed any ship in the vicinity to stand-by him in case he had to abandon ship as the fire took hold.

We answered his call, as we were the only ship anywhere near his position. We turned back on our course and made for his last given position. We did not have much of a problem finding him, there was clouds of dense, foul-smelling smoke coming from the ship. The smell of it was somewhat nauseating, so we steamed to the weather side of him so as to keep out of the way of the stink.

In the meantime, his crew had been fighting the fire and they seemed to be winning the battle. Whilst this was going on, both ships were steaming at full speed towards Freetown, the nearest port of refuge.

The Captain of the Finnish ship told us over the radio that he did not have any charts for the approaches to Freetown.

We gave him all the instructions he would need to get there safely, warning him, under no circumstances to try and pass between two certain buoys. Those buoys marked the ends of the underwater concrete barrier which the French had laid at the outbreak of the war. Any ship steaming over that barrier would have torn her bottom out.

We finally left the ship when she was near enough to make the port safely, we then proceeded on our voyage.

I did four voyages in a row on the "Rembrandt" before being sent home on leave again. During the time I was in her, she had three different Captains.

I left the "Rembrandt" at Middlesborough on the 19th June 1952, and was at home until the 14th October 1952, when I was sent to join the "Ribera" at Birkenhead. I was to be in her for three voyages running across the Western Ocean for grain from Canada to the U.K.

It was whilst I was in that ship that I learned that a Chief Officer much junior to me, had been promoted to Captain.

That promotion should rightly have been mine.

I mentioned this to one of the Captains of the "Ribera". The Captain was Captain Copping, the first one I ever sailed with in the company. He was sympathetic, and then went on to ask me if I had any idea why I had been shifted to sail with so many different Captains.

I told him I had no idea why, he then took me into his confidence. He told me that all the Captains had instructions from the owners, to monitor my reactions about the early promotion of a junior man.

He then said that he was pleased that he could report favourably about me to the owners. All this was because of the report made by that drunken bum of a Captain I'd sailed with earlier.

Because of him, I was under scrutiny as to my suitability to be made a Captain in the company. By this time I had been serving in the company for 9 years.

On leaving the Ribera, I was sent home on the 29th August 1953 until 19th December, when I had to join the s.s. "Ramsay" at Glasgow.

I was in her for the home-trade run down to Liverpool, where she was to load a full general cargo for the Shaw Savill, Albion Line.

The "Ramsay" had been chartered from the slipway by them for a period of four years to carry cargoes to and from Britain to Australia and New Zealand. General cargo out, and wool, hides and casings home.

Casings, by the way, is the correct name for sausage skins. These are the intestines of sheep and were shipped to Britain in barrels of salted water.

On arrival in Liverpool, we were all sent home on leave. The company had decided that the ship should remain in port for the Christmas holiday. I left her on the 20th December 1953 and rejoined her for the voyage on the 1st January 1954.

The voyage lasted four and a half months, and I enjoyed it because it was entirely different to any previous voyage.

I had plenty to do working out the stowage of the cargoes, which was in many small parcels and had to be stowed so that we could work as many holds as possible at any one time. This of course speeded our loading and discharging.

Shaw Savills showed their appreciation for co-operation by making generous monetary bonuses. I remember that I received £90 for the voyage. By today's standards that may not be much, but in 1954 it was the equivalent of two months wages to me.

On the way home via the Panama Canal, two things occurred, one during my morning watch, 4 to 8 a.m. I noticed a strong smell of seaweed, but at the time we were hundreds of miles off the coast.

Next I saw the water of the Pacific Ocean had suddenly turned from deep blue to a muddy appearance.

Considering that the depth of the ocean under our ship was something like 3,000 fathoms, (18,000 feet), something was obviously wrong.

Then I saw the water ahead of the ship boiling up and churning,

I didn't know exactly what to do in the circumstances.

I altered course as far away from the boiling area as possible, and made for what appeared calmer waters ahead.

I found out later, after we had reported the incident to the United States Weather Office, that there had been a subterranean earthquake, and we had sailed right over the area.

I saw loads of gnarled tree trunks being thrown to the surface of the ocean, and there was a strong smell of sulphur in the air.

The second incident, unpleasant for me, was the fact that going along the deck one morning to check on how the chipping of the decks was going with the use of electric scalers, I got a splinter of steel in my right eye.

I did not know it at first, but when my eye started to hurt and close, I knew something was wrong.

I asked the Captain to examine my eye, but he said he could not see anything in it. After a couple of days my eye was filmed over, so on my morning watch I rigged up a couple of mirrors from my sextant, and with the aid of a watchmaker's eyeglass, I was able to look at my eye. Stuck in the middle of the iris was the sliver of steel!

I knew then that I had to get rid of it before any further damage was done to my eye. I nipped down to my room and got some cotton wool, then back on the bridge in the chartroom, I wrapped a small amount of the cotton wool around a match-stick.

Then with the watchmakers eyeglass firmly held in my left eye, I was able, with difficulty, to see the offending item.

I then very gently swept across the eyeball with the cotton wool pad. At the first touch on the piece of steel, it hurt and I knew that I would have to sweep across the eye in the opposite way.

This I did, and praise the Lord, the sliver of steel got stuck in the cotton wool, and I was able to remove it without pain.

Shortly afterwards the Captain came on the bridge and I was able to show him what had damaged my eye.

As we had still several days steaming ahead before we reached Balboa, the port at the Western end of the Panama Canal, all I could do was to bathe my eye several times a day. This I am pleased to say cleared the infection and I was able to see properly again.

When we arrived at Balboa, Captain Kyne insisted that I should go ashore and see a specialist about my eye. I was taken by the Agent to the United States Army hospital, and there my eyes were minutely examined by a specialist.

He was re-assuring, and he said that there would be no staining of the eyeball, but they would as he put it, irrigate the eye.

To this end he injected copious amounts of some solution to wash the eye, and I am pleased to say that my eyesight was O.K. after that, and has been ever since.

By the time we got back to Hull, the voyage had lasted four and a half months. I was given a few days leave, then I had to re-join the ship in London.

About this time, Boltons were building a new cargo ship which was to go on a four year charter to Shaw Savill Line. The new ship was a little behind time and unable to make her scheduled maiden voyage between Australia, New Zealand and South Africa.

This was to be a brand new shipping service between those countries, carrying general cargoes.

As the prospectus of the loading and sailing had been publicised broadly, the "Ramsay" was, after delivering her outward cargo from the U.K. to Australia and New Zealand, to take over the South African run until the other ship was ready.

So when we arrived in Australia and discharged some of our cargo we then started loading in the empty spaces, cargoes for South Africa. This went on at each and every port of call in Aussie and New Zealand until we were full with cargo again.

When this was done we sailed to Capetown, which was to be the first port of call. At the final port in Australia, we had loaded about forty pedigree rams for shipment to the Falklands Islands.

These we carried on deck in specially constructed pens. One member of our crew was paid to look after the sheep, which meant cleaning them out and feeding and watering them each day.

I remember the shipper giving me instructions that if the rams got constipated, I was to see to it that they were given an extra dose of bran.

How the hell was I to know when a ram is constipated, did I have to stand and watch them holding on to the toilet straining bar!

Anyway, we got them safely to Capetown, where they were put ashore after much consultation with the local health authorities.

We then started the run up the coast to Port Elizabeth, East London, Durban, Lorenco Marques, Beira, Tanga, and finally Mombasa.

As loading and discharging went on all night at these ports, it meant that I had many nights out on deck supervising the loading of the cargo. On the day we arrived at Lorenco Marques, I was feeling very much under the weather, and by the time we had got the ship anchored in the harbour, I was feeling very ill indeed. I reported to the Chief Steward, who in turn told Captain Burns.

He came to my room to see me and said that as there was a Doctor coming on board to see another man, he would have him check on me.

That evening the Doctor came and saw me, and immediately diagnosed me as having pneumonia. My temperature at the time as 104 degrees. He ordered me to bed and gave antibiotics to be taken every three hours, and he said he would be back in the morning to see me. Before leaving my room he said that I must not get out of bed, as the tablets would knock hell out of me.

He wasn't joking when he said that!

That night I sweated buckets, my bed sheets were soaked by the time he came to see me the next morning.

The Doctor then prescribed some antipyretics, I think that was the word for it, to drop my temperature. From then on I started to recover, but was very weak. The "Quack" said that as we were going up the coast, he would not order me ashore into hospital, which he would have done if we had been sailing on a long passage.

He said, if necessary, I could be landed a day of two after if my condition did not improve.

When we go up to Tanga, the Captain asked for a Doctor to come out and see me.

The Agent requested the Doctor, but as it was a Sunday morning, the Doctor refused to come to the ship. However, he said he would see me if I was to go to his surgery.

To this end, the Captain told me to get ready to go ashore and report to his room when I was ready.

This I did with difficulty, and then tried to mount the stairs to his room. When I got to the door of the room I was in a state of collapse.

The Agent saw me in the doorway and immediately told the Captain that I was in no fit state to be taken ashore. He then left and brought the Doctor back with him. I was given more treatment and told to take things easy. Our next port of call was Mombasa, and there I had to go and see the Doctor every day, my chest was loaded, and he was not too happy about that.

He gave me a very large bottle of medicine and told me to take a drink of it every time I saw the bottle.

He said that when any phlegm I coughed up tasted of the stuff, then it was doing the job it was for.

After several days of drinking whatever it was, it did taste as he had said, my lungs were being cleared of the infection.

Before we sailed a week later, the Doctor had told me that if it had not have cleared, I would have spent my Christmas in hospital as he was concerned about the infection.

Leaving Mombasa, we sailed to the island of Mauritius, where we loaded several hundred drums of molasses for Australia.

So it was back to Australia and New Zealand to discharge and then load general cargo for home.

This voyage had lasted 11 months, far longer than I had expected.

It is worthy of note that I did have one or two brushes with that particular Captain during the voyage, all because I was doing my job to the best of my ability.

My job as Chief Officer was, apart from navigational duties and cargo planning, to keep the ship in good condition around the decks. To this end, I had a plan to get rid of a lot of rust that had accumulated around the steelwork.

As the Captain was partial to his gin drinking in the evening, he usually woke up with a shitty liver and wasn't fit to be near first thing in the morning.

I had given the Bosun strict orders that no chipping hammers were to be used before 9 a.m.. Then to my horror, one morning at a few minutes past 7 a.m. there was the rattle of chipping hammers.

I shouted at the top of my voice for the din to desist, but it was too late.

The bridge telephone rang, I answered it, it was the Captain, he was breathing tongues of fire because he had been rudely awakened by the noise of the hammers.

He'd have words with me after breakfast he said. He did, and they were very harsh words indeed. I learned later that he had been in ships with coolie crews, and he thought he could treat me the same way. I was a little brutal and told him a few home truths, after which he had a bit more respect for me. I pointed out to him that I intended that any ship I was Chief Officer of was to be the best kept ship in the fleet. He got the message eventually.

We signed off the voyage at Hull on the 10th May 1955, and again I was sent on leave.

Between then and the end of 1955, I was sent to stand-by the "Ramsay" whilst she was in the U.K. discharging and loading her outward cargoes.

A little more leave and then I was sent to Middlesborough to stand-by at the Smith's Shipyard, where a new breed of ship was being fitted out for the Bolton S.S.Co.

The ship was the "Redcar", a 15,000 ton iron ore carrier, one of the first of that class of ship purposely built for long term charter to the British Steel Corporation.

I was senior Chief Officer in the company, hence the reason I was sent to supervise certain things appertaining to the deck, bridge and chartroom fittings.

The job was interesting enough, but it was mid winter and I was almost frozen most of the time I was down at the shipyard.

I was staying at the Merchant Navy Hotel in Marton Road.

The accommodation was good and so was the food provided, and I was able to go home every weekend on a Friday night until Monday morning, all expenses being paid by company. Unfortunately, I was brought down with a bad bout of the 'flu which confined me to bed in the hotel.

The manager and his wife were concerned about me and sent for their Doctor, who gave me treatment. After several days he suggested that I should go home until I was fit enough to start work again. This I did, but was very ill when I got home, and had to call my own Doctor in. He said I was to forget about work for at least two weeks.

I'd informed my employers of the situation, but this did not stop the Marine Superintendent at Middlesborough ringing me up to ask when I would be back on the job. I told him I'd be back as soon as I was fit enough to climb hold and bridge ladders aboard the ship.

Some two weeks later I returned to Middlesborough and carried on with the job. Looking back, I realise what a fool I was at times, such as when the Super said I was to go down into the double-bottom ballast tanks and check that they had been grease coated. I was also to collect any debris such as bolts, washers, rags, waste or anything else that could foul the ballast pumps when they came into operation.

My stupidity was that I entered those tanks alone. There should have been a man stationed at the manhole of the tank in case anything happened to me. After all someone could have come along and sealed up the tank, not knowing that I was down there.

When it eventually dawned on me, I told the Super that I did not enter any further tanks unless there was a man to stand-by the open door of the tank for my safety. He wasn't too pleased with that, as I was the only man from the company there.

When it was near time for the trials of the ship, my worst fears were confirmed. The Captain was to be the one who had put in the bad report about me to the company.

I was going to have to sail with him again worst luck, and worst luck it was to be.

Chapter 20.
More than half seas over

Before proceeding further, I must revert to an earlier voyage in the "Ribera", one which will always remain in my memory.

I'd joined the "Ribera" at Birkenhead on the 14th October 1952 for a light ship voyage to Vancouver, where we were to load a full cargo of Canadian grain for the U.K.

The outward passage empty ship gave me plenty of time to have work done down the holds scaling and painting.

For years I had put up with placing rope lashings across the hatches when loaded. These I was always told were to stop the tarpaulins from billowing up when the ventilators were turned into the wind for ventilation of the cargo.

In actual fact, these lashings had a far more important job to do.

They were there to stop the wooden hatch boards from bouncing when heavy seas dropped on them.

Hardly a winter passed in the North Atlantic without some ship or other sending out a distress call saying that they had had a hatch stove-in in heavy seas.

When that happens, there is little hope for the ship, she is generally a doomed vessel.

This voyage I decided to have some wire rope lashings made to fit each hatch. I'd ordered the necessary wire for the job, and I gave the Bosun all instructions as to how I wanted them fitted.

The Bosun, a man skilled in the art of wire splicing made the lashings, complete with a bottle screw fitted at the centre of each hatch. This bottle screw was to haul the wires bar tight, far tighter than any rope lashing could have been. In fact they were like steel bars across the hatches when screwed up.

I was delighted with the results of his work, little knowing that later in the voyage they were to save the "Ribera" from a watery grave.

We loaded our cargo of grain in Vancouver and sailed on the 4th December 1952 for Hull.

We'd rounded Cape Flattery on the south western corner of the Straits of Juan de Fuca in my evening watch that night. Having cleared the Cape, we headed South down the West Coast of the U.S.A. towards the Panama Canal.

When I came off watch at 8 p.m. that night, I noticed the barometer was falling. I remember saying to the "Old Man", it looks like we are in for a bit of a blow.

How big a bit of a blow, I was to find out during my watch next morning between 4 a.m. and 8 a.m.

When I took over the watch at 4 a.m. the ship was labouring in fairly heavy seas, but she was riding them beautifully.

The 2nd Officer had stayed on the bridge to have a cup of tea with me. We discussed the weather and falling barometer.

Nothing to worry about was our decision, and with that the 2nd Officer went down to his room to turn in.

Around 5 a.m., I went into the chartroom to have a look at the barometer. The bottom was falling out of it, for it was reading 27.05 inches, the lowest I had ever seen at sea.

There was obviously something nasty around, and I didn't know how nasty.

I lit a cigarette and went back into the wheelhouse.

Snug in the wheelhouse, I stood looking through the front windows at the heaving seas. I was content, the ship was riding them well but taking some water over the fore deck. Nothing unusual in that. Then I noticed a very light streak in the sky ahead of the ship.

"Great", I thought, "There's break in the clouds, that's a good sign".

Then the alarm bells in my head started ringing, "At 5 a.m. on the 5th December, the sky could not be as light as that".

In a split second the awful truth dawned on me. What I was seeing ahead was the crest of a mighty sea lit up by the light of our foremast light some 70 feet above the level of the sea!

I shouted to the man at the wheel, "For God's sake, duck".
I turned my back to the windows and pulled my bridge coat collar over my head. Seconds later I felt the ship put her nose down and come to a full stop.
She had put her bow into the base of the sea.
The noise was terrifying as thousands of tons of the Pacific Ocean crashed aboard, sweeping along the full length of the ship.
The wheelhouse windows shattered, and I could feel the glass hitting my coat as the sea water filled the wheelhouse.
Fortunately, I had the starboard door open and the water went out almost as quickly as it had entered.
I asked the wheelman if he was alright. He said he was.
I next looked at the compass, and to my horror I found that we had been carried bodily round onto a course 90 degrees away from our course. We were now beam on to the seas.
I had to get her back on the right course, but in weather like that I would have to be careful.
Another sea like that, with us beam on to it would have been disastrous, it could have rolled us over.
I told the helmsman to try bringing the ship round ten degrees at a time then steady her before doing the same again until we were back on course.
I was too busy concentrating on that to worry about what had happened or what damage had been done to the ship.
When we were finally back on course I was then able to try and find out the worst.

The Foremast light was out, smashed by that wave.
Part of the noise I had heard was due to the reel holding the 5" insurance wire on the forecastle head, had been torn from the deck. The force of the sea had taken it through the guard rails and dropped it onto the No.1 hatch.
The ventilators situated on the top of the masthouse between No.1 and 2 hatches had been sheared off as clean as a whistle.
Apart from the wheelhouse windows being shattered, monkey island woodwork had been carried away.
The whole of the starboard side teak woodwork of the bridge was missing as I found out when I went to ring the telegraph to the engineroom.
The telegraph wasn't there, it was lying on the deck, flattened by the sea.
I made my way down the ladder to the lower bridge to go and call the Captain. I found all the woodwork on that bridge had gone.
Going into the alleyway to his room, I knocked on his door and then tried to open it.
The door opened about 6" and then refused to go any further, no matter how hard I pushed against it. I put my back against the bulkhead and my feet on the door and pushed with all my strength. The door finally moved enough for me to enter the room.
The room was a shambles, the steel safe was lying behind the door.
All the forward bulkhead polished wood panelling was hanging loose from the bulkhead. His desk was overturned on the deck.
The Captain was there, getting his trousers on over his pyjamas, a shocked expression on his face.
"What's happened Mate?" he asked.
"I don't know except that one hell of a sea hit us", I replied.
"For all I know, we could be steaming under".
"I'll be up in a minute" answered the Captain as I made my way back to the bridge.
As an afterthought, I said "Watch out as you come on the bridge, all the front of the bridge has gone over the side".
The "Old Man" finally arrived on the bridge and ordered me to go and call all hands to muster amidships.
I left the bridge and with great difficulty managed to get right aft to call the Bosun, Carpenter and the deck hands.

There was no need to actually call the deck crowd, they were all up. Their accommodation was a shambles.

Every bunk had been thrown onto the deck by the force of the whiplash effect of that tremendous sea crashing down on the foredeck.

I made my way back to the bridge. The Captain then left me in charge of the ship, while he went down on the deck to assess the extent of the damage. He returned an hour later, by which time I was nearly frozen, standing there in my absolutely saturated clothing. I asked his permission to go down to my room and change into some dry clothes.

When I got into our alleyway on the lower deck, I found the 2nd Mates room awash. The sea had bashed the steel bulkhead in and at the same time smashed the two portholes of his room.

The broken glass from the shattered ports was lying on his bed.

He had been lucky not to have been cut to ribbons with those 1" thick shards of glass.

Having changed my clothes, I then got out a bottle of brandy and poured two glasses of it out. I handed one to the 2nd Mate and I downed the other one. Under normal circumstances that amount of brandy would have made me pie-eyed, but it had no effect on me at all. That proved how badly shocked I had been by the ordeal.

Thank God there were no more seas like that one, and the ship rode the storm well.

We were able to cover the broken ventilators, and also to nail timber over the torn tarpaulins on No.1 hatch. This was only a temporary measure until the weather allowed us to put new tarpaulins on. It prevented any seawater entering the hatch.

The repairs to the woodwork would have to wait until we reached port and obtained the necessary timber to rebuild it. As we got further South the weather eased up and I was able to make a thorough examination of the damage to the ship.

Going under the forecastle head, I was amazed to see that the 3" diameter steel staunchions supporting the deck above, were bent like dog's hind legs!

Next I got the Bosun to open No.1 hatch so that I could go down and have a look at the cargo, to see if any of it had got wet.

Standing in the tween decks at the after end of the hatch, I could scarcely believe my eyes. The centre line partial bulkhead was also had a dog's leg in it. It dawned on me that it was a miracle that the "Ribera" was still afloat.

Without those steel wire lashings I'd had stretched across the hatches, the "Ribera" would have been consigned to the deep.

The hatches would have bounced and slipped off their landings and into the hold. No.1 hatch would have been "stove-in".

I have often wondered what it was that induced me to have those wire lashings made and fitted that particular voyage. That I shall never know. I only know that they saved me, and the rest of the crew from a watery grave in the North Pacific Ocean.

On arrival in Hull, the owners had Lloyds Surveyors down to the ship to assess the damage. Their considered opinion was that the ship had been lucky to survive such a sea.

Mr. Bolton, the owner, came down to see his ship and he would not believe me when I told him of the damages.

I hate people who do not believe my words.

I asked Mr. Bolton if he would be good enough to accompany me forward and see for himself that what I had said was true.

We first went under the forecastle head and I pointed out the bent staunchions. He then helped me to remove a couple of the hatch boards from No.1, so that we could get daylight into the tween deck space. Entering the masthouse we got into the tween decks, where I showed him the bent steel bulkhead.

He needed no further convincing, he'd seen for himself what the might of the seas can do to a ship. He too realised that it was a miracle that the "Ribera" had survived such a storm.

I went on leave, but the memory of that terrible night would not leave me in peace. I had nightmares over it. I would wake in the middle of the night screaming for men to take cover, that mountainous seas were charging towards the ship. I'd wake, covered in sweat, and then realise it was now only a dream.

Three months later I rejoined the "Ribera" for a further two short voyages, safe in the knowledge that she could take anything that Nature could throw at her.

In August 1953 I went on leave again until the middle of December, when I was sent to join the s.s. "Ramsay" at Glasgow for the Home Trade run down to Liverpool, where she was to load her outward cargo for Australia and New Zealand.

The ship was not to sail before the New Year, so all of us were sent home to enjoy our Christmas holiday.

I returned to the ship for signing on, on the 1st January 1954, and we sailed shortly afterwards. The voyage lasted five months, and on arrival back in Hull, I went on leave again. As the ship was going to be at least two months in the U.K., I had a nice leave before rejoining her for another Shaw Savill voyage. This one was to be a comparatively long one.

In fact it lasted ten months, returning to Hull to discharge, on the 9th May 1955. This was twice the length of the ordinary voyage to Australia and New Zealand, but we had had to stand in for the "Romanic" which was to have taken over the Australia / New Zealand / South Africa run. Her fitting out and trials had not run to schedule, and Shaw Savill were anxious to get the service under way after announcing the start of the service.

I shall never understand international trade, we took motor tyres out from Britain for discharge in New Zealand. In New Zealand we loaded tyres for South Africa. In South Africa we loaded tyres for Australia!

I suppose it made sense to someone!

Whilst loading bags of coffee beans at Mombasa, there was a bit of a flap when several bags were found to be missing from their respective hold of loading. In other words they had not been tallied into a certain hold.

The loading foreman came to me and said that they would have to start unloading the cargo to find the bags. As we had already loaded several hundred bags of the stuff, I thought it was mad to suggest that we unloaded it all. It was forcibly brought to my notice that each of those bags of beans was worth two hundred pounds sterling. It was therefore cheaper to pay the native labour than to lose one bag of coffee beans.

So the unloading began, and carried on until the missing bags were found in another hold. At that point it was accepted that the bags were on board the ship, but in the wrong hold.

That was of little consequence because the coffee was all for one port in Australia, and would be discharged regardless of the hold that it was in.

Whilst in South Africa, in East London, I was instructed by Shaw Savills, to take sufficient dunnage timber for dunnaging a cargo of second-hand barrels, full of molasses. These molasses were to be loaded at Mauritius, and apparently timber was at a premium there. I had to work out what quantity of timber would be needed for the job, remembering that the drums could not be stored more than two high.

I worked out what I thought would be needed for the job. This done, the order was given to a timber yard for supply.

Imagine my surprise, when the next morning, two lorry loads of timber arrived alongside the ship. I'd given the measurements in running feet. The yard had converted this to ton's weight, and I think they sent down about four tons of the stuff.

There it was, piled high on our foredeck, more dunnage wood than I had ever seen before. The good thing about it was, that when the timber firm brought their bill for my signature, they were very generous with a cash bonus for me.

The timber was used for the purpose of dunnaging the barrels, this made the Charterers happy because the drums all arrived without damage at their destination. I was happy because of the cash bonus, in other words everybody was happy.

I enjoyed the voyage, apart from my occasional brushes with the Master during the voyage over minor annoyances to him, such as him being rudely awakened by the crew's chipping hammers, or scrubbing the decks before he was out of his bed in a morning.

Chapter 21.
Trials and tribulations of the "Redcar"

The ship left the shipyard for her sea trials, and had the owner and all his staff with him, along with the all the shipyard boffins who would monitor the ship's performance at sea.

It was to be an all day and night session running up and down the measured course to ascertain her maximum speed.

It all ended up with a glorious piss-up for all concerned, as they were happy with the results. The ship was now accepted by the owners and would store and come into service immediately.

The maiden voyage of the "Redcar" was to be from the yard to Seven Islands in the Gulf of St. Lawrence, Canada and back to Glasgow with ore.

Little did I know at the time that Seven Islands was the fastest ore loading port in the world. Their loading rate was a little over 4,000 tons an hour. This they increased to 8,000 tons an hour later. Our loading time was very short and with a fairly high swell on the water it was difficult to get a good reading of the Plimsoll. Anyway, I loaded according to our marks, and that gave me a cargo of 15,050 tons.

When we finished loading we had to get off the berth immediately to allow the next ship in the berth. The captain sent for me and wanted to know how much cargo I had loaded.

I told him, 15,050 tons, he went berserk and said that I had underloaded the ship again.

He'd wanted more than that he said. I told him he had got all the cargo the ship could have and still be down to her legal marks.

He grumbled all the way back to Glasgow.

In the end I said "Look captain, they give you an outturn weight here, and I'll bet what I said is within a few tons on the outturn weight when we get it.

It was, the outturn was 15,020 tons, but even that did not satisfy the cantankerous old bastard.

My second voyage with him on the "Redcar" was to Wabana, Newfoundland, and on this voyage we had two passengers, relatives of the owners. As we neared the coast of Newfoundland the Captain was showing off to the passengers by taking the ship well inshore. It was during my 4 to 8 p.m. watch on the bridge that he was showing off. Suddenly I spotted that we were headed straight on to an outcrop of rocks right ahead. I yelled to the Captain, he hadn't seen the danger ahead. A quick hard-a-starboard and we just scraped by those rocks. At nearly 14 knots they would have torn the bottom out of the ship.

Navigators I have sailed with, or clever bastards I have known!.

Our cargo was for Middlesborough this time, and when we arrived there, the Marine Superintendent came to see me.

He told me that I was wanted for interview in the head office in London, and that I was to go home that day and be at the office next morning.

I packed my overnight bag and caught the train to Hull.

When I got home, my wife, not unnaturally, wanted to know why they wanted me to go to the office. I didn't know, so I could not tell her why. I was to find out the next day.

I caught an early train the next morning to King's Cross, arriving there around 10.30 a.m.. From there, I took a taxi to the company's head office in Houndsditch.

I entered the outer office and gave my name and business to the receptionist.

"Please take a seat, Mr. Mathison, I'll let them know you are here", she said. I sat down and waited, and wondered why I was here in the first place.

A cigarette later, the junior Director appeared and greeted me in a fairly amicable manner, as he guided me into the inner sanctum, the Boardroom.

There, seated around the large mahogany table, was the Managing Director, Mr. F. B. Bolton (now Sir Frederick Bolton), a Mr. P. B. Arthur, Senior, his son, another Mr. Arthur who had shown me into the room.

Mr. Bolton asked me to sit down at the end of the table facing him.

He brought out his gold cigarette case and offered me a cigarette, and in the nervous state that I was in, I accepted a fag.

After the usual salutations, Mr. Bolton asked me if I had any idea why they had called me to the office.

As I had no idea whatsoever, I replied that so far as I knew, men were only called to the office for one of two reasons.

Mr. Bolton then asked me what those two were.

"It is either to higher, or to fire a man", I replied.

"That is rather a blunt statement Mr. Mathison", said Mr. Bolton.

"I am sorry if my summing up offends, but I am a blunt person, so which of the two is it? There was complete silence in the boardroom, as they looked from one to another.

As there was this silence period, I carried on, "I cannot think that I am here to be highered, so I can only assume the latter applies".

Mr. Bolton then cleared his throat and started to tell me that he had had an unfavourable report about me from one of his Masters.

In view of that he said, he would give me the choice of either staying with the company to the end of my present contract, or I could leave the company as soon as I wished.

I suppose I could have defended myself, and have given my version about the drunken bum, Capt. Thomas, the man who had blackened my name in the company. But what the hell, I thought, they would only think that I was being malicious towards the man.

Who's word would they believe anyway? I am sure they would have taken his word against mine.

To me the saddest part was that I had no one there to defend me. Had I have known what was in front of me, I would have asked my union representative to be present at the interview. With him there, I think it would have been a different story.

I was instructed to go back to the ship and collect my gear, then go home on leave and consider the options they had given me.

I was to let them know in due course what I had decided, whether to stay to the end of my contract, or leave immediately.

As I came out of that office, I met the junior Superintendent.

He asked me what had gone on in the inner sanctum.

"Mr. Grierson", I said, "I have just been sacked after 12 years in the company".

"You must be joking!", he answered.

"I don't joke about things like that Mr. Grierson".

"Now I know we have not got on too well together, you and I, but I assure you, I have never said a word against you in this office", said the Super.

"I wish I could believe that Mr. Grierson, I really do", I answered.

With that I was about to leave the office when I decided to ring my wife and tell her what had happened. It was foolish of me, but I needed to talk to someone close to me.

I left the office and made my way to King's Cross for my train home. My head was full of so many things, and at the same time, I was humming softly to myself, "As you walk through the storm, hold your head up high, and don't be afraid of the dark", the song from Carousel. Since that day, whenever I hear that song my mind goes back to that fateful morning in London, when all my dreams were shattered.

Arriving back in Hull later that evening, I took a taxi back home.

After a nice cup of tea and a bite to eat, I told my wife what had happened in London. I realise now what a shock it must have been to her. Our livelihood taken away just like that, after all those years of what we thought was job security.

I was still in a state of shock, but I tried to hide my feelings. My wife was very supportive and did what she could to help me over the period.

For almost a week, I did not know how to get some sleep, and I remember my wife asking me something, it must have been about Boltons.

I rushed out of the living room and into the next room, there I broke down and cried as never before in my life.

I was shattered, my mind couldn't think straight. My wife came into the room and saw the state I was in and tried to console me.

When I had regained some semblance of composure, she suggested that I should see the Doctor, as I looked ghastly.

"Take a look in the mirror", she said.

I did, and I knew she was right, I looked like two penn'orth of death warmed up.

I made an appointment to see the quack, and his first reaction when he saw me was to ask, "When did you last have a sleep"?

"About a week ago", I answered.

"Next question, you don't have to answer it if you do not want".

"What big emotional shock have you had"?

I unburdened myself and told him the whole story of the past week.

The Doctor nodded, and said "I quite understand, this has been a hell of a shock to you."

I nodded in agreement.

"Your first priority is some sleep, therefore I will give you some sleeping tablets".

At bedtime that night I took the tablets as prescribed, and slept soundly for the first time in a week.

After several nights sleep, my mind was back to normal, and I could think straight again.

My old fighting spirit had come back, and I was going to show those officious pricks in the office what a mistake they had made.

I phoned the London office and told them of my decision.

I would stay with the company until the end of my contract. Their answer was that they were pleased to hear this. They further went on to say that they were prepared to review the situation in a year's time or so.

How magnanimous of them!

The year was the length of my contract still to run, and at least I would have an income for that period and if I so desired I could look around for other employment.

It might be worthy of note that when I left the London office, I had to go back to the "Redcar" to collect my gear.

Arriving back in Middlesborough about noon, I went straight to the agents, hoping to find the Captain there.

The agents said he had just left the office a few minutes earlier.

I left the office. I knew just where to find him, in his favourite pub, the Zetland, a few yards away from the office.

I was right, there he was, at a table with his favourite tipple in front of him.

As I approached the table he greeted me with "How are you my boy, how did things go in London"?

As calmly as my feelings would allow me, I answered, "Thanks to you, Captain, I have just been sacked after nearly twelve years in the company".

"Well my boy, if there is anything I can do, just ask".

"There is Captain, but you are not man enough to do it".

"Tell me boy, and I'll see what I can do".

"Right, at two o'clock when they are back in the office in London, call them and retract whatever you said against me".

He was dumbstruck, he couldn't answer that.

"No sir, you haven't got the guts, have you"?

I turned and left the bar and made my way to the ship at Eston Jetty.

Once aboard, I packed my gear ready to leave the first thing in the morning. Before leaving the ship I went up to see Captain Thomas. I told him that he had destroyed something valuable to me.

"What was that"? He asked.

"My faith in human nature, I wouldn't trust another man further than I could throw him", I answered.

Tears ran down his face, it was pitiful. Turning to leave, I said, "Captain, I'm leaving now, and I hope our paths never meet again".

They never did, I heard some years later that he had died.

I will not enlarge on my feelings when I heard that.

My hatred for that man stayed with me for a long time, until I released him from my hatred at a Billy Graham's Evangelistic meeting at the City Hall in Hull. Somehow I felt a great burden had been taken from my mind by that action that night at that meeting.

But the hurt of losing my job, after 17 years was still there.

Chapter 22.
A change of fortunes, and a flight from Japan

I was given about a month's leave after leaving the "Redcar", and then I got orders to join the m.s. "Ripon". She was the second of the four ore carriers which Boltons had acquired. This time I was to serve under Capt. Grugan. I was quite happy to sail with him, as I had had several voyages with him in other ships.

You may remember that he was the Master of the "Ribera" when we took that mountainous sea aboard in the North Pacific. Here we were again, to spend more winter voyages together, this time on the North Atlantic, and the North Atlantic can be murderous in heavy weather. Our runs were to be across to Seven Islands in Canada, and Wabana in Newfoundland for iron ore.

As the weather forecast was not very good, we ballasted to the full. That is, we filled every ballast tank, so that we were carrying something like 12,000 tons of salt water in the wing tanks and the double bottom tanks.

In the heavy seas on the way across the ocean, the ship tried to roll her guts out. We were sometimes rolling to just over 45 degrees from the upright, this made things most uncomfortable.

Sleep was almost impossible as you were thrown from one side of your bunk to the other. For the Cooks in the galley, it was a hazard. Despite the pans on the stove being held in place with the fiddles, (These are steel bars fitted on top of the stove), they slopped the boiling soup or whatever over the top of the pans. This got on to the galley tiled deck and made it into a skid-pan, if it didn't scald you first.

The ship was too "stiff", which made her come upright at a hell of a speed. As Chief Officer, I mulled over this problem, how could we overcome it?

Then it struck me, the answer was to pump out the double bottom tanks. This would help to make the ship more "tender" and she would roll a lot easier.

I went and had a word with the Captain. At first he wasn't very chuffed with the idea. Like me, he had been brought up with the idea of full ballast when empty ship.

I explained to him that the wing tanks went right down to the bottom of the ship, therefore she would still be very stable.

I explained that we would be getting rid of 4,000 tons of bottom weight, which was causing the violent rolling.

He finally agreed with me, and we pumped out the tanks.

The result was almost unbelievable, the ship went along as calmly as one could wish for. We'd solved the problem, and this was passed on to the company for the benefit of the other ore carriers.

On one run across to Wabana, we ran into bitterly cold weather, and all the fresh water pipes under our accommodation amidships, froze up. In so doing, the copper pipes burst or joints blew apart.

The net result was that we, the Deck Officers, had no fresh water, hot or cold for personal use. I had a word with the Chief Engineer about the situation. He came and looked at the pipes, his reaction was that there was nothing he could do about them.

That did not go down at all well with me.

I said," Well you give me the materials, a blowlamp, some copper binding wire, sheet copper, and some flux, and I'll repair those pipes". He agreed to give me the things I'd asked for, but there was a smirk on his face. I could read his thoughts, "A Deck Officer repair those pipes, some hope".

What he didn't know, was that I was a pretty skilled plumber and knew how to repair copper pipes.

In atrocious weather conditions, I got the Bosun to rig up some staging for me to stand on under the deckhead. I stripped the meagre insulation off them, in so doing cut my hand badly, but I was not aware of it due to the cold. Having had the hand attended to, I carried on with the repair. Several hours later, I had repaired all the pipes. I went along and asked for the water to be turned on again so that I could test the pipes.

Praise the Lord, they were all watertight again, and we got our water supplies back in the Officer's accommodation.

The Chief Engineer had a bit more respect for me after that episode. As far as I was concerned, no pig-iron polisher was going to tell me the job was impossible. When we arrived back in the U.K., the company had steam pipes fitted alongside the pipes to prevent any further freezing up in Arctic conditions.

On my second voyage to Wabana in the "Ripon", we had anchored in the bay to await the pilot the next morning.

During my watch, 4 a.m. to 8 a.m., I was on the bridge keeping anchor watch, when I heard a sound like a rushing train. I went outside the wheelhouse to have a look round, but I could not see anything, but there was this terrific roaring sound. Going back into the wheelhouse, I looked at the barometer, the needle was flickering madly and falling at the same time. It was going down like a stone. The noise I could hear was an approaching hurricane!

I rang "Stand-by" on the engineroom telegraph and then dashed down to call the Captain. "We'd better get out of here fast, Sir " I told him," There's a hurricane just about to hit us", With that I went back to the bridge and told the standby man to get the Carpenter and the watch out ready to go forward to raise the anchor.

The next moment the winds struck us and we started to drag anchor towards the rocky beach. By now the Captain had got himself onto the bridge. "Man for the wheel, Mate", he said,

"And you go fo'ard, we'll get under way".

I left the bridge and walked towards the Fo'castle head, but the wind had now reached hurricane force, and I was bent double trying to make my way forward. When I got to the ladder up to the fo'castle head, I had to grab hold of the guard rails to drag myself to the windlass. Chippy put the windlass in gear, and we started to heave the anchor up.

The trouble was that we had pumped out all the ballast ready for loading, and we were like a paper kite on the water, being driven ashore by the winds now reaching about 100 miles an hour.

The engines were started, but the propeller was churning fresh air and we were still being driven stern first, ashore.

I rang the engineroom and told them to start the ballast pumps at full speed and fill the after tanks so that the propeller could bite the water. Fortunately the ploy worked and we slowly got away from the beach with only a few feet to spare.

We headed out to sea, passing under the 600 foot high cliff at the entrance to the bay, almost touching it in the ferocious winds.

Two hours later, the hurricane had passed us and swept out to sea, and we were able to go back into the bay and alongside to start loading our cargo of ore.

The method of loading was the most primitive I had seen for years. The ore was tipped over the top of a cliff from lorries bringing it from the mine. It fell into a hopper at the foot of the cliff, from there it was fed on to an endless belt to the chutes that dropped it into our holds.

As we had a night alongside, I decided that I must have a look at the town of Wabana. I might as well have stayed aboard, I have never seen such a dilapidated place, the roads were full of potholes, the pavements were just wooden walkways full of holes, shops were almost non-existent. It was in fact a dying town.

I was glad to get away from the place, but I was to call there again in another ore carrier some time later.

I served six months on the "Ripon" and then went on leave again.

Shortly after going on leave, I was told to report to Smith's Docks at Middlesborough. I was to stand-by during the fitting out of another new ship for the Bolton S.S. Co.

This time it was a cargo ship, the "Ruysdael". It was the same procedure as before, only this time I had to draw up a store list of all the things needed on deck for a six months voyage. This job was to take me a couple of weeks, as I had to think of every single thing that we would be likely to need on a foreign-going voyage. That is, right down to the last nail, screw, cleaning materials, tools, world-wide charts, pens, ink, pencils, paper, note books, log books, paints, brushes, brooms, buckets, ropes, wires, oils, soap, greases, shackles, canvas duck and tarpaulin, torches, batteries. The list was endless and really tested my brains. I also had a lot of say in the fitting out of the equipment in the wheelhouse and the chartroom. In fact, I was kept fully employed during that standby period at the yard. The day came of course, when the ship was ready for her trials, by which time the Captain had been appointed for her, he was Capt. Roberts. I had sailed with him previously, I was happy to be sailing with him again.

As usual, the owner, Mr. Bolton and his retinue were on board for the trials.

It was whilst we were out on the trials that Capt. Roberts told me that I might hear something to my advantage before the ship docked again. He did not enlarge on that.

Some time later I was told that I was wanted in the Captain's room. I went up the stairs to the room and knocked at the door.

It was opened by Mr. Bolton, "Come inside Mr. Mathison", he said.

I stepped inside the room and he closed the door behind me.

I waited expectantly, for whatever was to come.

Mr. Bolton spoke, "I am pleased at the way things have turned out Mr. Mathison, and it is my intention to promote you to Master in the company at the next opportunity".

I stood there, flabbergasted. I had never in my wildest dreams expected to hear that I was to be made a Captain in the Bolton S.S. Co.

Mr. Bolton had kept his word about reconsidering my position after a suitable time.

When I had got my breath back, I thanked him for what he had told me.

He shook hands with me, and said, "Now, I think it is time to forget the past".

"Sir", I answered, "As an employee, I cannot afford to remember the past".

Maybe that remark of mine was not the most politic thing to say, but it just came out.

Later I was talking to one of the junior directors who had congratulated me at the news.

I remember saying to him, "What if the next command comes up when I am at the other side of the world on voyage?"

His answer was, that wherever I was in the world, I would only be a few hours flying time away from Britain.

I was a bit sceptical, and said, "Oh yes, I can see them flying me home from Japan to take command of a ship".

On completion of the sea trials, the ship was stored up for the possible six months voyage, the crew signed on and away we went.

The ship had been chartered by the Cargill Grain Co. to load the first cargo of grain at a brand new elevator at Norfolk, Virginia, U.S.A.. We were supposed to arrive on the very day that they had fixed for the opening ceremony of the elevator. This was not to be, as on the way across we encountered heavy weather which put us back two days. The grain company kept the opening ceremony, but used a large barge to pour the first grain into. Nevertheless, they gave us a good time while we were loading our cargo for the Continent. Cargill Grain Co. were also very generous with their bonuses. They gave me $150 at the end of that first voyage.

Our next employment for them, was to load a full cargo of grain, in umpteen dozen parcels, for consignees in Japan. If my memory serves me rightly, Captain Roberts had to sign 120 Bills of Lading for that cargo shipped at Durban, South Africa.

By law, three Bills of Lading, for each parcel of cargo, must be signed by hand. Any others that may be required can be stamped with a signature stamp.

For the uninitiated, a Bill of Lading is legal proof of the ownership of a cargo being carried in a ship.

When a ship arrives at her destination, the Captain of the ship must not release a cargo until the Bill of Lading has been presented to him by the person claiming the cargo.

That was the old time procedure, but today, consignees produce the Bills to the ship's Agents, who in turn give them to the Captain of the ship. This speeds up the discharge of the ship.

This cargo of grain was for discharge at Kobe, Japan. We had lovely weather all the way from South Africa into the China Sea.

On the way there I decided to make some ventilator covers from canvas during my lonely watch on the bridge.

To this end, I carried a bolt of green tarpaulin up to the bridge one afternoon. It was a foolish thing for me to do, because in so doing I slipped a disc, though I did not know it at the time. I only know that the next day, I could hardly walk without being in excruciating pain, and I was forced to take to my bunk.

It was several days before I was able to walk again without pain.

Little did I know then, what devastating effects that was to have on me later.

Just before we arrived in Kobe, Captain Roberts had a cable from the owners.

It said that I was to be flown home from Japan to take command of one of the company's ships!

That junior director had been right, he obviously had known what they had in mind for my future.

On arrival at Kobe the relief Chief Officer came aboard and took over from me. I was signed off there and put on the night train to Tokyo. I shall never forget that journey from Kobe to Tokyo.

It was an all night journey, and the heating was on full blast on the train. The Japs seemed to thrive in that heat, but I felt absolutely wrung out with sweat by the time we got to Tokyo. The company's agent met me at the station and took me to a hotel close to the airport. I had hoped that I would have been put up at one in the centre of Tokyo, so that I could have seen some of the sights of the place.

I was miles from the city, and to get a taxi there would have cost me a fortune, so I had to make do staying at the hotel.

Come the evening meal, I chose what looked good on the menu, Chicken al a American. What a disappointment that turned out to be. What I didn't know was that the Japanese like their cooked meats more or less raw. When I tried the chicken, I could have been sick, it was only half cooked. That was the end of the meal for me.

For the remaining two days that I had to stay there, I lived on coffee and biscuits. I was damned glad when the Agent came to take me to the airport. I was able to buy something there in the cafe that I could eat, and believe me I was famished.

We left Tokyo airport for Hong Kong, but on the way there we experienced very strong head winds, and the Pilot announced that the aircraft would be touching down at Iwo Jima for further fuel supplies. I had never thought that I would land on an island so fought for during the war with Japan, but I did.

On landing, all passengers had to get off the plane during the re-fuelling operations.

I made my way to the restaurant there, but it turned out to be an American Airforce canteen. I tried to buy a Coke and a sandwich, but they would not accept my Sterling, which was the only money I had. They only took American Dollars. The attendant behind the counter took pity on me and gave me what I had asked for, saying,

"Take it buddy, the treat's on me". I couldn't thank him enough for that generous gesture.

Shortly afterwards we took off for Hong Kong, and arrived there safely. There was a short break here before we left for Delhi.

This was the first time in my life that I had flown in an aircraft. I must admit my nerves were showing, my stomach was upset and I couldn't face the meals brought to me on the plane, the air hostess was quite concerned about me. I stuck with the tea and biscuits. We touched down at Delhi for a short spell, and I went into the cafe there, hoping to get something substantial to eat, but standing near the counter I saw cockroaches running around the showcases putting me off having anything in the place.

Back aboard the plane, we took off for Karachi, on the way there I was able, because of my seat at the window, to see the Himalayas. Something I never ever thought that I would see. It was a magnificent sight to see the world's highest mountains, snow clad.

Our call at Karachi should only have been a short one, but as things turned out, it ended up as an overnight stay in the magnificent Karachi Hotel for all the passengers.

After the normal stay, we boarded the aircraft for take off.

The plane started the take off run down the tarmac, but failed to reach safe take off speed. The Pilot turned the 'plane round and went back to the starting point and tried again.

Still no joy, one of the engines would not rev up to full speed, so it was back into the airport for the engineers to have a look at the faulty engine.

We were told that there would be a delay of about an hour, so it was off the plane and into the cafe to await boarding orders. One hour became two hours and still no signs of taking off.

Then it was announced that the delay would be at least another three hours. This was in the middle of the day and the temperatures were pretty high. By this time I'd been travelling for three days and I had not had my clothes off. I was hot and sticky and most uncomfortable.

I got talking to one of the hostesses, and I said to her that I would love to go and have a shower and change my clothes.

She said she could arrange that, if I followed her. I did, and she took me to their accommodation where they stayed overnight.

She showed me the bathroom, and said "Go ahead, have your shower and shave, there's soap and towels in there".

I felt like new man after that refreshing wash down and a change of clothes. They certainly try to look after you, these airline companies.

Next it was announced that the flight would not take place until the following morning, as they were having to replace the faulty engine. The air hostess explained to me that the faulty engine would be flown back to Britain for the manufacturers to repair.

This is apparently done when the repair is beyond the scope of the ground engineers at the airports.

We were then all taken to the hotel for the night, and it was there that I had the most satisfying meal I had had since I left the ship some four days earlier. I really enjoyed that meal, after which I went to bed and had a good sleep ready to face the next day.

Shortly after breakfast the next morning we were all taken back to the plane to take off for Beirut, Lebanon. All went well this time and we were soon airborne again.

As we approached the airport at Beirut, we struck an air pocket in the turbulence. The plane dropped like a stone several hundred feet. It went down like an express lift, many of the passengers were sick. My heart felt as though it was in my mouth, but I wasn't sickened by the experience. I was used to that sort of thing at sea, when the ship suddenly fell away under your feet.

I was apprehensive when I watched the planes wings flapping like those of a bird. How much would they flap before they fell off the plane?

A short stop over at Beirut and then we were on our way to Zurich, and finally London.

I remember when we left Zurich, flying above the clouds, it was like looking down on thousands of balls of cotton wool, a remarkable sight.

Next, all the lights of London came into sight, the journey was nearly over now, and when we landed at Heathrow I know how Columbus felt when he knelt and kissed the earth when he made land after crossing the ocean. I was glad to be back in England.

It had been a very long flight from Japan.

The nervous tension of that flight had played havoc with my stomach, I was ill for a few days after I got home.

On the 12 May 1958, I was sent to join my first ship as Master.
The ship was the ore carrier m.v. "Ribblehead", I joined her at Middlesborough for the usual runs across to Seven Islands, Canada for ore.
Aboard the ship, I met the Marine Superintendent, George Lockley, who congratulated me on my promotion. Then to spoil the day, I met the assistant Super, Mr. Grierson, the man with whom I'd had so much strife whilst Chief Officer.
His words were not of a congratulatory nature "Captain, don't think that I shall kow tow to you now you are Master".
To which I answered, "Mr.Grierson, you treat me with the respect due to a shipmaster, and I will treat you with the same respect".
After that we seemed to get on quite well whenever we met.
He'd got the message!
The ship was then duly handed over to me by the outgoing Master,
I signed for all the ship's documents, and then went with the Agent to the Custom House.
There, on the production of my Master's Certificate, my name was entered on the ship's register.
I was now officially the Master of the m.v. "Ribblehead", I'd finally reached the peak of my profession, on a salary of £117 per month! I felt on top off the world, that is until I said cheerio to the Pilot as we sailed on my first voyage in Command.

I suppose all first trip Masters suddenly feel the weight of the responsibility now on their shoulders.
They are responsible for the safe navigation of their vessel, an item probably worth several millions of pounds.
They are responsible for all the crew aboard the ship, for their health and safety. To see as far as is possible that they are well fed and cared for, and if perchance one falls ill, then you make a quick reference to the Shipmaster's Medical Guide.
This tells you how to treat the pox, boils, scabs and crabs.
Whatever you've got wrong, this book tells you the treatment thereof. Fortunately, seamen are a naturally hardy and healthy breed, and serious illnesses are few and far between.
I settled into my position fairly well. As soon as we were clear of the British coast and on our way across the Atlantic, I set a pattern for keeping up with my clerical work, of which there was plenty. There was the inevitable Portage Bill to be got under way.
The Portage Bill is the account kept of all seamen's wages, overtime, leave pay and any other payments made on behalf of the owners of the ship.
One side of it lists all the monies due the Ship owner, and the other side, all the monies due the Master. When the ship finally signs off, this sheet has to be balanced. If all is correct, there will be a balance of money due to the Master of the ship, that is his salary plus whatever profit he has made from the sale of the bonded stores aboard the ship during the duration of the voyage.
As the bond can cost several hundred pounds, few first trip Masters have that kind of money to pay the ship chandlers.
I asked the shipping company if they would pay it for me, and I would credit them with the amount on the Portage Bill. They agreed to do that, so I had no trouble, but of course I was in debt to them until the settling of the Portage Bill.
There was one occasion when I lost some money, even though I was in credit with my Portage Bill. It happened when on a long voyage, I had to ship some more bonded stores, (that is tobacco cigs and beer and spirits).
The price of these abroad was higher than in Britain, and we, the Chief Steward and myself, forgot to raise the prices accordingly.
The result was that I could not understand how I came to be £300 short of my expected balance on the Portage. It took me a long time to find the error.

All the money from the sale of the bonded stores did not come back to me, some of it went to paying the Chief Steward for handling the sale of it. His cut was 5% of the sales, which over a long voyage could add up to a tidy sum of money. At that time it was handed over to him free of income tax, whether he declared it or not was entirely up to the individual. I, of course had to account for such payments on my income tax returns to keep me straight with the Inland Revenue Authorities.

These days, ships bonded stores are now run by the shipping companies, it is no longer in the hands of the shipmaster.

The old, old story, more money in the shipowner's pocket, they even begrudge the Master making a few extra Pounds as they did in the good old days. Believe me, a competent and conscientious Master earns every penny he gets. It is he who when the ship is in peril on the high seas, spends the nights out on the bridge, pitting his skill against the forces of Nature at her worst, whilst the crew for most part are snug and warm in their bunks.

I know from experience, what it like to go 96 hours without sleep bringing your ship through a hurricane, and doing it without loss of life or limb, and / or damage to your ship.

I did six month's stint as Master of the "Ribblehead", and then was relieved for my leave. The average spell on the ore carriers was six months at a time.

Chapter 23.
s.s. "Reynolds"

I had left the "Ribblehead" on the 10th November 1958, and was home until the 27th December, when I was ordered to take over as Master of the "Reynolds". She had arrived in Liverpool. I packed my gear and went to join her there. Her Master at the time was Capt. Roberts, who I had last sailed with when I was Chief Officer, he was very pleased to see me. However, he wanted to know what I was doing joining the ship so early. He apparently had told our office to leave me at home 'til the Christmas holidays were over.

As he pointed out, he had no children to share his holiday with, and he didn't mind staying on the ship for a few more days to allow me to have whatever time I could with my family. Having gone through all the palaver of handing the ship over to me, he went on leave.

The ship had no further employment, and was to be in the Huskisson Dock for nearly a month before the company could get a Charter for her. In consequence, we only had a skeleton staff of the essential people on board. There was myself, three Deck Officers, Chief Engineer and three other engineers, the Chief Steward and a couple of Assistant Stewards, the Cook and Assistant Cook.

These Assistant catering ratings, I think were on a scam. They would be sent down from the local Pool office for a job, stay for about a week, and then leave the ship.

As Master, in other words, the employer, I had to stop National Insurance from their wages, and had to buy the stamps for their Insurance Cards. When I used to ask them for theirs so that I could stick the stamp on it for the week they had worked, they came up with the answer that they had left it at home. They would they said, bring it to me. They never did so, and I had several pounds worth of stamps on hand. This did not please me, so I wrote to the local Unemployment Office, gave the details of the person who had worked on the ship, and enclosed the stamps to be attached to their cards. I can well imagine the surprise those guys would get when they were accused of working whilst drawing the dole. I don't mind moonlighters, but when it causes me aggravation, I do!

As our stay in Liverpool was obviously going to be a long one, due to the collapse of the freight market, I had my wife, daughter and son come to the ship for a few days. In the meantime we had shifted into the drydock, this made the toilet arrangements a bit awkward. For instance you were not supposed to use the lavatories aboard the ship. Being mid winter the toilets on the dockside were a bit out of the question. Besides, they were the most unhygienic places that you could imagine.

My steward, the 2nd Steward, a seasoned seaman, gave us the solution to disposing of our bodily waste via the ship's toilets.

So that was that problem solved, and we had no complaints from the dock authorities.

One night we decided to go to the pantomime, at I think it was the Empire Theatre. When we came out of the show to go back to the ship there was the worst smog I have ever seen. There were no taxis running, for traffic was at a standstill.

I estimated that the distance back to the ship was about two miles, so we set off to walk back. Well I don't know Liverpool topography all that well, and we were plodding along with scarves over our noses and mouths.

After a while we heard someone shout out, "Hey, were the 'ell do you think you're going"?

"Back to Huskisson Dock", I replied.

"Well at the moment you are heading into the Mersey Tunnel".

I thanked the man for warning us, and he pointed out the direction we should be going.

An hour and a half later we arrived at the dock gates, and the policeman on duty asked us how the hell we had got there.

We told him we had walked from the city centre. He gave us strict instruction how to avoid falling into the dock, and bade us good night.

Once back aboard the ship we removed the scarves, they were black with the soot and pollution we had been breathing in on our way back. A bit of supper and a cup of tea and we were all ready for bed, particularly the children. My family stayed for a week and then went home as we were now getting ready for sea.

The owners had managed to secure a charter for the ship, on rock bottom rates of freight. We were to proceed to Ancona, Italy, where we were to load a cargo of ammonium phosphates for China.
I signed on my crew for the voyage, stored, bunkered and took fresh water for the passage. My crew was of course nearly all Liverpudlians, and a great bunch they turned out to be once we had got over the teething troubles.
The run to Ancona was a nice pleasant one as the weather was fine. Our cargo was to be the first from a new factory that had just opened, producing fertilisers.
It was here that the first troubles began with the crew. There was, unfortunately, a bar right alongside us on the quay.
Come dinner time each day the lads would make their way into the bar and stay there until late in the afternoon. This did not please either the Chief Officer nor the 2nd Engineer both of whom wanted to have some work done aboard the ship.
The two Officers concerned came to see me and asked me to do something about the absentees. I did, I called them all up to my office and read the riot act to them, then logged them for being absent without leave. This cost each of them 5/- as per the Articles of Agreement. The entries were made in the Official Log Book, then read out to each of them, they were then asked if they had anything to say.
The law requires that the entries had to be read to the men and any reply they made had to be written in the Log Book. Their answers were the usual, "Nothing to say".
Entries having been made and duly signed by myself and the Chief Officer, that was that.
(For the uninitiated, the Log Book is a legal record of all incidences aboard a ship, which must be recorded according to law). Accidents, births, deaths, marriages, strandings, collisions, illnesses and treatment, breakdowns if serious, cargo damages, all must be Logged for future reference.
Having logged the men, I then gave them a pep talk. I pointed out to them that the fine doubled with each breech of conduct, and that in the long term it could be very expensive for them.
Before they left my office, I pointed out to them that they could have a pleasant time aboard the ship or a rough time if they didn't play ball.
I indicated that we would probably be away for several months and it would be to the advantage of all, if we got on well together.
I think my approach came as a bit of a surprise to the miscreants, because they all agreed that it would be nice to be "pally". I made a suggestion to them, with the agreement of my two senior officers, that if they behaved themselves and gave a good day's work for their pay, I would see that they got sufficient time off at each port to do their shopping, drinking or screwing, etc.
They heartily agreed with my suggestion, and from that day on I can honestly say those men were the best crew I have ever had on any ship under my command.

We did have one further bit of trouble when several of the crew had been ashore and came back a bit worse for wear. They played about with the dock gate policemen's motor scooter, knocking it over and damaging it.
The man was able to identify the wrongdoers and came down to the ship with the Agent. The position was explained to me and I had all the crew mustered for recognition. They were picked out and asked to pay for the repairs to the vehicle. This they refused to do, whereon the man said he would have them arrested.
The Agent them explained to them if this happened they could be locked up for several weeks before the case went to court, by which time the ship would have sailed.
The damage claim was for a few thousand lira, but with the exchange rate about 1,400 to the Pound Sterling, it worked out about five pounds per man.

After a lot of argy-bargy, they agreed to pay the money and keep out of trouble. I instructed the Agent to pay for the damages and debit me with the sum of money as "Cash to Master". This was after each man had signed the sub book for his share of the damages. In that manner, I got the money back from the men when they paid off the ship at the end of the voyage.

My next headache was when the engineers were pumping out the water ballast. One of the tanks had previously, unknown to us, been used to carry fuel oil for the boilers. As soon as the water went overboard from the pumps, it fouled the harbour water and there was a great furore from the Harbour Authorities. The pumping was stopped, but we still had to get rid of the oily water, some two hundred tons of it, so that we could load the amount of cargo we were chartered to carry. Apparently our oily water separator was not able to cope with the amount of oil in the water.
What to do, that was the question now.
The only answer was to see if the local refinery would have any use for the retrieved oil.
The answer was yes.
This however meant hiring a small tanker from them to come alongside and have all the oil and water pumped into the tanker.
This of course was going to cost a fair sum of money.
I had to telephone my owners and get their permission to do this.
At first they demurred, and wanted to know why the separator could not cope with separating the oil and water. I told them that the Chief Engineer had informed me that the oil was too thick and there was too much of it in the bottom of the tank.
The owners finally agreed to the idea of the tanker at their expense, and when the Harbour Authorities heard what we were doing, they dropped all charges against the ship for pollution of the harbour.
So we got away lightly in this case.

As we were the first ship to load at this new factory, the local TV company came down and asked me to appear on TV to give a brief description of the voyage with the cargo to China. Fame at last!
In the studio they had a huge wall chart on which I had to point out the route which the ship would take to reach China. Of course, an interpreter told them in Italian what I said.
After my pep talk to the crew, everything went well, no more skiving off for a quick bevvy at the local bar at dinner time. The only other bit of trouble I had at Ancona, was having to hospitalise one of my sailors who fell and broke an ankle. I had to pay him off and leave him in hospital as it was near to sailing time.
I made a point of going to see him in hospital before we sailed, mostly to assure him that he would be returned home as soon as he was fit to travel. Whilst I was there, I noticed how his ankle was strapped up, little did I know that that would be of great use to me later in the voyage.
On sailing from Ancona it was the usual run to the Suez Canal, then down the Red Sea, through Hell's Gate and into the Arabian Gulf, then Eastwards towards Singapore.

In my Charter Party was a clause that on passing a certain Longitude, I was to cable Sinofrac, the Chinese Government charterers, for my discharge port orders.
This I did via Colombo Radio station, and back came the answer,
"Disport Sing Kiang". I acknowledged receipt of the orders and asked the 2nd Officer, our navigating officer, to dig out the charts for the port.
He got all the charts we had of China out and nowhere could he find such a port as Sing Kiang. I had a look at the charts, such a name did not appear on any of our charts.
Now here was a problem, I was bound for a port of which we had no knowledge of its position. I radioed Colombo and asked if they knew its location, they replied that they had no idea, and would I, when I found out, please advise them for future reference!

I was now in a quandary, I didn't fancy their idea of cabling my owners and letting them know that I did not know where I was going! I would have looked a fool in their eyes.
In the end, I cabled the Chinese Agents and asked them to give me the geographic location of the port, as it did not appear on any of our Admiralty charts of China.
Back came the reply, Sing Kiang is the new name for Taku Bar.
Now Taku Bar has been on the charts for donkey's years, so I now knew where I was going. It appears that they had just changed the name the day before I cabled in for my instructions. How the hell did they think I would know they were changing the name of the port?
I let Colombo Radio know for future reference.

When we finally arrived at Taku Bar, the Pilot and a load of armed soldiers came aboard, this smacked of real communism. The Pilot took the ship to anchorage and then as all the crew had to be mustered on the boat deck whilst the soldiers rummaged through every room. Some of the crew had maps of the world posted up in their rooms, on which they plotted our progress each day.
Some of the maps showed China as Imperial China, and these were torn down by the soldiers. Only maps showing China as The Peoples Republic of China were allowed.
I could see that we were going to have to be careful what we did or said in China, otherwise we could be in dead lumber. I was later, through no fault of my own.
We berthed and started our discharge, There were armed guards on the quay day and night, who kept a close eye on everybody coming and going from the ship. Crews were allowed ashore but had to be back on board their ships by the curfew time of midnight. Woe betide those who weren't. My 2nd Steward overstayed one night and when he came back to the ship in the early hours of the morning, he was whisked off to the local lock-up.
They returned him 24 hours later, and he was a nervous wreck. They had brain-washed him for hours, wanting to know what he had been up to, was he a spy for Britain or any other country. Why had he broken the rules of The Chinese Peoples Republic, and so it had gone on.
Needless to say, he never went ashore again, he'd had a bellyfull.

There wasn't much to see in Sing Kiang anyway, there were only two places that crews could go officially, one was the State run bar and restaurant and the other the State run shop.
I was taken on a tour of inspection by our agent. The highlight of it was the pride with which he showed me around the massive cold store, stacked with hundreds of tons of frozen meat.
Big deal!
I noticed that the quays were kept scrupulously clean, women with small whisk brushes swept it every day after the loading or discharging was done. We were allowed freely ashore, but only within the city limits, and we all had to be back aboard by midnight. To be honest, there wasn't much to keep you ashore anyway. Booze was good, cheap and plentiful at the State bar.
At the State shop, clothing and shoes etc. were good and cheap.
I'm always sorry that I did not buy a Teinsin washed carpet which was on sale in that shop. The price of it in the shop was about £120, but in Britain that would have been something around £1,000 by the size of it.
I had to keep my owners fully informed of the progress of the discharge of the cargo so that they could find another Charter for the ship. About three days before the last of our cargo was out, the owners cabled me and said that they had fixed the ship to load a cargo of grain there in Sing Kiang. There was however a very tight cancelling date for the charter. They also said that it was imperative that I made the cancelling date. By that, they meant that I was able to hand in my Notice of Readiness to load before the expiry time.

The expiry date was two days after the end of our discharge of cargo. This meant that we had to have the ship's holds cleaned out and fitted with shifting boards, (to comply with the British grain carrying laws). The Chinese couldn't understand this. They thought that we would just drop the grain into the holds until we were full up.

I had to explain the procedure to them, and that the shifting boards were to stop the cargo from shifting when the ship rolled in heavy weather.

My problem was, that two days is hardly enough to erect these boards in five holds.

At first I engaged some Chinese carpenters to help with the job, but they were a dead loss. None of then spoke a word of English, so it was impossible to give them instructions. In the end I appealed to my crew, I pointed out what it meant if we did not have the ship ready by the cancelling time and date.

I promised them double overtime if they would work right through and get the ship ready. They jumped at the chance of some extra cash, and worked like demons. The ship was ready for acceptance just two hours before the expiry time, when I handed in my Notice of Readiness.

My next job was to cable the owners and tell them that my Notice had been presented and accepted. The ship was now on Charter to the Chinese Government to load a full cargo of grain for Bulgaria. I could almost hear the sighs of relief when my cable arrived in the London office.

Back came a reply expressing their relief at the news.

An item I had almost forgotten, was that on our passage across the Indian Ocean to China, the main injection pipe in the engineroom split, and this entailed stopping the ship for repairs. This pipe carried all the sea water for cooling purposes. The Chief Engineer told me that the position was serious and would I go down the engineroom with him and see for myself what the repair entailed.

It turned out that at the bend in the 15" bore copper pipe, it had been scoured so thin by sand and silt over the years, that it was paper thin. I know because I pressed my fingers on it and the metal gave way. The ship's side valve had of course been closed so that the water in the pipe could drain away and no more could enter.

It was decided that the area was too big to repair with Thistlebond, (that is a fibreglass and resin), A cement box was the only answer. This entailed the Carpenter building a wooden box around the area to be repaired. This box was then filled with cement, so that there was a coating of at least six inch thick all around the pipe. This in itself took several hours to do, and of course we were stopped and drifting, two black balls having been displayed on the forestay.

This to let any approaching ship know that we were " Not under Command ". At night two vertical red lights are shown, with the same meaning.

That cement box was so large that we had to remain static for 24 hours to allow the mass of cement to set before water could be allowed to flow through the pipe again.

In the meantime I had to inform my owners of the stoppage, as all time such as this had to be accounted for in the Charter.

The owners asked me to inform them as soon as we were under way again, and that I was to have the pipe repaired permanently on arrival at Singapore.

This was of course a job for a Lloyds engine surveyor, who was called in on arrival at Singapore. His summing up was that the pipe would have to be renewed in its entirety over the damaged section. Shipyard workers came and removed the damaged pipe and took it ashore. Now, 15" copper piping is not a plentiful commodity. This meant that they would have to fabricate a new pipe for the ship. This they did, by taking a large sheet of copper of the required thickness, slowly heating it over a forge and slowly shaping it to the pattern of the original pipe.

I was taken to the metal workers shop and watched part of the process. It was fantastic to see how they slowly shaped that copper into a pipe. When the job was done they brazed the end flanges back on to the new pipe and brought it back to the ship for fitting.

With nothing better to do, I went down the engineroom to watch the fitting. When it was in place and the gaskets inserted, the pipe was an exact fit. All that remained to be done was to bolt the whole lot together. It was truly a fantastic piece of engineering.
It had however, taken five days to do.
Anyway, we were able to proceed on voyage. We kept a piece of the pipe to show the owners the state it was in when it punctured. It was just like a bit of tissue paper. That could have happened when the ship was in dire need of the engines, such as in a storm.
We were lucky - it had happened in fine calm flat seas.

Chapter 24.
An apology to the People's Republic of China

Our stay in Hsing Kiang lasted a month, discharging phosphates and loading the cargo of grain. I think all hands had a reasonable time whilst we were there. There was however, one occasion when I wish I had not been there.

This occurred one morning.

I had just finished my breakfast when the agent came aboard and informed me that I was in serious trouble.

Me, what had I done wrong I asked myself? I'd spent most of my time aboard the ship.

The Agent explained that the Chief Officer had been taking the depth of the water around the ship at 6 a.m. that day.

This, he explained gravely, was strictly forbidden by the Harbour Authorities. In view of that, I was to be taken before a panel of interrogators to explain why I had allowed this to happen. I was still in my bunk at 6 a.m., how the hell was I to know what the Chief Officer had been up to?

That cut no ice, I had to go before this court, and he arranged for me to be picked up by a taxi at 10 a.m..

Arriving at the office, I was ushered into a room, wherein there were three men dressed in the standard blue denim uniforms.

They made me sit down and then started the interrogation.

There was an interpreter present.

The first question was "What was my name?"

I told them, " Arthur Mathison. "

Next question, "What qualifications did I possess".

My answer to that was that I held a Master's Foreign-going certificate issued by the Board of Trade in Britain.

"Ah, so Captain, but what other qualifications have you?"

"I have no other qualification but that, that is all that I need to be Master of a British ship".

So the questioning went on for about an hour.

"Did I not know that I was liable to ten years in prison for breaking one of the rules of the Peoples Republic of China."

"Had I not read the rules that were put on board when we arrived?"

I pointed out to them that the rules had been posted up for every crew member to read, to keep them out of trouble.

"Then why did I let the Chief Officer take soundings of the harbour, which is strictly verboden?"

"How could I have stopped him when I was asleep when the incident happened"? I asked.

"Ah yes, but you are the Captain of the ship, and are responsible for the actions of all your crew ".

I was beginning to get a bit hot under the collar by this line of questioning, and my temper was wearing thin.

"If there is a question of a fine for breaking the rules, I am sure that my owners will agree to pay such fine", I told them.

They then went on with the spiel that it was not as simple as that, and that I was liable to 10 years in clink!

I had no answer to that, so I shut up.

"Can you use a typewriter Captain?" I was asked.

"Of course I can type", I answered, whereupon they put a typewriter in front of me on the desk.

A clerk brought several sheets of typing paper, and inserted a sheet in the machine.

The interpreter then started to dictate what I was to type.

An apology to the People's Republic of China.

"I, Arthur Mathison, Master of the British ship "Reynolds", do hereby apologise to the People's Republic of China, for having broken one of their rules. I agree to abide by all and every rule of the said Republic, now and on any future visit to this country.

I am aware of the harsh penalty which will be imposed, should I break any further rules of the People's Republic of China".

I then had to date the sheet and append my signature to the apology.

This done, I was told that I would now be returned to my ship, the generous shower!

All this had taken nearly three hours, and I was in a grim mood when I got back to the ship.

My first call was for a cup of tea, and my second call was for the Chief Officer, Mr. John Parslow.

I gave him the thin edge of my tongue, and made it plain that if he did anything stupid like that again, he'd be out on his ear.

I can laugh about it now, but at the time it wasn't so funny with 10 years jail sentence hanging over your head, when you are totally innocent. The outcome was that I vowed I would never take another ship to China, and I never did, even though I was sent to a ship that was destined to go to China.

I phoned my owners and told then of the incident in 1959, and that I was "non persona gratia" as far as China was concerned. When they heard what had previously happened to me there, they took me out of the ship and put another Master in Command of her.

On leaving Sing Kiang with our cargo of grain for Bulgaria, we ran into a fairly heavy aftermath of a recent typhoon.

The Chief Officer had been down the forepeak for some reason, and he came to my room to report that he had noticed the bow plating panting. (Panting is an expression used to indicate that the plating is moving in and out).

I went along with him to have a look at this phenomena, and sure enough I sighted the bow plates moving, and they were not supposed to so do.

A careful examination revealed that several of the frames, the vertical steel ribs of the ship, were fractured.

I put a matchstick in the fracture of one of them when the plate panted inwards, as it went back outwards, the matchstick was cut in two!

Initially we counted ten such fractures, and a close watch on them every day showed more appearing with the stresses set up by the panting.

I cabled my owners and put them in the picture about this. They came back with a cable saying that I was to keep a close watch on the situation, and if need be, have repairs done at Singapore.

By the time we reached Singapore, the number of fractures had increased to 20. This was a job for the Lloyds surveyor, who was called in on arrival. He inspected the job and then gave orders to the ship repairers we had called in.

The job was to take about ten days to repair, as all the fractured frames had to have doubling plates fitted to them.

It turned out that all this was inherited from the time when the ship had collided with a steel dolphin when she was leaving the oil terminal at Curacoa in the West Indies. She must have put hairline fractures in the frames, but these had gone unnoticed in the past.

Repairs done, we sailed on the next stage of our run to Bulgaria.

The repair at Singapore had been imperative, because we would be sailing into the south west monsoon in the Indian Ocean, and the seas off the African coast can be pretty heavy. Heavy seas for any time could have caused plates to fracture. As everyone knows, if you bend a piece of metal sufficient times, it will break.

My orders were for Varna in Bulgaria as the discharge port, and when I arrived at the cape off Varna, I radioed in for the Pilot.

I was to get closer in to the port first they said.

I pointed out that my Admiralty charts showed the approaches to Varna as being a mined area, (aftermath of the war).

After a lot of argument I got the Pilot boat to come out to us some twenty miles from the port. No way was I going to take my ship in waters that were declared minefields. There may or may not have been mines on that run in, but I had no way of knowing. Like China, Bulgaria was a Communist state, though a bit freer in their outlook towards foreign seamen.

Not that there was much to attract people ashore there.

The local radio station came and begged some records from me, as they were unable to obtain records for the benefit of their listeners. I remember that one of the records was "Three coins in a fountain". I heard it played over their radio station later.

I had been instructed by my owners that I was not to release the grain cargo until I was presented with an accomplished Bill of Lading. This was the first and only time I have had an original Bill of Lading, signed by me at the loading port, being brought back to me as proof of ownership of the cargo. I kept that Bill for many years, and then somehow it got lost when we shifted house.

I had intended to give it to my old Nautical School so that other students could see what an accomplished Bill looked like. A Bill of Lading is accomplished when it is sold to the final buyer. Bills can change hands many times before a ship arrives at a given port with a specific cargo. This is part of the money making business of ship's cargoes en route from the loading port to wherever.

I only went ashore once in Varna, and I did not find it at all interesting. It was very drab, everybody seemed listless.

My owners cabled me and said that they had ordered 20 tons of extra bunker oil to be shipped at Varna. They also stated that to ensure that there were no delays, they had double banked the money to pay for the oil, one payment to the Bank of Bulgaria in Sofia, the capital, and one payment into a bank on the Continent.

We shifted ship and took the oil, and as we were ready for sailing, I ordered the Pilot.

I waited all day but no Pilot appeared.

The next morning I saw a launch approaching the ship and I thought this must be the Pilot. It wasn't, it was only the agent. When he boarded the ship I asked him why no Pilot to take me out.

"I am sorry Captain, but we cannot let your ship sail until we have the money in the bank for the oil".

"But I told you, my owners have double banked the money to pay for it, and I want to sail on my next employment".

"Until we hear from the bank in Sofia, we cannot let you sail".

With that he went back ashore in his launch, while I sat in my room fuming at being held against my will. However, there was nothing I could do about the situation. The next time he came aboard, and no Pilot with him, I asked to be put in touch with the British Ambassador in Sofia. He wasn't very keen on that.

On the third day of waiting, the Agent came with my clearance and the Pilot. After he had given me my clearance papers and was about to leave the ship, I gave him a piece of my mind.

I told him that I had been impressed with the country when I arrived, but in view of the treatment of holding me up when payment had been guaranteed for the oil, I thought nothing of Communism. I pointed out that in the free world, I could go into a port, and take on board a 1,000 tons of oil and it would be given just upon my signature on the bill, which was then transmitted to my owners. I stressed the point that Communism would die a natural death because it could never work. Strangely enough, it has died in many parts of the world, notably Russia where it all started after the revolution in 1917. China and Cuba are probably the only two countries still holding on to Communism.

Leaving Varna we sailed for the Red Sea, to the port of Quosier to load a cargo of phosphates for Japan.

This was to be my second visit to that port, and I nearly came to grief when approaching the place light ship. There was a stiff easterly breeze blowing and as I got nearer to the port, it got really strong and was driving my ship ashore.

I ended up putting my engines full astern on emergency ring.

That is a double ring on the engineroom telegraph. This tells the engineer to give the engines all the power he can.

This had the effect of bringing the ship to a standstill, only a few yards off the beach, and I was able to get her turned round and head away from the shore, much to my relief.

As I had seen what little there was of Quosier I wasn't interested in going ashore, other than to see how they weighed the cargo as it left the works on the endless belt to the ship.

Three days later we sailed for Japan, down the Red Sea out into the Gulf of Aden and into the Indian Ocean.

The weather was hot, so hot on passage that the deck composition on the decks in the crew accommodation was soft to walk on.

This was the summer of 1959, which I heard on the radio was the hottest in Britain for a considerable number of years. Here we were in the tropics, I had the coolest room in the ship and yet the temperature in my room was still 90 to 100 degrees, even at night.

One night at just about midnight, I was getting ready for bed when there was an urgent knock at my door. I answered it to find one of the engineers there. He explained to me that one of the firemen had fallen down the stokehold, and despite the fact that they had got him up to his room, he was in a bad way.

I quickly dressed and went to see the man, he was lying on his bunk, moaning about the pain in his ankles.

I had a look at them, and I could see them swelling even as I looked at them.

He'd broken both of them.

It appears that he was coming off watch and climbing the stokehold steel ladder, when he slipped, losing his grip on the ladder. He had tried to land on his feet, but in doing so had landed flatfooted on the steel plates below. That had shattered both ankles.

Remembering how the hospital at Ancona had dressed the sailor with the broken ankle, I did exactly the same for this poor devil.

This eased the pain for him a little. To help him rest I gave him a Morphine tablet, that way he got some rest without pain.

Whilst I was down there in his room, I was appalled at the heat the men were living in. I was sinking into the deck composition whilst standing there attending to the injured man.

This made me determined to do something to lower the temperature in those rooms, but what I asked myself?

In the morning I went up on the boat deck to view the intakes of the blower system, and I discovered that they faced inboard, right over the stokehold grating. The net result was that the air being pumped down into the rooms was heated up by the rising heat from the stokehold.

I got hold of the Chief Officer and explained to him that I wanted a duct building away from the stokehold. He was to get the Carpenter to build a square duct framework at least six feet long, then cover it with some old blankets from the store room, the far end of it being left open of course. When this was done I got the Bosun to find an old hose pipe, block the nozzle of it, puncture the hose with a number of small holes, then attach it to the deck service water line.

The hose was then suspended over the blanket covered framework duct, and the sea water turned on so as to spray the blanket covering. Air of course, was being sucked through the duct all the time, but passing through a water cooled blanket, the temperature was dropped considerably. Several hours after the start of this experiment, I went down into the crew accommodation, and what a difference!

The place was warm, but it was a hell of a lot cooler than it had been for weeks. The crew were really grateful for my ingenuity. All I had done was to apply Nature's way of cooling things down. It was a throw back to the old water chatties we used when I was in the fo'castle. We'd make a water bag of canvas and hang it in the wind. This cooled the water down until it was nearly ice cold. That was the only way we could get a drink of cold water in the tropics when we didn't have a fridge.

It was simply using Nature's way of cooling by evaporation of water. I later cooled my own room down by hanging a wet towel at my open port holes and letting the wind blow through it, my only problem was how to keep the towel damp all the time.

The whole experiment gave me a great idea for cool air through a ship, at very little cost to the shipowner, but unfortunately I did not pursue the idea.

Our discharge port in Japan was a place called Nigata, on the West coast of Honshu, here I landed the injured Fireman for treatment in hospital. With two broken ankles, I had to leave him there when we sailed a week later.

I quite enjoyed our stay in Nigata, it was a clean modern town with plenty of shops.

Just before our discharge was completed, I received my new orders from the owners, I was to proceed to Cairns, Queensland, to pick up a full cargo of sugar for the U.K.

Loud cheers from all hands when they heard the news!

By now we had been away from home for the better part of eight months. Before leaving Nigata, I was speaking to another ship's Captain, and he asked me which way I was going to take my ship. I said by the shortest route, down the eastern side of the Philippine Islands. He advised me against taking that route. He pointed out that it was the Typhoon season and if one came along I would be trapped on a lee shore.

In other words, the hurricane force winds would be driving me ashore. I took his advice and went via the Western side of the Philippines. I'm glad I did, because a typhoon did come along, but I was sheltered by the islands and experienced no trouble whatsoever. I had a lot to thank that shipmaster for, without it I might well have been in dire trouble.

Incidentally, the deepest part of the World's oceans, the Mindano Trench, is just off the east coast of the Philippine Islands.

The depth of the ocean is 5,736 fathoms, (34,416 feet deep)!

Deep enough to drop the Mount Everest in and lose it!

After a pleasant run from Japan I picked up the Barrier Reef Pilot off Cape York, Australia, for the run down through the Barrier Reef to Cairns, our loading port.

Out stay in that port was to be a long one, as the sugar was brought down to the ship in bags. These were lifted aboard with the ship's derricks, and then cut open to allow the sugar to drop into the holds. As there were umpteen thousand bags needed to load the ship, all the crew enjoyed a three weeks stay in Cairns.

The people of Australia are probably the most friendly and hospitable to be met anywhere in the world, and they go out of their way to make visitors welcome and at home. They will come aboard and invite you to their homes for an evening out. As I said, we all enjoyed our stay in Cairns.

The Chief Officer and myself went out with the local Scout troop to their camp, we stayed most of the day and into the early evening.

We watched them pitch tents then start the camp fire, and when it had burnt down to a heap of hot ashes, they dug into it and placed the joints of meat, to be left all night to cook in the hot ashes.

I'll bet that meat was really tender and tasted good the next day when they had it for dinner. I don't think I would have been too keen on sleeping in a tent at the camp, because there were snakes around. The scouts had great fun chasing one away whilst we were there. As the Scoutmaster said, the snake had no chance when those kids went after it.

They thought it was great fun, but not my scene.

Come the time for sailing from Cairns, a large part of the people of Cairns turned up on the quay to say goodbye to us.

I had the record of "Now is the hour, when we must say goodbye" the Maori song. I had it played through the ship's loudhailer system as we pulled off the quay.

The result was touching, there were people on the quay wiping the tears from their eyes. I must admit mine too were a bit misty, I was leaving Australia for the last time, though I did not know it at the time.

I have often regretted that I did not visit Australia any time in the remaining years I spent at sea. I had previously spent a lot of time there and had got to like the people and the country. Given the chance, I would have settled there in my younger years.

I was almost persuaded when I was offered the job as Assistant Harbour Master, but my wife would not leave Britain to come and join me, so that job went out of the window.

Leaving Cairns for the homeward passage, we were under Pilotage from Cairns to Cape York via the Great Barrier Reef, where we dropped the Pilot.

Then we went on a westerly course through the Torres Strait into the Arafura Sea, past the island of Timor to the South of us, and on into the Flores Sea. Still steaming westerly we went past Flores and Sumatra, (now Indonesia), and on to Singapore for oil fuel and water.

I had a quick run ashore there to the Agents office and then had a shopping spree. I bought innumerable mechanical toys made in Japan, which I was to give as presents when we arrived home, as it was to be close to Christmas when we did arrive in the U.K.

I was proud of the state of my ship and of my Officers and crew, all had functioned in the best traditions of the British Merchant Service throughout the voyage. We had achieved a great amount of ship maintenance during the voyage by the removal of rust from about 100 steel plates overside. However, rust was now showing through again and I wanted to bring the ship home looking as good as new. To this end, I arranged with the Chief Engineer, to ease our speed down a little so that we arrived at Suez too late for the evening convoy through the Suez Canal.

I further got the Chief Officer to offer the Deck crew double overtime to go over the side at anchor and paint the ship around.

The crew were only too willing to oblige, and they set to with gusto and made a marvellous job in a very short time.

When they had finished it looked as though we had just come out of drydock.

As the crew had behaved themselves so well, I decided to waive all the fines imposed on the defaulters, (with the agreement of my Chief Officer and Chief Engineer). I had the men involved sent to my office. As we waited for them to arrive, we could hear their conversation as they came up the stairs.

One said, "What do you think he wants us for whack? "

To which one of them answered "He'll be wanting us to sign for our fines and forfeitures".

"Aye, that'll be what he wants I guess".

This rather amused me, because they didn't have to sign for such things, even if I had let them stand.

When they arrived in my office, I told them that I was waiving the fines, which in some cases, amounted to ten pounds. They all thanked me for my generous gesture, and as they were about to leave, I said "Well men, as I have saved you some money, how about a little donation to the Royal National Lifeboat Institution"?

I placed the donation sheet in front of them.

Each of them made a donation, which would be deducted from their pay. I thanked them and they left my office.

I heard them laughing on their way down the stairs.

I glanced at the donation sheet, each of them had donated the £10 saved.

No wonder they were laughing, they knew that I as Captain, I would have to subscribe a greater sum than theirs!

They had the last laugh, at my expense!

We finally sailed into Greenock in late November 1959, and were met by one of the company's Director. On boarding he said that he had never seen one of their ships come home after such a long voyage looking so good.

I suggested to him that he should go and congratulate the Chief Officer, Mr. John Parslow, as he was the man in charge of the upkeep of the ship. We paid off the next morning, this being done in the dining saloon. As each man signed off the Articles and drew his pay, they all, without exception, shook hands with me and thanked me for a pleasant voyage. This in front of the Director!

When we had finished the business, the Shipping Master said he had never in all his days seen a crew shake hands with the Master of a ship when they signed off.

His summing up was "Captain, you must have been one hell of a fine man to sail under". My answer to that was "A happy ship is an efficient ship, and that's the way I like it".

I was sent on leave for three months after that voyage, before being sent to the "Ruysdael", one of the company's latest ships.

I was as familiar with her as when I had sailed in her on her maiden voyage as Chief Officer. It was from her that I was flown home from Japan to be promoted to Master.

My voyage as Master of her was a short one across to the States for a cargo of grain for Hull. On the passage home we ran into dense fog in the English Channel, this persisted all the way through the Channel and up into the North Sea.

With the aid of our Radar I was able to keep going until I got up off the Norfolk coast. There, there were too many buoys showing up on the Radar to be sure where we where, so I dropped anchor. It was no use going any further without knowing my exact position. I lay on my bunk for a rest for about an hour, then the Second Officer called me to tell me that the fog had temporarily lifted. I shot onto the bridge and was able to see Haisbro Lightvessel. We got a bearing off it, and then we were able to get the distance off from the Radar. That gave me my ship's position. I was now able to plot my course for Spurn Light vessel. We hove up anchor and got under way again, and I made it safely to the Pilots for the Humber. The Humber Pilot wanted to know how the hell I had got there, as he said, "Captain, you are the first ship to arrive here for five days, all ships are fogbound around the coast".

We docked in the early hours of the morning, and after dealing with the Customs and Port officials, I went home for a few hours.

I really should have gone to bed, as by this time I had been on my feet for almost 96 hours. I returned to the ship to attend the pay off of the crew, and at the end of that I suddenly felt unwell.

I nearly blacked out. A visit to my Doctor was indicated. After examining me he wanted to know what had brought this on. As he said, I had always been in good health. Well, I told him I hadn't had a sleep for 96 hours.

His summing up was that my heart was taking too much strain and that I must slow down or Nature would slow me down permanently.

I was to rest for at least two weeks, and then go and see him again.

I had to report his findings to my employers, who of course said that any deterioration in the health of one of their Masters, was of grave concern to them.

I was to go on leave and rest, and that at some later date, would I submit myself to examination by a Doctor of their choice, after consultation with my own Doctor.

I replied that I was agreeable to such an arrangement, but that I was sure that their Doctor would agree with mine that my condition was simply due to me overstretching myself on this homeward passage, and all would be well after I had rested for a while. This proved to be the case, and the next time I saw the Doctor, he said that things were back to normal again.

I phoned my employers and let them know this. They appeared very happy about it. However they left me at home for two months before re-appointing me as Master of the "Ruydael" for another voyage.

Chapter 25.
The end of an era

I cannot remember where I rejoined the ship, but I remember the voyage very well. I sailed from the U.K. for the United States. I was to load a cargo of coal at Norfolk, Virginia. The cargo was what is known in the trade as peas and beans, that is, very fine coal, usually used in power stations for fuelling the furnaces.

At Norfolk, the coal was loaded by more or less spraying it into the holds with a mechanical device which shot it in at a hell of a lick and at the same time plastered it down hard in the holds.

Our cargo was for Montevideo, Uruguay.

When we arrived there and started to discharge the coal, using grabs and the ship's derricks, the coal was so solid that it seemed to stand on end as they dug down with the grabs.

We ended up with a deep hole in each hold, with the coal standing shear like a cliff. Getting it to fall down was a dangerous business, too unsafe for anybody to venture into the hold in case of being buried in a fall of coal.

Whilst we were in Montevideo, the Chief Officer broke the bones in his right foot, and of course was unable to carry on his duties.

I cabled my owners about this and they decided to fly a relief Officer out to the ship. This is where I made a grave mistake, I should have paid the Chief Officer off, and then carried him home on the ship as a D.B.S., (a Distressed British Seaman).

This, as the owners pointed out to me later, would have saved them paying his National Insurance contributions. They would also have received 30 shillings a day from the Government to pay for his keep on the ship from the time of his pay off to arriving home. I wish they had told me this when they sent the other Officer to join the ship.

I was in the doghouse over that incident.

After discharge of the coal we were ordered to proceed up the River Plate to Rosario, to load a cargo of grain for the Continent. This entailed getting the holds cleaned out and washed down and dried out to receive grain, no easy job when on a tight cancelling date.

Entering Argentinian waters, we had the Customs come aboard and they sealed up the Bonded stores, after they had had their share of the goodies. We then went up river to Rosario to load, and our stay there was to last almost two weeks.

In this time all the crew were short of cigarettes and tobacco.

I asked the Agent to get the Customs to come aboard and make an issue from the Bond. They eventually turned up and when they went to the Bonded store they saw the seal placed on the door by the Buenos Aires Customs officers. This they said very gravely, was most difficult. I conferred with the Agent, he in turn had words with the Customs Officers, all conversation being in Spanish so I couldn't make out what was being said. Finally the Agent told me that it would cost me to have them open the Bond.

It did, in all they took away from the ship 10,000 cigarettes, about a dozen bottles of whiskey, tins of salmon and other tinned products, half a dozen paint brushes, and tins of sweets.

Talk about graft, the Argentinians live on it, all Government officials are very poorly paid, so they prey on ships.

After this, I was put wise by the Agent. He pointed out to me that the Customs thought that the Bond was the shipowner's. But it was not, it belonged to me, I had bought all there was in it.

It seems that under the Argentinian law, I should have declared all the contents of the Bond as my own property and then the Customs men dare not have touched it. They would have had to have relied on my generosity for any perks they got.

Unfortunately I did not know that when I arrived in Argentine!

I wrote home and advised my owners to tell any of the Masters in the company about this procedure, so that they would not be stung for exorbitant amounts of cigs and spirits. I didn't lose out on the deal because my owners reimbursed me for all that was taken from me in the course of business dealings on their behalf.

We had been chartered to do a certain speed on voyage, but had failed to reach that speed, and I got a cable from the owners wanting to know why we were not doing the chartered speed.

I consulted the Chief Engineer on the matter, and the answer I got was that the oil fuel shipped at the bunkering port was of poor quality.

This, however was not the cause, as I found out later.

Our Chief Engineer was on his first voyage as Chief, and he had thought he could improve the engine performance. He had been messing about with the timing of the engine. This had increased the oil consumption greatly. When I got into radio range with the owners on the way back home they instructed me to run the engine at the maximum revs. I pointed out to them that this would greatly increase the fuel used. They said never mind that, so long as I had plenty to see us to our discharge port of Rotterdam.

I ordered the Chief Engineer to give the ship maximum speed.

He did, and coming up the English Channel, you would have thought that we were a coal burning ship instead of a motor ship.

There were clouds of thick black oily smoke coming out of the funnel. On arrival in Rotterdam, our Engineer Superintendent came aboard to find out what was wrong with the engines.

A careful examination showed that the Chief had badly upset the timing gear, and the ship was not fully burning the fuel in the engine. That was the end of his reign as Chief Engineer, they demoted him back to Second Engineer, to get more experience with Doxford Diesel engines.

I went on leave again from Rotterdam. I had about seven weeks at home before being sent to join the ore carrier "Reivaulx".

Little did I know when I joined her on the 10th January 1961, that she was to be my final command with the Bolton S.S. Co.

I was on the usual run to Seven Islands, Canada for iron ore.

All seemed to be going well, but one Sunday morning when I was making my inspection of the crew's quarters, as required by the Merchant Shipping Acts, I found a flick knife under the pillow of one of the Somali engineroom hands. As this man had been in one or two nasty brushes with some other member of the crew, I told the Chief Engineer that I wanted that man paid off on arrival in the U.K..

I was not going to have any crew member in possession of a flick knife. I had seen what can happen in a fight when a knife is used, and I had no intentions of it happening again.

Some hours later, after I had finished my inspection, the Chief Engineer came and told me that the Second Engineer was resigning.

This announcement came as a surprise to me, I had always understood that the 2nd Engineer liked the ship, so why his notice of resignation? I asked the Chief, and he told me it was because I had told them to get rid of the Somali possessing the flick knife.

I explained to the Chief Engineer my reasons for his dismissal, I'd seen what can happen aboard a ship when a knife is drawn in anger. I wasn't going to take the chance of it happening on any ship of which I was the Master.

The Merchant Shipping Acts clearly state that it is a punishable offence to carry an offensive weapon aboard a ship.

The Chief left my room, to return about an hour later. He was in a solemn mood.

"What's on your mind Chief?" I asked him.

"Well, it's like this Captain, if the 2nd Engineer leaves the ship, then I am going as well".

I was dumbfounded by this statement, then a thought struck me.

I'd heard unofficially, that the Somali engineroom hands were buying their jobs in the ship. The little bird that told me, also said that they handed over some of the excessive overtime cash they drew. I had noticed the amount of overtime payments were particularly high in this ship, but as the engineroom was kept spotlessly clean, how could I interfere in the running of the department?

When I was Chief Officer on another ship where this Chief Engineer reigned, he had once said that he would get his new house paid for in double quick time.

He had said this at the tea table in the saloon, to the Captain and myself. When he had left the saloon, the two of us tried to figure out how he could raise the cash so quickly.

I had also noticed from the Bond issue book, that bottles of spirits were down against the names of some of the Somali men.

I knew that Somalis do not drink spirits, it is against their religious upbringing. Those bottles of spirits, my informant said, were appearing in the rooms of the Chief Engineer and the 2nd Engineer.

All this was of course hearsay, so I was powerless to do anything about it. However, there is no smoke without a fire.

"So, Chief, because I want to fire a man for carrying a dangerous weapon, you and the 2nd want to resign".

"Yes, Captain", was his answer.

I took the bull by the horns, "Well Chief, the whole thing stinks, two responsible Officers will resign over the sacking of one seaman".

No reply was forthcoming, so I continued, "There is something more sinister to this action than just that".

"I don't understand what you are getting at", he replied.

"I think you do Chief" I said.

There was complete silence for a few minutes.

"What are you getting at?" said the Chief.

"Look Mr. do you want me to spell it out to you what has been going on in your department"?

With that the Chief turned round and left my room. What I had heard was obviously true.

Now I was on the horns of a dilemma, Captains for ships were ten-a-penny.

Good Chief and second engineers were at a premium.

If I cabled my owners and said that I wanted replacements for two senior engineers, I was going to be on the hot spot.

In other words, I had to let the matter drop, even though I was seething with anger.

When we arrived in the U.K., our Engineer Superintendent came on board, I just had to tell him of the entire incident of the two engineers handing in their resignation.

At least I'd got it off my chest.

I did another voyage on the "Reivaulx" and back to Britain, after which I was sent on leave.

A few days after I arrived home I had a call from our London office, asking me to present myself there on the 21st May 1961, as they had things to discuss with me.

I made my way down to London, arriving at the head office at the appointed time. I took a seat in the foyer, to await being called into the inner sanctum, the Board Room.

Eventually one of the junior Directors came out and called me into the room.

Seated at the table were the owner, Mr. F.B. Bolton, other directors and the company's secretary.

Mr. Bolton was the first to speak, "Be seated Captain", he pointed to a seat. I sat and waited for whatever was to come.

"Captain" said Mr. Bolton "I regret that we must ask you for your resignation".

I sat there, my world lay about me in ruins, the bottom had dropped out of it. I lit a cigarette, to try and compose my thoughts before replying.

"Sir" I said addressing Mr. Bolton "Will you please tell me what I have done so wrong to warrant this"?

Mr. Bolton looked at his minions before answering me.

"We find you temperamentally unsuitable to us", was his reply.

I still had no idea what he meant by that statement, was he trying to suggest that I was "nuts", or soft in the head?

"Please tell me what I have done wrong, don't let me leave this office wondering where I failed in my position as a Shipmaster".

Again Mr. Bolton looked at the others, and then said, "Captain, it would be difficult to be specific on the matter, wouldn't it, gentlemen".

Of course they all heartily agreed with their Managing Director, whatever their thoughts might have been on the subject.

I then tried to press home my side of the meeting.

"Mr. Bolton, I am now 45 years old, I have served you for 17 years, during which time I have served you to the best of my ability at all times, now you want me to resign".

He nodded his head, "We think it best for all concerned".

"But don't you realise that at my age, my chances of another job as things are these days, are negligible", I said. "Also, I have a wife and two children to provide for".

"Yes Captain, we have taken that into consideration, and therefore we shall keep you on full pay until the end of your contract, you will not be appointed to any more of our ships during that period, but stay home on leave".

He paused for breath before continuing, "In addition, we shall pay you for a further six months after the expiry of your contract, during which time you will be allowed to take further employment with any other shipping company".

"You cannot however do this until the expiry of your contract".

I nodded my head in acceptance of what he had said.

"Further" said Mr. Bolton "We have decided to give you the total amount of money accrued in my non-contributory pension fund, which was the said £1250.

This meant that I would be receiving one year's salary, plus the sum from the pension fund, a total of £2654 as the pay-off.

I was asked if I thought this fair. What could I say, except that it was reasonable.

"Then that is all there is to be said, you are now free to go home." said Mr. Bolton.

"Sir, before I leave this room, will you please tell me where I went wrong, so that I shall never make the same mistake a second time".

"I am sorry, but that is not possible, so now I bid you good day".

There was nothing more to be said, so I took my leave of the meeting, and made my way to King's Cross for a train home.

My wife was shattered by the news when I told her what had happened. After 17 years, I was going to have to build a new way of life, where did one start, I asked myself?

This happened in May 1961, and I wrote no less than 50 letters to various shipping companies in the hopes of finding another job.

Some of my letters were answered, saying that they did not have any vacancies. Many of my letters were ignored and no replies were made.

The future looked grim indeed, and apart from that, my will to return to sea had faded.

I felt that I could not face it again, ever.

Chapter 26.
I become a shopkeeper

I thought long and hard about my future.

How was I going to make a living if I didn't go back to sea?

Why not become self-employed, buy a shop and be my own boss?

The more I thought about it, the better I liked the idea. So my search through the local newspaper each day brought me to a shop that was in my price range, which wasn't very high, I was not a wealthy man.

The shop was a general store situated on a council housing estate in Froghall Lane, Hull. I went to view the place, and found that it was the only general store on the estate, which was a good sign, and there would be no opposition, so I thought.

After a talk with the present owner, we discussed the price, and I decided to buy it. Prior to signing the contract to buy, I was given the opportunity to man the shop to learn something of the trade, the customers, and be introduced to the various wholesalers who supplied the shop. I was favourably impressed by what I saw during my week at the shop before taking over. I thought I could make a living from the deal.

So I became a shopkeeper.

The premises were a bit dingy, so I made a point of re-decorating the shop. A coat of fresh emulsion paint on the walls made a world of difference to the outlook. I had new fluorescent lighting fitted, all the shelves washed, and the stock displayed so that it could be seen easily by customers.

My first week's takings were not what I had expected, £80, and most of this was in groceries which only returned 12.5% profit. I wasn't going to make a living on that.

At that time, for some reason which escapes me, fruit was at a premium, apples, pears, oranges and bananas, were expensive.

I noticed that the women customers were a bit embarrassed when they asked me the prices, in case they felt that they could not afford such luxuries for their children.

To save them further embarrassment, I started packing the fruit in clear cellophane bags, say two or three apples in each bag. These I marked with the price on them and put them on display. It worked wonders, the shoppers knew what they could afford, and chose whatever suited them without having to ask me the prices. My fruit and vegetable trade increased four-fold.

I also got a good reputation for the quality of the cheeses and bacon I sold, I had a good supplier for these items, always of first class quality.

My fruit supplier was most helpful too, he gave me many tips on how to look after fruit and veg.

For instance he told me never to leave the box of bananas on the concrete floor of the shop. Bananas, he said, were very susceptible to cold, and would go black if left overnight in the box on the floor.

He also showed me that pears ripen from the centre outwards, which led me to cut a pear picked at ransom from the display each morning to make sure that the customers could not complain.

He further showed me how to make a head of lettuce appear freshly picked. You cut a sliver off the base of the stalk, leaving it as though it had been newly harvested.

All tricks of the trade, but at least honest.

In a few weeks my turnover had increased to about £180 a week, with a gross profit of about 25%. This was still nothing like what I had earned as a Shipmaster, and out of that I had the rent and heating and lighting of the shop to meet.

I still had my mortgage on my house to meet, my family to provide for, and through too much enthusiasm and too little business acumen, I found myself going into debt by the end of a year as a shopkeeper.

I could see bankruptcy staring me in the face, so I decided it was time to get out whilst I was still solvent.

I put the shop up for sale, but what was I going to do next?

One of my male customers gave me an idea.

He was a taxi driver. Why he asked, seeing that I had a car, didn't I take up taxi driving?

He explained the ins and outs of the game, and then said if I was interested, he would introduce me to the boss of the taxi office from which he worked.

Clutching at straws, I jumped at the idea, what had I to lose?

I got a buyer for the shop, at a price less than I had paid for it, plus the stock at valuation. When the sale was completed, I ended up with £175 left of my original £2000.

At least I had not gone bankrupt, I was still solvent but with very little in the bank.

I went and saw the owner of the taxi office, and he accepted me as a runner-in, as they are called. That is a man who owns the car, but works from an established taxi office.

I would have to apply to the Police for a Hackney licence as a private hire taxi. My car had to be tested and inspected by the authorities to see that it was fit for use as a public conveyance.

It passed muster and I was issued with a Private Hire licence No. 325, a red and white plate was given to me to attach to the rear of my car.

Thus I became a taxi driver, a reliable one to boot, so much so, that the boss of the office, to whom I paid a weekly sum for the use of his office, used to hand me some good jobs.

For instance he knew that he could depend on me to do the hospitals run, carrying doctors from one hospital to another.

Or call me out on my time off to transport blood samples for examination at the Haematology labs in urgent cases.

All those runs were at a fixed agreed fare, according to the distance involved.

I stuck this for a year, and it gave my family a living, but it was wearing out my car, and repairs needed to be done.

The time had come when I would have to go back to sea, if I could find a job.

I did, as Chief Officer of one of Trinder Anderson's ships, the "Ajana". I had written an application to the company, in the hopes that they might have a job going. They did, and they sent for me to go down to their office in London for an interview. At the office I met their Marine Superintendent, who wanted to know all about me, my certificate, my experience etc.

I gave him all the details of my years with Bolton S.S. Co., and how I came to be dismissed after 17 years with them.

He asked me if I had taken legal action against them, as he thought that I had a good case.

I told him that I had consulted the M.M.S.A., our union, but they had been as good as useless.

M.M.S.A., by the way stood for Mercantile Marine Service Association, the Master's and Officers Union.

He left me a while as he went to have words with his superiors, and when he returned, he said that I was to join the "Ajana", at Tilbury the following week. I would, he said be on pay from the time of leaving their office.

I left Trinder Anderson's office feeling very much elated.

I now had a job as Chief Officer in a reputable company. Maybe I could further my career at sea with these people.

On the appointed day, I travelled down to Tilbury, complete with my gear for sea. On boarding the ship, lying in Tilbury Docks, I reported my presence aboard to the Captain, one Captain Hastings.

We had a long conversation, in which he told me that he knew all about me. The head Office had filled him in on all my details.

He asked me what salary I had been receiving as Master in Boltons.

I told him £117 per month. That he said was a good salary.

I agreed with him that it was. Then he shocked me by saying that if he heard me bragging aboard the ship that I had been a ship's Captain, he would have me out of the ship faster than you can say rubber buggy bumpers!

I instantly knew that I was not going to get along with this man too well.

The ship still had cargo on board for Rostock in East Germany, It was a stinking cargo of bags of fish meal from Luderitz Bay in South Africa. On sailing from Tilbury, we had clear fine weather down the Thames and out into the North Sea. Then came the fog, and when I saw it close in, I went to the Radar machine and started taking the cover from it, prior to switching it on.

Captain Hastings asked me what I was doing.

I told him I was getting the Radar ready for switching on.

He promptly ordered me to replace the cover, saying, "I'll tell you when to put the Radar on, it does not go on without my permission".

I was dumbfounded, but I replaced the cover and went outside the wheelhouse to keep my bridge watch.

Funny man, funny peculiar, not ha ha.

Come eight bells, 8 p.m. the end of my watch, I handed over to the 3rd Officer and left the bridge after filling in the Log Book.

At 4 a.m. the next morning I went on the bridge to take my watch, and the Captain was still up there, his eyes going square with watching the Radar screen. It was a glorious summer morning, but still dense fog, and we were steaming along at 14 knots!

I heard a shout from the lookout man on the fo'castle head.

He was waving franticly away to port. I looked in the direction he had indicated, and there was a ship heading straight into our No.2 hold.

I yelled out to the man at the wheel, "Hard a port", the man responded instantly, and at our speed, the ship started to turn immediately. My theory was that if we were going to have a collision, it was best to do it head on.

Captain Hastings froze in his footsteps, as he saw the other ship bearing down on us.

The lookout man on the other ship was running like hell from the fo'castle head, thinking we were about to collide.

My action had saved the collision.

We passed alongside each other at about two yards apart. So close in fact, that had I reached out, I could have shaken hands with the Captain of the other ship.

As soon as we had cleared each other, I ordered the wheelman to go back on his course, then I resumed my walking up and down the bridge.

I never said a word to Captain Hastings, it was he who spoke first. He said "I thought that was one of the buoys showing up on the Radar".

"Captain", I answered "It doesn't pay to make mistakes like that".

On arrival at Rostock, he told me that he wanted some horrible paint runs on the ship's side cleaning off and repainting.

I gave orders to the Bosun for this to be started. Stages were rigged overside for the man, and they set to work with scrapers on the offending runs.

I had noticed them when I joined the ship at Tilbury, and thought what a hell of a nasty job the sailors had made of it.

It turned out that the stuff on the ship's side wasn't paint, but tar. Being hot weather it stuck to the men's skin and faces, and it burnt them. They all complained about the job.

I went and explained to the Captain that he had better order some lanolin for them to rub on their skin, if he insisted on them carrying on with the work.

He wouldn't listen to me, so I told the Bosun to knock off the job.

I didn't want men getting their eyes and faces burnt by the tar.

The Captain was none too pleased at my action, but there was nothing he could do about it.

Some days later, I was sat in my office working something out when he appeared in the doorway.

He was holding an object in his hand "What's this?" he asked.

I looked at what he was holding, before replying.

"It looks like a half inch nut to me", I said.

"Well what the hell is it doing lying in the bed of No.2 starboard winch?"

"I wouldn't know Captain, I don't make a habit of diving under winches to see what's under there".

A growl from him and then away he went, I wasn't going to get into a slanging match with him, but I knew that we could never get on together as Captain and Chief Officer, a great pity because I needed that job.

Completing our discharge, we sailed for Stettin, Poland, for a full cargo of coal for Dublin.

The weather was still fine and hot, and as we had armed guards at the gangway, passes had to be shown every time you stepped ashore.

Poland was still under the Communist regime at the time.

We started loading the coal, and after we had shipped a good quantity, the Captain came to my room and wanted to know why I was not down the holds checking on the loading and stowage of the coal.

"The company provides boiler suits for you to wear, so get down those holds and see to it!"

I'd loaded many thousands of tons of coal in my time at sea, but never had I seen an officer go down the holds to see how the cargo was going in.

This man must be paranoid, to want his Chief Officer go down into the holds and watch the loading.

I wasn't going to argue with him, so I donned a boiler suit and made my way to the most loaded hold.

I went down into it and had a look at the heap of coal, getting well and truly covered in dust at the same time.

I had a look into each of the five holds, and then, as black as hell, I went and reported to him that all was well with the loading. This was an act of sheer devilment on my part.

On completion of loading, we sailed for Dublin.

Our stay in that port was quite pleasant, and I was pleased to be able to get away from the ship each evening.

The discharge was slow, because the stevedores used large steel buckets, filled in the holds, and then lifted and dumped into trucks on the quay. Invariably there was a lot of coal spilled in this procedure. Some of it was shovelled up and put into the trucks or lorries. However, a fair amount of it was left each night when the dockers knocked off for the day. It was then that women and children came with prams or bags and picked up all the coal left on the quay. I spoke to the Foreman the next morning, about this unusual procedure. He informed me that it was the practice in the port, to allow the poorer people of the fair city to come and glean whatever coal they could. This struck me as a very nice gesture on the part of the owners of the cargo.

On completion of discharge, and around sailing time, the weather had changed and it was blowing hard.

As we were making a light ship, (empty ship) passage, I decided that we might have to fill the deep tank with ballast water.

To this end I instructed the Carpenter to screw down the deep tank lid. This entailed screwing down about 80 bolts which held the lid down. He had no sooner finished the job when the Captain came to me and asked why the tank had been closed and screwed down.

"Well Sir, as it's blowing hard out there, I thought you might want to ballast the ship a bit more for the passage across the Irish Sea to the Bristol Channel".

"Get it opened up again Mister, I 'll give the orders when the tank has to be closed", he snapped.

This man didn't want a Chief Officer, he thought he could run the whole sheebang by himself!

When we got to Cardiff, I told him that I was leaving the ship.

I explained to him that I had hoped that I could have settled in the ship and maybe serve in the company for a long time, but under the circumstances on that voyage, where the Captain had no faith in me as a Chief Officer, it was better that I leave the ship.

He then said that he had great confidence in my ability.

"I haven't forgotten the speed with which you acted to avert that collision, that was superb seamanship".

"Without boasting Captain, you realise that I have commanded bigger ships than the "Ajana", and I know how to handle them". He then went on to explain to me that he didn't have too many years to do before he could retire with a nice company pension.

That he explained was why he was so concerned about everything aboard his ship.

My answer to that was, that if he did not learn to delegate, he would not live to enjoy his retirement.

I was sorry to leave the ship, as I had hoped that I might have had permanent employment for the foreseeable future.

Captain Hastings gave me a lift in his car, which his wife had driven down from Hartlepool, to the station.

As I got out at Cardiff station, he wished me all the best for the future.

It was only when I had boarded the train for Hull, that I recalled where I had seen that man before.

It also gave me the answers to why he had taken such a dislike to me. He had been an Able Seaman in a West Hartlepool ship by the name of "Lilburn", owned by Smith Hoggs of West Hartlepool.

We had sailed together in the fo'castle, and I had held my Master's certificate longer and had more command experience than him. If only I had remembered that aboard the ship, I could have asked him if the name "Lilburn" meant anything to him.

So ended another hope.

Chapter 27.
Klondyke, but no gold!

On returning home, it was a case of searching for another ship. I heard of one from the Pool office. A Newcastle shipowner, Witherington Everett, needed a Chief Officer. I wrote to them immediately, and got a reply saying that they had a vacancy for a relief Chief Officer for their ship, the "Chevychase", due in West India Docks, London.

As instructed, I travelled down to London, and took a taxi from King's Cross to the ship. She was a fine modern ship, but much smaller than I had been used to. She was engaged on a regular run with general cargo from the U.K. to ports around the Mediterranean.

This sounded like the answer to a dream.

However, on reporting to the Captain, he informed me that I was only there for one voyage whilst the Chief Officer had leave.

Another dream gone up in a puff of smoke!

We loaded a mixed general cargo for several ports in the Medi.

Amongst them, Tripoli, Malta, Benghazi, where after discharging, we loaded personal luggage of troops returning to Britain.

Among the heterogeneous cargo loaded, was bags of sweet almonds, these were for Britain, and the Captain told me that I should watch them carefully, or they would be pilfered by dockers at other ports en route. We discharged drums of chemicals for I.C.I. in the Grand Harbour at Malta, and loaded materials produced at their factory there.

From Malta, we sailed into Salerno, Italy, to load barrels of pickles and hundreds of cases of tinned tomatoes for Heinz in Great Britain.

So now you know where all your pickled onions and gherkins come from!

Salerno is not too far from Pompeii, a place I had always wanted to see. I can remember the stories we were told about the place, when I was at school. How it was covered in volcanic ash when Mount Vesuvius erupted centuries ago, and encased everything with molten ash. This was too good a chance to miss, so I asked the Captain if he minded if I had the afternoon off to go and see the ruins. He agreed, and away I went on a hair-raising bus journey from Salerno to Pompeii. On arrival at the gates of the area that had once been a city, I found that you had to pay to go into the grounds. However, there was a party of American tourists all going in, so I joined on to their group and was let in free of charge as just another member of the party.

They had arrived by a chartered coach, and so were not limited to time spent there. I had to rely on the local bus service, so I was restricted to the amount of time I could spend looking at the ruins. In three hours I saw as much as I could and I got some very good photographs of the place. It was most interesting to see so much so well preserved after hundreds of years since the eruption of Vesuvius, that had covered the city in molten ash.

In the museum in the grounds, were the mummified remains of people, encased in the solidified volcanic ash. In all, I had a most educating and enjoyable day out, but I was glad to get the bus back to the ship and arrive there safely.

We sailed the next morning for home with our cargo, docking on the Tyne, where of course I had to leave the ship to let the permanent man back into his job. I went to the offices of the owners on Newcastle Quay, to see if they had any other job that they could offer me.

Unfortunately, they did not have anything further to offer me, so it was back home and out of a job again.

I was in the offices of the M.M.S.A. in Hull one day when the secretary said to me that if I wanted a job, why not try Klondyke Shipping Co.? They were a local company. But, he added, you might get a job, but you won't keep it long.

I'd heard of the company and their antics, but I was desperate for a job, so I went along to their offices in Scale Lane, Hull.

On entering the office, I introduced myself, and was shown through to the Director's office.

I told him why I was there, and on request showed him my Master's certificate and my Seaman's Discharge book. He perused them and then said he could give me a job as Chief Officer of their ship, the "Kirtondyke".

She was due to arrive in Barry two days later and he wanted me to join her there. I accepted the job and went home elated that I was in work again. For how long, I did not know, but whatever length of time it was, I would be earning money to keep my family.

A few days later I got instructions to join the ship in Barry.

I left home on the evening train to South Wales, arriving in Cardiff about 8 a.m., a change of trains, and then on to Barry.

I took a taxi down to the ship with my gear, and when I saw the ship, I was in two minds to get back into the taxi and go back home.

The Kirtondyke was the smallest ship I had ever gone to join, and I wasn't at all chuffed with the sight of her. She was a ship of about 1,400 tons deadweight, having two hatches, but only one long hold, served by the two hatchways.

I went aboard and reported to the Captain, he arranged for me to sign on as Chief Officer.

We took a load of coal from Barry to Le Havre, and after discharging at Le Havre, we then went to Caen, where we loaded iron ore for Flixborough, up the Humber.

When the ore had been discharged we then went up river into Goole to load more coal, this time for East Yelland power station in the Bristol Channel.

What a drab place that turned out to be.

Leaving Yelland, we then sailed to Mousehole in Cornwall for a load of granite chips, used for road surfacing. These were for Southampton.

It was there that the Captain's wife came aboard for a break, and the run aboard the ship to Swansea. It was then that the Captain asked me if I would be prepared to take over command while he had some leave, as he had not had a break for about seven months.

I said I'd be glad to take the ship to let him have leave, so when we got to Swansea he got on the phone to the Hull office, and put the proposal to the Director, Mr. Atkinson.

He came back aboard and said that the office had agreed that I should take over from him for the voyage, whereon he took me to the Customs House, where my name was entered on the ship's register. I was now the Master of the "Kirtondyke" for the next, and I hoped, subsequent voyages.

I loaded a cargo of coal for Nantes, in the meantime the office had sent a replacement Chief Officer to the ship.

I don't know where they dug him up from, but he proved to be a dead loss to me as a Chief Officer.

On completion of loading, the weather had deteriorated badly, and I was advised not to sail until the weather got better.

There was a storm blowing out in the Irish Sea and the "chops of the Channel". That's the sea area between Land's End and N.W. corner of France, Finisterre.

Two days later I decided that the weather had eased down enough for me to sail, which I did, but was sorry afterwards that I had.

I went down with a bad bout of 'flu, and the Chief Officer was as drunk as a lord, though I didn't know it at the time.

On clearing Land's End for the run across to France, we ran into a very heavy westerly swell, and being a small ship, we were tossed around like a cork. I wasn't feeling seasick, but I was so under the weather from the 'flu, that I could hardly keep my eyes open.

Thinking that the Chief Officer and 2nd Officer would be keeping their watches of the bridge, I had a little nap.

Waking a little later I decided to go on the bridge, I needed some fresh air anyhow. When I got into the small wheelhouse, there was only the helmsman there.

I asked the man at the wheel where the Mate was, and he told me that he had left the bridge about an hour earlier and hadn't been back!

This was a right state of affairs, the ship going along, with only the man at the wheel, and no officer on watch on the bridge.

I checked the compass, and saw that we were on the right course for Nantes, then I went to look for the Chief Officer.

I found him in his room, dead to the world, and I thought that he too, was a victim of the 'flu. I left him in his bunk and made my way back to the bridge but I knew that I was not in a fit state to try and keep his watch for him.

What to do, that was the question?

The only answer I could come up with was to switch on the two vertical red lights, as it was night, to indicate to any approaching ship, that we were "Not under Command". This is the international signal for use at sea, and respected and obeyed by other ships, to keep clear of the ship displaying the signal.

We were not strictly "Not under Command", but it made life easier for me, I was able to tell the man at the wheel to ring the bell to my room if he saw a ship approaching. In the meantime I was able to go down to my room, and dose myself with Aspirin and have a rest. I was having catnaps, then having a look around on the bridge until the 2nd Officer took over the bridge watch. I told him the Chief Officer was flat out with the 'flu in his room.

I was now able to go down to my room and have a four hour sleep, which I badly needed. The sleep and the Aspirin seemed to work miracles, because when I woke up, I felt a 100 % better. We were now nearing the coast of France, and I was able to get in touch with the local coast station on the radio-telephone to give my E.T.A. at the Pilot station. The station was Brest le Conquet.

We eventually arrived and picked up the Pilot for Nantes.

On berthing the Agent came aboard, and I told him I had a sick man aboard, could he get a Doctor to come and see the man.

On arrival, the Doctor examined the Chief Officer, and then told me the man was hopelessly drunk, not ill.

That was all I needed, a piss artist for a Mate!

I immediately went on the phone to our office and reported this. I told them that I wanted him replaced as soon as we came back to the U.K.

We discharged our cargo of coal, and sailed back to Goole for another load of the stuff, this time for Dover. This suited me fine, as I am well versed in the coastal run around Britain.

Then it was back to Goole again for more coal. On arrival there, the Captain returned, and I went down a step to Chief Officer again.

I did one more voyage as such, and then was asked to take over as Master again.

This was so that the Captain could attend to the sale of his house, as he was moving from Goole to Cheltenham.

I was glad of the opportunity to be the Master again for the voyage with another cargo of coal for Le Havre.

After the Le Havre discharge, it was to Caen for iron ore for Flixborough, from there back to Goole as usual. By this time I had some leave due me, and was not surprised when the Director came aboard and said that the Captain would be returning and I was to take the leave I had due me.

I was, he said, to contact the office when my leave was up. This was heartening news, so I was all ready to leave the vessel when the old Captain arrived.

I handed the ship over to him and away I went on leave, happy in the knowledge that I had a job waiting after my leave.

I had saved a little bit of cash from voyages, this I was able to spend on my family during my leave.

At the expiry of my leave I contacted the company, and was told to hang on a day or two. The days passed and there was no word from Klondyke Shipping Co., so I made my way down town to their office in Scale Lane.

On arrival I asked to see Mr. Atkinson, the Director. I was taken to his office, whereon he asked me what I wanted to see him about.

"Well Sir", I said, "You told me to contact you when my leave was up, which I did, but have received no instructions as to what I am to do".

His reply shattered me, "I'm sorry, but I have nothing further to offer you."

"Why, when you were aboard in Goole, didn't you say you would not be giving me further employment, that way I could have saved my cash and looked for another job".

He made some lame excuse, which made me really mad at the way I had been treated.

"You know Mr. Atkinson, I was warned about your company many years ago. I was told that I would get a job with you, but not hold it very long, and the person who told me that knew your company very well indeed".

I stormed out of the office before I said something I might regret.

Here I was, out of work again, with little hope of further employment, I had reached the end of the line. There was only one thing left to do, something that I had dreaded ever having to do, join the dole queue for the first time in my life.

It seemed to me that the last shred of self-respect would go if I had to do that.

I told my wife that I would have to go and sign on at the dole office the next morning.

Coming down stairs next day, I heard the letter box flap, and a letter fell to the floor. I went and picked it up.

That letter was the answer to my prayers!

It was from Messrs. R.S. Dalgiesh, the Watergate Shipping Company of Newcastle. It was a reply to a letter I had written them weeks ago, hoping to get a job with them.

They could, they said, offer me a job as Chief Officer on one of their ore-carriers, the "Pennyworth".

If I was still available and interested, would I phone them immediately, reversing the charges.

Was I available and interested, I'll say I was!

At ten a.m., I phoned their Newcastle office and asked to speak to the Marine Superintendent, Capt. Philips.

He came to the phone and spoke to me, giving me details of the ship, and the date of her arrival at Eston Jetty, Middlesborough.

He went on to say that the job was only temporary, but after he had met me personally, there might be a permanent job for me.

As the ship was due two days later, he said that I would be on pay from the time I was speaking to him on the phone.

They would he said, send me a rail ticket for the journey to Eston Jetty. I was over the moon, I had another job, and prayed that it was one that would last for a long time to come.

I joined the "Pennyworth" at Eston Jetty, as instructed.

She was just the sort of ship I was looking for, another 15,000 ton ore-carrier on regular runs back to the U.K.

Reporting aboard, I met the Captain, Captain Gault. He was unshaven and had a piece of sticking plaster on his face. He looked a real rough character to sail with.

In fact, he turned out to be one of the nicest chaps I have ever sailed with. I met the Superintendent when he boarded, and he got all details about me during our conversation.

He said he hoped that our relationship would be a long one, I told him, I too hoped it would be so.

After my first voyage on the "Pennyworth", I submitted a deck work report to the Superintendent when he came aboard.

He was very surprised at this, but I pointed out to him, that that had been the procedure when I was in Bolton S.S. Co., and I assumed that it would apply in this company.

I did two or three more voyages, and then I met Mr. Peter Dalgliesh when he came down to the ship.

He made a point of seeing me in private in my room. He said he knew that I had been

Master for some years, and he wanted to know what kind of ships.

I gave him full details of my experience at sea.

He was impressed.

He also wanted to know why I had left Boltons after 17 years with them.

I told him the whole truthful story of my dismissal from that company, and that I was not told what I had done wrong to warrant such treatment.

When I told him that they blankly refused to give me a reason for getting rid of me, he said that was an inhuman thing to do.

I asked Mr. Dalgliesh if he knew Mr. Tim Bolton.

He said that he did.

"Well Sir, if you contact him, you will find that everything I have told you is the absolute truth, and I still do not know why I was dismissed, I'd be a happier man if I did".

We had a very long talk, during which I told him that if any shipowner had the courage to give me another job as Master, I would prove that they would have no regrets for so doing. Mr. Dalgliesh said he would bear that statement in mind for the future. After the next voyage, on arrival at Newport, I was instructed to leave the "Pennyworth" and travel to London, to take over the "Tamworth" as Master for the coastal voyage to the Tyne.

This was the first step to becoming a permanent Captain in the company.

After sailing into the Tyne and handing over the ship to the permanent Captain, I went back and joined the "Pennyworth" again as Chief Officer.

The next thing was that I was asked to take over as Master of the "Ravensworth", one of the small 9,500 ton ore carriers, running mainly to Port Talbot and Workington in Cumbria.

From then onwards, I was Master in Watergate Shipping Co., and my sojourn with them was to last twelve years, the final twelve years of my career at sea.

A great deal of my time was spent going up to Murmansk for iron ore. Some of those voyages up to Murmansk were hair-raising to say the least.

One such voyage during the middle of winter, almost scared the pants off me. I was bound from Port Talbot to Murmansk, and had just passed the northern tip of the Shetland Isles in worsening weather. The wind and seas were getting more ferocious by the hour. It was time for me to bring the ship head to wind and seas.

Knowing that we would do some tremendous rolling in this operation, I warned all hands to secure everything, including everything in the galley.

The "Ravensworth" was a Doxford Diesel economy engined ship, that is, she had a three cylinder engine which could be very temperamental when set at slow speeds. If set at speeds below 65 revolutions per minute, it tended to stall.

With this in mind, I asked the Chief Engineer to stand by at the engine when I signalled for a low speed, whilst I turned the ship around into the wind and seas.

I instructed the Chief, that when I rung the telegraph for full speed, I wanted every ounce of power he could give me to get the ship out of the trough of the swell.

At the appropriate time, when there appeared to be a lull, I slowed the ship down and started my turn. She soon dropped away into the trough of the swell and started to roll. She rolled over to a degree that I had never before in all my years at sea known. Oh, my God, I thought, she's going to turn herself right over, I rang the emergency signal, a double ring on the telegraph for maximum speed to try and drive her round head to the wind and seas.

The Chief Engineer responded instantly with full throttle, and the ship slowly started to come out of the trough and meet the seas head on. All went reasonably calm when she was fully around and "hove to", to ride out the storm.

Whilst I was carrying out this procedure, a small Danish fishing boat passed us, heading away to the North.

What a fool, I thought, for a vessel so small to be tempting fate in that sort of weather!

Four hours later, our radio operator handed me a note saying that the small vessel was in a sinking condition some 50 miles to the North of us. There was nothing I could do for him, I was too far away, and in any case was having difficulty with my own ship.

Fortunately, there was a Russian ship close to where the stricken craft was, and he was able to save all the crew of the trawler before she sank in those horrendous seas.

Even though we were "hove to", we were making our way slowly to the North, and unfortunately at that time, the Decca coverage did not extend that far North, so we did not know our position.

Come the early evening, the skies cleared and stars became visible.

The Chief Officer and myself got our sextants out to try and get "sights". I took one star and the Chief took another. When worked out, we were able to plot our position on the charts.

We were miles past the Lofoten Islands, which was where we were heading for, to enter the Lofoten Fjord to take the inside route to Murmansk. It was a case of turning Southeast for the Islands.

We ultimately made it safely to Lodingen, where we shipped the Pilots for the run through the fjords to Honningsvaag, which is just south of the North Cape. There we dropped the Pilots and proceeded on our way to Murmansk.

As Murmansk was, and probably still is, a big Russian naval base, the entry into the harbour had to be rigidly followed as it was supposedly a mined area. There was a track laid down on the charts which had to be strictly followed, failure to do so brought warnings from the shore signal station that you were doing wrong.

You didn't argue with the Russians, you did exactly as you were told, otherwise you could be in big trouble.

I notice my Discharge Book is stamped with entry and exit at that port at least a dozen times.

I spent a whole winter sailing to Murmansk, and had some hair-raising weather experiences in so doing. The Atlantic can be bad, but so can the seas between Britain and the coast of Norway.

I did one voyage across the Western Ocean in the "Ravensworth" to Seven Islands for ore. As it was late in the year, the weather was anything but good, we had a hell of a passage through tremendous seas all the way across the Atlantic. I wasn't at all happy about that sort of voyage and was damned glad when they switched us back on to the Murmansk run.

The big trouble was, that at Port Talbot, they started the discharge in the morning, and they finished in time to get the ship away in the evening. This went on for several voyages and I was getting a bit tired of being pushed out of the port the same day as arrival. I noticed that some of the other small ore-carriers always seemed to get a night in port, using engine trouble as the excuse. So one day I expressed my anger in the quay superintendent's office.

He was very understanding "I take it that you would like the night in port" he said to me.

"Too damned right I would" I answered.

"Well, there's no need to get stroppy about it, it can be arranged".

He picked up the 'phone and called our agents.

"It doesn't look as though we shall finish the "Ravensworth" tonight Mr. Poley".

The voice at the other end of the 'phone said "you must have had a word with the Captain".

"Yes I have, in fact he is here with me right now".

"That's O.K. with us, we will arrange for pilots in the morning".

From then onwards we always got a night in port at Port Talbot, and all it cost me was a few cigarettes and a bottle of spirits each time.

This sudden change in sailing didn't go unnoticed by my Owners, and one day Nicholas Dalgliesh asked me how come the "Ravensworth" was getting an overnight stay in Port Talbot every time she stopped there now.

I told him that it was all done by kindness and a few words in the right ears. He laughed when I said that, after all it was nothing in or out of the shipowner's pocket, and in any case it made for a happier crew.

161

In all, I was Master of the "Ravensworth" for five sets of Articles, totalling some sixteen months of sea service, running to Canada, North Russia, and West Africa for iron ore.

On the voyage to West Africa, which followed the bad passage to Murmansk, when I thought the ship was going to turn herself over in heavy weather, the engineers reported that some of the "floors" in the engineroom were fractured.

This was serious, as the engine itself was bolted to those floors.

"Floors", by the way are the transverse steel beams across the bottom of a ship.

We managed, with difficulty, to have them all welded up when we got to Point Noire, in Mauritania, our loading port.

It struck me later, that that damage was probably caused by the tremendous strain imposed on them in that violent rolling. They would be taking the whole weight of the engine, a matter of some hundreds of tons.

I did not tell the owners that, of course.

Chapter 28.
Final years at Dalgliesh Shipping Co.

On checking through my Seaman's Discharge Book, I find that I served on the "Pennyworth" through 10 sets of Articles of Agreement, a total of 36 months service on her as Chief Officer and Master, before I was shifted to another ship.

After some leave I was appointed Master of the company's largest ship, the "Silksworth", a vessel of 20,000 tons cargo capacity.

She was mainly on the grain trade from the United States and Canada to the Continent, usually Amsterdam, Rotterdam, or Antwerp.

It was in her that I had my first taste of the "Ice Race" into Port Churchill, in the Hudson Bay at the start of the grain season from there.

The sight of the ice floes and the icebergs on that run are something that I shall never forget.

There is a fixed date, before which ships must not try to navigate the waters to the West of Resolution Island at the entrance to the Hudson Bay.

If arriving there before that date, you had to wait for the ice-breaker to arrive to escort your ship through the ice.

The breaker would go ahead of your ship and you were supposed to follow astern of him at a distance of one cable, that is roughly one ship's length behind him. I tried following him, but as quick as he broke the ice, it closed up again behind him and we were hitting hard ice. As our ships were not "ice-framed", that is specially strengthened, I could not risk damaging my ship.

The Master of the ice-breaker understood my concern and said he would wait until the next day, by which time he thought the conditions might be a little better for us.

It wasn't, and he said that he would have to leave us as he had to deliver stores to some place that was in dire need of them.

Away went the breaker and there we were stuck in the middle of nowhere, thick ice all around the ship.

When I say thick ice, I mean ice that was anything up to three or four feet thick.

The stuff that would tear a ship's steel plating apart as though it was paper if you hit it at too much speed.

Left to my own devices, and with no knowledge of navigating under ice conditions, I decided that the best way to make progress without damage to my ship, would be to put the nose of the ship gently up against an ice flow and then push that ahead of me.

The idea worked, we would put the stem of the ship slowly against the ice flow and then go ahead with the engines, pushing the ice ahead of us. The beauty of this idea was that it saved my ship from damage, as the iceflow acted as a buffer when we ran into more iceflows. The man on the look-out would warn me when the iceflow started to break up with the impact.

I would then stop the ship and find another flow to push ahead of me. It was slow progress, but at least I finally got to Port Churchill without incurring any damage to my ship.

I was however, not to be the first ship of the season to arrive at Port Churchill. The "Tamworth", commanded by Captain K. Jewell, beat me to the Pilot, so he got the award as first ship.

This was a great disappointment for me, as I had hoped to be first ship of the season that year. Ken Jewell was one of Dalgliesh's seasoned ice navigators and used to the ice, I wasn't.

That made all the difference. Ken got the soapstone carving award presented by the harbour authorities, and as a booby prize, I was given a water colour painting of scenery at Churchill, painted by a local artist.

I still have that painting at home.

That same season, getting near the closing date for Port Churchill, Dalgliesh's ship, the "Tamworth", was to be the last ship to load before the port closed for the winter.

Due to some freak weather conditions, heavy ice formed on the river surface just before she finished loading. As she was due to sail the next morning, there was no undue alarm. The "Tamworth" finished her loading and was ready for sea the first thing next day. She was assisted off the quay and swung round head out to sea by the local tug and under the supervision of the Pilot she headed for the entrance to the harbour.

Just a few hundred yards inside the harbour is a nasty outcrop of rocks which have to be avoided. These rocks are marked by a buoy anchored over them.

As a ship brings that buoy abeam, she has to go at full speed and with the rudder over to hard-a-starboard, to make a right angled turn to the right. Failure to do so would end up with the ship high and dry on the rocky shore ahead.

Unbeknown to anyone in the harbour authorities, the flow of the ice during the night had shifted the buoy from over the rocks.

The result was that the "Tamworth" ran slap bang into the rocks, tearing a massive hole in her No.1 hold.

Here was a major disaster, a fully loaded ship, no major ship repair facilities at Port Churchill, and winter setting in very fast. In the Hudson Bay, winter comes more or less overnight, so if the "Tamworth" was not to be iced in for the winter, she had to be got out of Port Churchill fast.

The nearest drydocking facilities were at St. Johns, Newfoundland. It was from there that a massive salvage tug came with high power pumps to cope with the water in the hold, and to stay with the ship until she reached St. Johns, which she successfully did a few days later. There, she was repaired in the drydock, but it took several weeks to get her out to sea again with her cargo of grain. Whilst in drydock, the grain from No.1 hold was discharged and taken ashore to silos where it was dried out and aired ready to be put back when the repairs were completed.

In this manner, very little of the cargo was lost, but it had been a very costly incident.

The shipowner was alright, insurance took care of his losses, but for Captain Beatty, it cost him his job.

He was sacked when the ship returned to the U.K.

I know for a fact that the Superintendent of the company tried hard to help him keep his job by telling him to say that at the time the accident happened, he had just popped into the toilet to answer the call of nature. Had that been true, it would probably have saved his job, after all the Pilot was still in charge on the bridge.

However, Captain Beatty was too honest, and would not use this excuse. He lost his job as Master with the Watergate Shipping Co.

I went to Port Churchill the next open season and had it drilled into me that I was to make absolutely certain of my ship's position at all times whilst entering or leaving the port.

During the closed season the harbour authorities had set up a series of beacons, one set to guide a ship into the entrance of the harbour, and a second set, which as they came abeam on your right hand side, you then turned sharply to put a third set dead in line ahead. This kept the ship clear of all dangers and led you right into the harbour towards the loading quay.

I was watching the Pilot like a hawk as we approached the entrance to Churchill that season. I wasn't going to be another Capt. Beatty through someone else's mistake.

We berthed safely, loaded our cargo and got out with the same degree of safety.

A costly lesson had been learned.

I later did another voyage to Port Churchill, this time in command of a new ship, the "Oakworth". She was one of the latest ships of the company, a fast 32,000 ton ship. My Chief Officer had never seen ice conditions such as we experienced, and was not in any way used to such conditions.

Early one morning, I was still in my bunk, having had the night on the bridge, when I was awakened by an almighty crash. I jumped up and found that the ship was going far too fast, and had hit a blue ice growler.

Now blue ice is ice that is very old and as hard as rock. I dashed onto the bridge and eased the speed of the ship down.

As tactfully as I could, I impressed on my Chief Officer that you did not ignore the danger of those ice flows. Fortunately, we had so far as I was aware, not suffered any material damage, but we were lucky on that occasion, it could have meant a hole in the bow.

The most harrowing conditions, were when you got a gale with snowstorms as you sailed through the Hudson Straits. Even with Radar and clear-view screens, it was almost impossible to sight ice flows or growlers in the choppy seas. It was a truly nerve-wracking experience sailing under those conditions, and I was damned glad to get out into the open waters of the Davis Straits, clear of the most dangerous ice.

The size of some of the icebergs can be judged by the fact that I have seen them aground in 600 feet of water. Just imagine the hundreds of thousands of tons of ice that represented. I remember one that we passed on our way home and it was still in the same position when we passed it on the next voyage. It was still aground and would remain so until sufficient of it had melted to let it float off again to become a danger to shipping around the Grand Banks of Newfoundland. There the effect of the Gulf Stream, and the comparatively warm water would help to disperse the berg slowly.

In early 1973, I had my usual several months in command of the "Ravensworth", carrying iron ore from Murmansk to Workington, and throughout most of my stay in that ship, the weather was atrocious each voyage. In May, I was sent home on leave as my son was getting married the next month. The company was going to launch a new ship called the "Naworth" at Cammell Lairds, Birkenhead.

The date was ideal, it was the day following my son's wedding in Nantwich, near Crewe. We were to attend the wedding and then stay overnight before going on to Birkenhead for the launching,

Two days before the wedding, we were out shopping in Hull, and I realised that I had got rid of a pain in my left leg that had troubled me for some time.

I remember saying to my wife that I was walking without pain.

Little did I know what was to follow later that evening.

It was late when we went to bed after a busy day, and at midnight I was crippled with the most unholy pain in my chest.

It is strange how you can sense that you need urgent medical attention. I knew that I had had a heart attack, and without quick aid, I was a goner.

I woke my wife and got her to phone for the Doctor, he arrived in record time. A quick examination and he rang for the ambulance.

15 minutes later, I was in the intensive care unit at Hull Royal Infirmary.

I'd had a massive heart attack.

I remember begging them to give me something to ease the pain, they would they said, when they had finished their examination. They did, and it put me to sleep. When I woke up some time later, at least the pain had gone and I found myself wired up to the visual heart beat monitor, and being fed intravenously by a drip.

The wedding, and the launch of the ship, went ahead without the presence of my wife and I. I was released from the hospital two weeks later, almost too scared to walk even a few yards.

Slowly my confidence returned, and I was able to get about again, but at a much slower speed than my usual one.

My employers gave me six months at home in which to recover, then I was given a medical check and pronounced fit to go back to sea.

This was heartening news both for me and Dalglieshs, and they appointed me Captain of the "Oakworth", which was due at the cement works at Greys on the River Thames.

Arriving at the gangway of the ship, I started to carry my cases up the steep gangway and was met at the deck level by the outgoing Captain.

"You shouldn't be carrying those cases, I'll get an A.B. to come and bring them aboard for you".

I had to assure him that I was not an invalid, and I was quite capable of carrying the cases myself.

I don't know who he expected was going to relieve him, I can only think he expected to see a worn out decrepit old man.

I was far from that.

The ship had been chartered by a Norwegian company called Taigland, to load a bulk cargo of cement for Palm Beach, Florida.

It took several days to load the 30,000 tons of cargo, this was the first time I had ever loaded cement in bulk.

The only other time I loaded cement, it was in bags for Malaya.

To facilitate the discharge of the cement powder, the ship had been fitted with special pipelines and pumps, to pump the cement ashore into the storage warehouse.

At Palm Beach, the stevedores fitted large funnel shaped hoppers into which the grab loads of cement were dropped and thus pumped ashore.

The loading of the hoppers was to be done by the ship's crew. They received extra payment from the consignees for driving the electric winches handling the grabs. For the crew this was money in the bank, paid to them tax free in American Dollars.

It was just the sort of job that most seamen welcome.

The consignees were a bit mercenary and wanted the crew to work until midnight every night. I had to draw the line on that idea.

The agreement in the Charter Party, was that the electric winches had to be shut down for several hours each day to allow them to cool down, and so that the engineers could keep them in good order.

The consignees offered me all sorts of bribes to allow the work to go on longer, but I was adamant.

I pointed out the terms of the Charter Party, and I was sticking to them. I had been warned by my company that they would try to get more working hours per day, and that I was not to give in to them on the matter.

On completion of discharge, we were ordered to Fort Lauderdale to take bunker oil, and there, the Charterer, Mr. Michael Taigland, joined the ship as passenger.

From what I learned, he was in financial trouble and he had to pay for the bunkers in hard cash in American Dollars.

We sailed from Port Lauderdale for Jamaica to load bauxite for the Mississippi. Whilst in Jamaica, Mr. Taigland took me ashore on a sightseeing tour. It was a very interesting day out, I enjoyed it.

As we were discharging at the port on the Mississippi, I got orders that we were to load grain a couple of miles downstream.

The trouble was that the holds would have to be cleaned out and washed down before we could pass the grain inspectors to load.

Given ample time, this would have been no trouble, but we were on a very tight cancelling date.

This meant that I had to have the ship ready to present my Notice of Readiness to load within 48 hours.

Enquiries as to the cost of getting shore labour to do the cleaning came up with a sum of several thousand dollars.

This did not please the Charterer, Mr. Taigland, in view of his financial state.

He asked for my advise, so I asked him if he would be prepared to pay my crew a lump sum of $1,000 to have the ship ready in time. He agreed, he would willingly pay them that amount if they could have the ship ready in time.

I called for the Bosun and put the proposition to him, $1,000 to be shared amongst the members of the deck crew to get the holds washed down and dried out in 48 hours, would he ask the crew?

He came back and said that they had jumped at the chance to make $100 each, and with that they all turned too after tea and worked until nearly midnight, before knocking off for the day.

The next morning they were at it again, and by the evening they had finished the job.

I was able to tell the grain inspectors that we were ready for inspection, and they passed the ship as fit to load grain, so I put my Notice of Readiness in immediately.

True to his word, Mr. Taigland handed me $1,000 to be shared out amongst the crew. He was happy and so were they.

Perks of that nature seldom arise for the average ships' crews.

I wish there had been that sort of chance to make some extra cash when I was a deckhand. In my days on deck, the ship would have paid a few measly hours overtime at 9d an hour for the job, (2.5p an hour).

How times had changed!

We loaded our full cargo of grain for Rotterdam, and sailed with the Charterer still aboard as a passenger. On passage he must have had news via the radio that he could make money if we could get to Rotterdam by a certain date.

He approached me and asked if it was possible for me to get the ship to Rotterdam by a certain date, which was ahead of my expected time of arrival.

The Charterer said that if we could make it, he would give both the Chief Engineer and myself, a bonus of $1,000 each.

I put this to the Chief, and he agreed that he could give us a little more speed, which we figured out would get us to Rotterdam by the required date.

The Chief opened the engine up to her maximum speed and we made Rotterdam in very good time. The Charterer honoured his promise and handed us both $1,000 each.

That at the time was worth about £550, so as far as we were concerned, it had been a very profitable voyage for us!

I could have done with a lot more voyages like that, but they are few and far between.

I was relieved and sent home for leave at Rotterdam, and had four months at home before my next ship, back to the "Ravensworth" for another spell of ore carrying from Russia to Workington in Cumbria.

This time, it was only for two months, before I was on leave before returning to the "Tamworth" for a voyage to the States, to load grain for the Canary Islands. That was a great voyage, as we had about 10 days in Las Palmas discharging and then we went to Teneriefe to discharge the balance of the grain.

It was just like being on holiday at those two ports!

Had I have known the length of our stay in the Canary's, I would have got my wife to have flown out to join me for a holiday.

From there we sailed to Albany, in the State of New York, there we were to load a full cargo of sorghum, a form of millet seed.

This seed is extremely fine and when stowed as it was in great heap in the warehouse, it tends to stick together, and form a wall when it is dug away for loading. Owing to the very hot weather at the time, this is what was happening, and the shippers considered it too dangerous for men to approach the heap in case they collapsed and buried the workmen.

This held up the loading for several days until they managed to get the wall of seed to fall.

The local population consisted of a great number of wealthy people, who came down to the ship and invited most of the Officers to their homes for evenings out. So a good time was had by all.

Waste disposal was one of the great problems we experienced at the port. By the harbour rules, we were not allowed to dispose of galley waste into the river. It had to be stored in bins on the deck. These soon become full to overflowing and with the heat maggots started crawling from the putrefying waste.

I asked for the local council to come and take it away, but they refused to do so. So despite the possibility of a massive fine on the ship, we dumped the stuff into the river about midnight each night.

At least we got rid of a serious health hazard.

We finally sailed with the cargo of millet for Ghent in Belgium, I was taken off there for some more leave, returning to the "Tamworth" at Aarhus in Denmark some ten weeks later.

I did a further three months in command of her, and then was relieved by another Captain, as we steamed through the Skaggerack into the Baltic. I was landed with the Chief Engineer at Copenhagen by the Pilot cutter, and we were put up for the night in a hotel and then flown home the next day.

I appear to have had another 5 months at home before being sent to my next, and final command.

I did not know at the time that it would be my last voyage to sea.

I joined the "Naworth", the company's newest ship, at Zeebrugge, for a voyage as usual across to the United States for grain.

This time it was to load for Poland, at some God-forsaken spot on the River Mississippi.

The day we started to load the cargo I had been ashore to the Agents, and on returning to the ship they had just poured about 100 tons of grain into one of the holds.

I stepped aboard and went to look at the hatch, and the smell from the grain struck my nostrils.

I called for the Chief Officer to immediately stop the loading, as that grain was faulty, it was sweating and unfit to be carried.

There was a hell of an outcry from the shippers, who said what the hell, it was only feed grain after all.

I went down to the barges alongside the ship, and plunged my hand down into the grain, it was hot.

No way was I going to load that muck, and I told the shippers so in no uncertain terms.

They argued with me, so in the end I called for the Polish representative to come and inspect the grain. He came with an expert, who agreed with me, the grain was not fit to be carried.

The outcome was that the 10,000 tons of grain contained in the ten barges, was all dumped into the river and new fresh grain was brought to the ship.

The crooks of shippers had thought they could get away with the lousy grain and no one would be any wiser.

They hadn't reckoned with a Captain who had had as much experience of grain loading as I had.

When we arrived at Gydinia, in Poland with the grain, there were complaints about it. So in the interests of my owners, I went down each hold and got samples at varying depths of the cargo as it was discharged. These I put into sterile bottles and sealed them up with a label giving the depth of the cargo, the temperature and the air temperature. I collected twenty such bottles, these I handed over when I arrived home, to the owners.

They had these samples analysed by grain experts, who found the grain at fault. My action saved our company a massive claim for faulty grain, for the shippers in the States had to meet the cost of the huge financial claim.

Chapter 29.
I'm forced to swallow the anchor

On completion of discharge, the "Naworth" was chartered by a Canadian outfit called Case, and we were to load timber in Sweden, then proceed to Antwerp to load general cargo for the Persian Gulf. During the loading I had a lot of trouble with the Case superintendent, who took it on himself to plan all the loading without consulting either me or the Chief Officer. This led to a haphazard loading. I complained to my owners and to the charterers about his highhandedness, but without success.

After leaving Antwerp we came across to Sheerness for a final bit of cargo, and there I was taken off the ship.

As the owners said, there was a clash of personalities and it was better that another Captain should take over. As things turned out later, I am glad that I was taken out of the ship.

Our personnel manager drove me home from Sheerness, and took the sample bottles with him when he went back to Newcastle.

Some little time later whilst I was at home, I had a call from our head office.

Could I tell them if there was any dangerous or noxious cargo down No. 2 hold? As I pointed out to them, I had no cargo plans of the cargo at home, and as far as I was aware, no dangerous stuff had been loaded aboard the ship.

I then asked them why they enquired, and I was told that some of the crew had gone down into one of the holds when the ship arrived in the Persian Gulf, ostensibly to bring out some rope slings. The boy who had been sent down failed to come out, so two more men went into the hold to find out what was wrong.

They too didn't come out, they had all been asphyxiated, and were dead when found.

I was asked if I could give any explanation of such a tragedy. I did, I told them about a similar incident aboard a ship where a superintendent went down a tank which had been closed for several months. All the oxygen had died, and in my opinion that is exactly what had happened in this case.

The holds had been closed and sealed for several weeks, and the ship had been in the high temperatures in the Persian Gulf, all the oxygen would had been expelled, hence the reason for the men's collapse and death in the hold.

I heard later that the men had been down the hold to pilfer some of the general cargo, not on official ship's duty at all. I don't know what the outcome of the claim for compensation would have been in this case, I never heard any more about it.

During my leave, I overexerted myself one day and brought on a mild heart attack which put me in hospital for nine days.

That spelt the end of my career at sea, as I was classified as unfit for further sea service by the Merchant Navy Pool Doctor, his report being based on the findings of the hospital.

It was a sad day for me, I was 61 years old, what future had I at that age?

The company kept me on full pay for three months, and then said that they were sorry to lose me, and they would pay me a further three months sick pay as per the National Maritime Board rules.

As they were deducting income tax from this pay, I asked them if they would pay me the three months money in a lump sum as medical severance pay. That way, I pointed out to them, I would not have to pay any tax on it, I would get the gross amount.

They agreed and paid me the sum of £3,000, and advised me to apply for the severance pay from the Pool Office.

This I did, and surprise, surprise, the board allowed me £235 for the 37 years sea service after the start of the Merchant Navy Pool in 1940.

Big deal, that's how much the country valued its seafarers who saved this country from defeat between 1939 and 1945.

If only I could have stayed with Dalglieshs another few months, I would have come out of it very well. They went bust shortly after I left them, and as one of the longest serving Captains

in the company I would have come out with several thousand pounds in redundancy pay.
All income I now had was the Merchant Navy Pension, which was paid in full to me on medical grounds, after a lot of enquiries and doctor's reports to them.
Fortunately I had got my house paid for, so financially we were not too badly off.

One morning my phone rang. It was the Merchant Navy Pool office. The voice at the other end asked me if I would care for a temporary job cargo surveying on the docks.
I said I would welcome the chance, and they gave me another phone number and said ring a Captain Holmes up.
I did, and he said that he wanted me to go down to King George Dock in Hull, to No.7 quay and there I would see several hundred cars on the dock. Amongst them he said I'd see a chap in a white boiler suit, I was to report to him and he would tell me what to do. He wanted me there immediately, so I had my dinner and took off for the dock.
I found the man he had described, one Mr. Stan White. I introduced myself and said that Captain Holmes had sent me down to give him a hand, so what was the job?
Stan White showed me that we had to survey all these Lada cars for damage in transit or even before they were shipped at Leningrad.
If I remember aright, there were 700 of these cars to examine. It took the two of us about three days to survey them all. At the end of the job I went back to the office to get paid for my work. It was then that Captain Holmes asked me what I was doing.
I told him I was out of work, and why. He said he could give me a job, but the pay wouldn't be very good.
He'd pay me £35 a week, and give me petrol allowance each time I had to go down to the docks on his business.
My pay at sea had been £163 a week, so it was a hell of a come down, but at least I would be earning something to supplement my pension pay. I stayed with Captain Holmes for the next four years, doing survey work on the docks and at Carnaby, where the main distributor for Lada cars was based.

Then came a slack time and survey work was scarce, so Captain Holmes wanted Stan and I to work short time.
He wanted me to work each morning and Stan to work each afternoon.
I disagreed with this arrangement. I said that if he would let each of us work a whole day alternatively, we could then claim the dole for the days we did not work. He wouldn't agree to this, so I went to the dole office and asked what they thought.
Their reaction was that he should work us as I had said, and if he didn't, I could claim redundancy pay as I had been with him for 4 years, and had been put on short time.
They also rang Captain Holmes up about the matter, and this did not please him.
We had a bit of a row in the office and I said that he didn't value his staff and therefore I was leaving him at the end of the week.
I was sorry to go, but I could not put up with such an arrogant man as my boss. It would have cost him nothing to have us work one full day each and then claim unemployment pay for the rest of the week.
That was the last work that I did that brought me near to the sea and the ships that I loved.
The year was 1981, I was 64 years old and I settled down to a land-lubbers retirement.

Lightning Source UK Ltd.
Milton Keynes UK
19 March 2010

151577UK00001B/7/P